한눈에 보이는
무료 글꼴 가이드 - 영어편

KB170958

DIGITAL NEW

머리말

디자인 작업에서 문자를 화면에 표현하는 폰트는 매우 중요합니다. 상상한 디자인을 구현하려면 디자인에 어울리는 폰트를 사용해야 하기 때문입니다.

폰트는 전문적인 훈련을 받은 전문가들이 오랜 시간을 작업해야 만들 수 있는 프로그램(단순한 이미지가 아닙니다)이므로 꽤 비싼 가격에 사거나 매달 혹은 매년 라이선스 비용을 내고 사용해야 하는 것이 현실입니다.

이렇게 힘들게 만든 폰트를 무료로 사용할 수 있도록 배포하는 것도 있는데, 이들을 무료 폰트 혹은 공개 폰트라고 부릅니다. 일반적으로 무료 폰트는 유료 폰트에 비해 품질이 좋지 않습니다. 하지만, 매년 더 많은 폰트들이 나오고 품질 경쟁이 일어나면서 무료 폰트의 품질도 점점 더 좋아지고 다양해지고 있습니다.

한글 폰트는 최소 2,350자, 많으면 11,172자나 되는 문자의 자형을 만들어야 하며, 이렇게 많은 문자들을 특정 스타일로 일관성을 유지하도록 만들어야 합니다. 여기에 한자까지 더해지면 폰트 하나를 만들기 위해 정말 많은 노력을 기울여야 합니다. 그래서 무료로 사용할 수 있게 공개된 한글 폰트는 많지 않습니다.

반면에 영어 폰트는 글자수가 적게는 몇 십자, 많아도 몇 백자에 불과해서 비교적 쉽게 만들 수 있습니다. 그래서 영어 폰트는 한글 폰트에 비해 엄청나게 많고, 무료 폰트도 더 많습니다.

한국인의 입장에서 영어 폰트는 주로 사용하는 폰트가 아니고 보조적으로 사용하는 폰트입니다. 수 십개의 패밀리 폰트로 구성되는 영어 폰트는 사용하기 복잡하고 가격도 비싸 우리의 관심 대상은 아닙니다. 그보다는 다양한 유형의 폰트들로 구성된 무료 영어 폰트 컬렉션이 더 실용적입니다. 영어 폰트를 본문용으로 사용하기 보다는 제목, 캡션, 장식용으로 사용하는 경우가 더 많을 것이기 때문입니다.

무료로 공개하기 위해 오픈 폰트 라이선스로 선언하고 공개된 영어 폰트들도 있지만, 무료 영어 폰트의 상당수는 유료 폰트를 홍보하기 위해 공개된 것입니다. 폰트를 홍보하는 가장 효과적인 방법은 폰트를 무료로 공개하는 것이기 때문입니다.

가끔 사용하는 영어 폰트를 구입하는 것은 부담이 되므로 비용을 절약하기 위해 무료 영어 폰트를 찾게 됩니다. 하지만 상업용으로 사용할 수 있는 괜찮은 영어 폰트를 찾기란 쉽지 않습니다. 당장 편집 작업을 해야 하는데 프로젝트에 맞는 적당한 폰트부터 찾아야 한다면 곤란합니다. 이런 내용들을 잘 정리해서 인쇄한 결과를 제공한다면 참 좋겠지만 그런 자료나 책은 발견하지 못했습니다. 그래서 직접 만들어보기로 했습니다.

실제로 작업을 해보니 지면은 한정되어 있고 무료 영어 폰트는 너무 많습니다. 어쩔 수 없이 다양한 종류의 폰트를 깊게 다루지는 못했습니다. 상당히 마음에 드는 영어 폰트인데 자세히 살펴보니 무료 사용 범위에 제한이 있어서 다루지 못한 것들도 많습니다.

이 책은 타이포그래피 이론이나 디자인 방법론을 다루지 않습니다. 디자인 작업을 할 때 사용할 수 있는 무료 폰트 중에서 적당한 것을 고르는 일을 도와주는 역할을 합니다. 무료 폰트의 참고 사전이라고 할 수 있습니다. 다양한 폰트를 다루고 있어서 폰트의 특성에 따라 표시하는 몇 가지 방법을 고안하여 사용했습니다. 인쇄를 하기 위해 폰트를 고르는 경우에 큰 도움이 되리라 생각합니다.

독자 여러분이 무료 폰트를 사용할 수 있는 기술적인 지식과 능력이 있다고 가정합니다. 그래서 웹사이트나 웹페이지에서 글꼴 파일을 내려받아 압축을 풀고 적절한 작업을 하여 운영체계 혹은 어도비 어플에서 글꼴을 사용할 수 있게 준비하는 방법은 따로 설명하지 않았습니다. 만약 이 책을 사용하는데 어려움이 있거나 질문이 있다면 네이버 카페 cafe.naver.com/1fontguide를 이용해주시기 바랍니다.

무료 영어 폰트 중에서 무료 사용 범위가 까다로운 것들도 있습니다. 그래서 무료 폰트를 선택할 때는 무료 사용 범위를 자세히 살펴보아야 합니다. 예상하지 못한 조건을 요구하는 경우가 있으므로 주의하기 바랍니다. 이에 대해서는 다음 페이지에서 자세하게 설명하고 있으므로 참고하시기 바랍니다.

차 례

6

Modern, Futuristic Font 308

Special Font 346

Font Index 398

무료 폰트의 사용 범위

무료 폰트는 폰트를 만든 사람이나 회사가 폰트의 소유권을 포기한 것이 아니라 폰트를 무료로 사용할 권리를 제공하는 폰트입니다. 그런 의미에서 보면 무료 폰트보다는 공개 폰트가 더 정확한 표현입니다. 그런데 저작권자가 폰트를 공개한 목적에 따라 무료 폰트의 사용 범위와 조건이 다릅니다. 따라서 무료 폰트를 사용하려면 먼저 그 폰트의 사용 범위를 파악해야 합니다.

현재의 법으로는 폰트 디자인은 저작권이 인정되지 않습니다. 문자의 형태는 인류의 공유 재산이라는 인식 때문입니다. 그래서 다른 방법으로 폰트 디자인의 권리를 보호하고 있습니다. 나라에 따라 다를 수 있습니다만 아날로그 상태의 글씨 모양은 저작권을 인정하지 않고, 디지털 상태의 폰트 파일은 프로그램 저작물로 보호하고 있습니다. 그래서 유료 폰트의 파일을 무단으로 복사해서 사용하였다면 저작권 위반으로 보는 것입니다.

무료 폰트는 크게 두 가지로 나뉩니다. 개인적인 용도로 혼자 사용할 때는 문제가 없지만 상업적인 목적으로는 사용할 수 없는 무료 폰트가 있고, 상업적인 목적으로도 사용할 수 있는 무료 폰트가 있습니다. 이 책에서는 당연히 상업적으로 사용할 수 있는 무료 폰트들을 소개합니다.

상업적으로 사용할 수 있는 폰트에도 몇 가지 종류가 있습니다. 폰트 파일을 판매하는 것을 제외하고는 모든 것이 가능한 진정한 무료 폰트가 있고, 일부 제한이 있는 무료 폰트가 있습니다. 예를 들면, 판매하는 제품이 아닌 경우에만 사용할 수 있다거나 판매 수량 25,000개 이하인 제품에만 사용할 수 있는 폰트가 있습니다. 예를 들어, 유튜브 동영상에 자막을 넣거나 무료로 배포하는 책자에 폰트를 사용하면 판매하는 제품에 사용하는 것이 아닙니다.

홍보 목적으로 유료 폰트의 일부 혹은 데모 버전을 무료 폰트로 배포할 때는 폰트 파일을 마음대로 재배포하는 것을 허용하지 않습니다. 재배포를 허용하지 않으면 해당 사이트를 방문하여 다운로드해야 하는데, 자연스럽게 그 사이트의 주소와 내용이 홍보되는 것입니다. 외국의 회사나 개인이 한국에서 재배포했다는 사실을 알기는 어렵겠지만 이런 사항은 지켜서 무료 폰트에 대한 보상을 해주어야 하겠습니다.

무료 폰트 라이선스

가장 많이 알려진 무료 폰트 라이선스는 오픈 폰트 라이선스*SIL Open Font License*입니다. 저작권을 설명하는 내용에 이 단어가 있다면 글꼴을 판매하는 것 이외의 모든 것이 허용된다는 것입니다. 반면에 오픈 폰트 라이선스라고 명시되어 있지 않다면 뭔가 사용 범위나 사용 조건에 제약이 있다는 뜻입니다.

퍼블릭 도메인 *Public Domain*

저작권이나 지적 재산권 등의 권리가 소멸되었거나 포기된 상태를 말합니다. 이런 글꼴은 어떤 용도로도 자유롭게 이용할 수 있습니다.

GPL *General Public License*

1985년에 자유 소프트웨어 재단*Free Software Foundation*이라는 비영리단체가 만들어졌습니다. 자유 소프트웨어 재단은 소프트웨어를 누구나 복제, 수정, 공유, 배포할 수 있도록 하자는 '자유 소프트웨어 문화'를 장려하는 운동을 하고 있습니다. GPL은 가장 널리 알려진 강력한 카피레프트*Copyleft* 라이선스입니다. 무료 글꼴에 GPL 라이선스를 적용하면 해당 글꼴을 누구나 마음대로 복제, 수정, 공유, 배포할 수 있게 됩니다.

오픈 폰트 라이선스 *SIL OPEN FONT LICENSE*

SIL International*(www.sil.org)*이 글꼴을 배포하기 위해 만든 라이선스입니다. 이 라이선스가 적용된 글꼴은 누구나 자유롭게 사용할 수 있습니다. 다만, 글꼴 자체를 단독으로 판매하는 것은 허용되지 않는다는 점에서 GPL과 다르며, 다른 프로그램과 함께 배포하거나 판매하는 것은 허용됩니다. 오픈 폰트 라이선스*OFL*의 목표는 전 세계에 걸쳐서 글꼴 공동 프로젝트를 활성화하고 학계 및 언어 공동체의 글꼴 제작을 지원하여 글꼴을 공유하고 협력하는 환경을 구축하는 것입니다. 오픈 폰트 라이선스가 적용되지 않는 무료 폰트는 폰트를 수정하거나 재배포하는 것을 허락하지 않는다는 뜻입니다. *www.olis.or.kr/license/Detailselect.do?lId=1086&mapcode=010068*

조건부 무료 폰트 라이선스

구글에서 'free font'를 검색하면 우수한 무료 영어 폰트를 소개하는 많은 링크들을 만날 수 있습니다. 하지만 'free'가 우리가 생각하는 '무료'는 아닐 수 있습니다. 폰트 사용자로서 알아두면 좋을 조건들을 살펴보겠습니다.

판매 제품에 사용 금지 혹은 판매 수량 제한
상업적으로 무료로 사용할 수 있는 폰트를 찾는 입장에서 안타까운 제한입니다. 동영상에 자막을 넣거나 무료로 배포하는 PDF 파일에 임베딩하는 것은 허용하지만 티셔츠나 패키지와 같이 물리적 실체를 판매하는 제품에 사용하는 것을 금지합니다. 이 제한을 풀기 위해서는 폰트를 사거나 연락하여 허락을 얻으라고 합니다. 이 책에서는 이런 폰트는 제외하였습니다.

조금 나은 조건은 판매 수량에 제한을 거는 것입니다. 예를 들면, 500개 이하 판매하는 것만 허용하는 식입니다. 이건 좀 애매합니다. 반면에 25,000개까지 판매를 허용하면 괜찮은 조건이라고 할 수 있습니다. 이런 무료 폰트는 소개하였습니다.

출처 표시 의무
무료 영어 폰트에서는 아주 보기 드물게 보는 조건입니다. 책에 사용할 때는 괜찮지만 출처를 표기할 공간이나 방법이 없는 제품에 사용하려면 곤란한 조건입니다. 그런데 사실상 이 조건은 웹사이트에 폰트를 사용할 때 링크를 걸어달라는 의미인 것으로 보입니다.

재배포 불가, 번들 불가, 서버 업로드 불가
홍보를 목적으로 공개하는 무료 폰트는 거의 대부분 재배포를 허락하지 않습니다. 예를 들면, 여러분이 운영하는 블로그에 폰트를 올려놓지 말라는 뜻이며, 커뮤니티에 공개하는 것도 금지합니다. 그대신 다운로드 링크를 소개하여 폰트에 관심이 있는 사람들이 그곳을 방문하도록 해달라는 것입니다. 또한, 하드웨어나 소프트웨어를 공급하면서 폰트를 함께 제공한다거나(번들) 웹사이를 운영하는 서버에 폰트를 두는(업로드) 것을 금지하는 경우가 있습니다.

저작권 및 사용 범위에 대한 언급 없음

free에는 'free for personal use'와 'free for commercial use'가 있습니다. 따라서 단순히 'free'라고만 표시되어 있다면 어느 쪽인지 잘 살펴보아야 합니다. 보통은 아주 작은 글씨로 혹은 별도 문서에 구체적인 무료 사용 범위가 적혀 있습니다.

간혹 정말 아무런 힌트도 주지 않는 경우가 있는데, 조건 없는 무료 사용이라고 봐도 좋을 것입니다. 하지만 역시 어떤 댓가를 받고 판매한다거나 제공한다는 것은 피하는 것이 좋습니다.

독자적인 라이선스

무료 영어 폰트의 사용 범위는 대부분 몇 줄의 간단한 문구로 설명할 수 있습니다. 하지만 간혹 매우 길고 복잡한 라이선스를 들이미는 곳도 있는데, 그 대표적인 곳이 픽셀부다*pixelbuddha*입니다. 꽤 큰 사이트이고 멋진 무료 폰트들을 보여주는데 이곳의 독자적인 Pixelbuddha Freebie License *pixelbuddha.net/Pixelbuddha-Freebie-License.pdf*를 읽어보면 'commercial projects that are not intended to be sold on markets, stocks, etc.'라는 문구가 나옵니다. 판매하지 않는 상업적 프로젝트에만 사용이 허락된다고 합니다. 이 프로젝트 초반에 픽셀부다의 폰트가 상업용인 줄 알고 모으다가 나중에 알고 제외하였습니다.

이에 비하여 픽셀설프러스*www.pixelsurplus.com*는 픽셀부다와 같은 꼼수를 부리지 않고 처음부터 명확하게 1. Free for personal use, 2. Personal & Commercial Use, 3. Free for personal & desktop commercial use를 확실하게 구분하기 때문에 편리합니다. 2번은 판매 수량에 제한이 없는 라이선스이고 3번(desktop 단어가 표시된 라이선스)은 25,000개까지만 판매할 수 있는 라이선스*www.pixelsurplus.com/freebie-licensing*입니다.

이들에 비해 폰트패브릭*www.fontfabric.com*의 FFF EULA *Fontfabric Free Font End User License Agreement* 라이선스는 훨씬 더 관대해서 판매, 재배포, 수정 배포을 제외하고는 거의 대부분 허용됩니다.

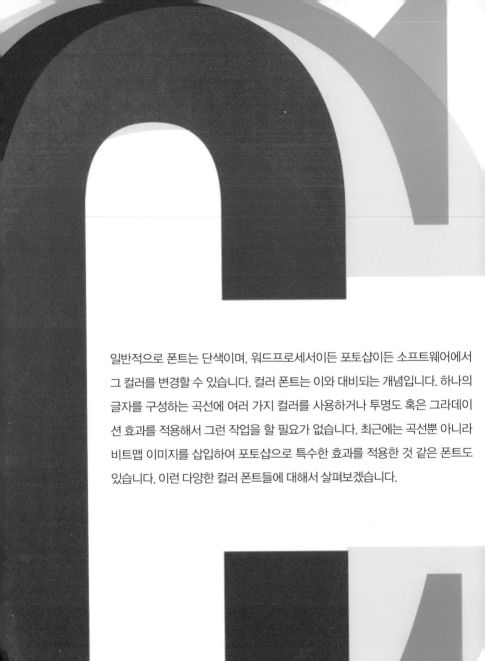

일반적으로 폰트는 단색이며, 워드프로세서이든 포토샵이든 소프트웨어에서 그 컬러를 변경할 수 있습니다. 컬러 폰트는 이와 대비되는 개념입니다. 하나의 글자를 구성하는 곡선에 여러 가지 컬러를 사용하거나 투명도 혹은 그라데이션 효과를 적용해서 그런 작업을 할 필요가 없습니다. 최근에는 곡선뿐 아니라 비트맵 이미지를 삽입하여 포토샵으로 특수한 효과를 적용한 것 같은 폰트도 있습니다. 이런 다양한 컬러 폰트들에 대해서 살펴보겠습니다.

CMYK Regular

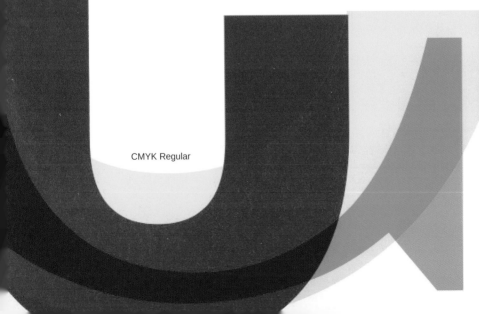

컬러 폰트

SVG 폰트 – 컬러

최근 폰트에 다양한 컬러를 구현한 새로운 유형의 폰트가 등장했습니다. 이것을 SVG 폰트라고 부릅니다. 기존의 폰트로는 구현할 수 없는 화려한 컬러를 손쉽게 얻을 수 있습니다. SVG 폰트는 워드프로세서 등 사무용 소프트웨어에서는 사용할 수 없고 SVG 폰트를 지원하는 전문가용 그래픽 소프트웨어의 최신 버전에서만 사용할 수 있습니다. 아쉬운 점이 있다면 무료 폰트의 수가 매우 적다는 것입니다. 28~63쪽에 25개의 무료 SVG 폰트를 소개하였습니다.

SVG 폰트 – 이미지

폰트 내부에 비트맵 이미지를 넣은 SVG 폰트는 폰트 파일의 크기가 커서 컴퓨터 메모리가 충분하지 않으면 그래픽 소프트웨어의 작업 속도가 느려질 것입니다. 그럼에도 이런 SVG 폰트를 사용하는 것은 곡선과 컬러만으로는 구현할 수 없는 화려하고 특별한 효과를 얻을 수 있기 때문입니다. 비트맵 이미지가 내장된 SVG 폰트는 그 수가 더욱 적습니다. 만들기가 어렵기 때문에 거의 대부분 유료입니다. 64~77쪽에 7개를 소개하는 것에 그쳤습니다.

Layered 폰트

SVG 폰트가 등장하기 전에 하나의 글자에 여러 가지의 컬러를 구현하기 위해 사용했던 폰트가 레이어드 폰트입니다. 모양이 유사한 여러 벌의 폰트를 만들고, 그 중 몇 개를 선택하여 각각 다른 컬러를 지정한 뒤에 겹쳐서 컬러 폰트를 구현합니다. 아쉬운 점이 있다면 글자들을 겹쳐서 사용하는 과정이 복잡하고 까다롭다는 것입니다. 레이어드 폰트를 만들기가 쉽지 않아서 폰트의 수도 많지 않습니다. 따라서 무료 폰트도 희귀합니다. 장점은 기존의 폰트를 다룰 수 있는 모든 프로그램에서 사용할 수 있다는 정도입니다. 78~89쪽에 4개의 레이어드 폰트를 소개하였습니다.

What is SVG Font?

Gilbert Color Bold Preview5 43p

SVG 폰트는 어떤 폰트인가?

SVG 폰트는 새로운 포맷의 폰트입니다. 벡터 곡선만으로 구성된 기존의 폰트와는 달리 폰트 파일 내부에 컬러, 음영, 이미지, 투명도 정보도 들어 있습니다. SVG 폰트를 컬러 폰트라고 부르기도 하는데 컬러 폰트는 정확한 용어는 아닙니다.

일반 폰트

비트맵이 없는 SVG 폰트

비트맵이 있는 SVG 폰트

기존의 폰트는 글자를 외곽선만으로 표현했습니다. 사람들은 글자의 모양뿐 아니라 컬러나 질감 같은 다양한 표현을 더하고 싶었습니다. 그 방법을 연구해서 나온 폰트 포맷이 애플의 SBIX(맥, 아이폰), 구글의 CBDT(안드로이드), 마이크로소프트의 COLR(윈도우), W3C의 SVG(맥, 아이폰, 윈도우)인데 현재는 SVG 방식이 대세가 되었습니다. SVG 포맷은 벡터 곡선과 비트맵 이미지를 모두 포함할 수 있습니다. 그래서 현재는 컬러 폰트라고 하면 SVG(Scalable Vector Graphics) 포맷의 데이터를 가진 오픈타입 폰트(OpenType SVG font)를 말하게 되었습니다.

SVG 폰트의 크기와 비트맵 해상도

SVG 폰트는 내부에 비트맵 이미지를 포함할 수 있기 때문에 일반 폰트에 비해 파일의 크기가 커져서 수 메가에 달하기도 합니다. 비트맵 이미지가 포함되지 않은 SVG 폰트는 일반 폰트처럼 크기를 조절해도 아무런 문제가 없습니다. 하지만 비트맵 이미지가 포함되어 있는 폰트를 그 이미지의 해상도가 감당할 수 있는 수준을 넘게 확대하면 계단 현상이 발생하게 됩니다. 따라서 비트맵 이미지가 포함된 SVG 폰트를 사용할 때는 너무 큰 크기로 사용하지 않아야 합니다. SVG 폰트의 파일 크기가 충분히 크면 비트맵 이미지가 큰 것이므로 다소 안심할 수 있습니다. 물론 견본 인쇄를 통해서 확인하는 것이 좋습니다.

color font

SVG 폰트의 장단점

SVG 폰트는 컬러 혹은 비트맵 이미지로 디자인이 된 상태이기에 소프트웨어에서 별도의 작업을 하지 않고도 글자를 입력하는 것만으로도 멋진 효과를 얻을 수 있습니다. 이론적으로는 SVG 폰트의 컬러를 변경할 수 없습니다만 이 문제를 해결할 방법이 없는 건 아닙니다. 매우 큰 비트맵 이미지가 포함된 SVG 폰트를 사용하면 그 처리 속도가 느려질 수 있습니다. 해결책은 컴퓨터의 메모리를 충분히 많이 확보하는 것입니다.

SVG 폰트를 지원하는 소프트웨어

SVG 폰트는 새로운 포맷의 폰트이기 때문에 이를 사용하기 위해서는 소프트웨어가 SVG 폰트를 지원해야 합니다. 그래서 워드, 파워포인트와 같은 사무용 소프트웨어에서는 사용할 수 없습니다. 또한, 그래픽 소프트웨어라 하더라도 오래된 버전, 예를 들면 포토샵 CS6은 SVG 폰트를 지원하지 않습니다.

 아래의 표를 보면 알 수 있듯이 가장 널리 사용되는 어도비의 3대 소프트웨어가 SVG 폰트를 지원하고 있습니다. 따라서 현실적으로 SVG 폰트를 사용하려면 최신 버전의 Adobe Creative Cloud를 사용해야 합니다.

소프트웨어	지원하는 포맷	지원 시기
Photoshop	SVG, SBIX	Photoshop CC 2017부터
Illustrator	SVG, SBIX	Illustrator CC 2018부터
InDesign	SVG, SBIX	InDesign CC 2019부터
QuarkXPress	SVG, SBIX, COLR	QuarkXPress 2018부터
Pixelmator	SVG, SBIX	macOS 10.14부터
Sketch	SVG, SBIX	macOS 10.14부터
Affinity Designer	SVG	macOS 10.14부터

Color fonts! WTF?

¶ What are color fonts?
¶ What's inside?
¶ Where's the catch?
¶ Where can I use them?
¶ Where can I get some?
¶ How can I make color fonts?

¶ What are color fonts?

- They are **the next big thing** in graphic design
- They bring **multiple colors, shades, textures and transparency** to type
- They include **vector shapes, bitmap images or even both** into font files

Standard vector font   Color vector font   Color bitmap font

Color fonts represent a key evolution in digital typography, introducing rich graphic features into font files. Thanks to new font formats, color fonts are finally becoming a reality for millions of creatives.

Color fonts can impact any type of text, since they may contain any type of characters, including emojis and icons.

Note that colors fonts are sometimes referred as chromatic fonts, which is actually a bit more accurate since they may include multicolored, grayed or even single-tone characters.

OPENTYPE

OPENTYPE

OPENTYPE

* SVG 폰트에 대한 자세한 내용은 www.colorfonts.wtf 사이트를 참고하기 바랍니다.

SVG 폰트를 윤곽선으로 바꾸고 컬러 지정하기 (인디자인)

SVG 폰트의 컬러를 변경하려면 글자를 윤곽선(패스)으로 바꾸고 컬러를 변경하면 됩니다. (인디자인과 일러스트레이터에서는 되지만 포토샵에서는 안됩니다) 하지만 이렇게 되면 글자의 내용을 수정할 수 없게 되므로 주의해야 합니다. 다만, 비트맵 이미지가 포함된 SVG 폰트는 윤곽선으로 바꿀 수 없습니다.

❶ SVG 폰트(55쪽 Pixel 폰트)가 적용된 글자가 들어 있는 텍스트 프레임을 선택합니다.

❷ 메뉴에서 [문자〉윤곽선 만들기]를 선택하면 텍스트 프레임이 사라지고 패스의 그룹으로 바뀝니다. 이때 SVG 폰트 내부에서 사용된 컬러가 색상 견본으로 등록되는데 이것은 RGB 컬러이므로 적절하게 CMYK 컬러로 변경해주어야 합니다.

❸ 메뉴에서 [개체〉그룹 해제]를 선택하여 그룹을 해제합니다. 현재의 상태는 패스(path)들이 합쳐져서 한 덩어리가 된 상태입니다. 이것을 컴파운드 패스*compound path*라고 합니다.

❹ 컴파운드 패스를 풀어서 각각의 패스로 해체할 수도 있습니다. 컴파운드 패스를 선택한 상태에서 메뉴에서 [개체〉패스〉컴파운드 패스 풀기]를 선택하면 됩니다.

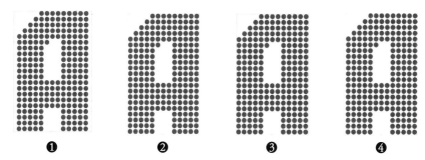

컴파운드 패스일 때 그라디언트 색상(방사형)을 적용하면 아래 왼쪽 예처럼 됩니다. 컴파운드 패스 전체를 하나의 패스로 간주하여 적용되는 것입니다. 반면에 컴파운드 패스를 해제한 뒤에 그라디언트 색상을 적용하면 아래 가운데 예처럼 각 패스마다 적용됩니다. 아래 오른쪽 예는 패스들을 3개의 컴파운드 패스로 만든 후에 색상을 적용한 것입니다.

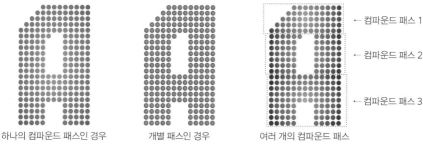

하나의 컴파운드 패스인 경우   개별 패스인 경우   여러 개의 컴파운드 패스

← 컴파운드 패스 1

← 컴파운드 패스 2

← 컴파운드 패스 3

앞에서 예로 든 Pixel 폰트는 구조가 매우 간단하여 윤곽선으로 변경하면 서로 분리된 한 종류의 패스들이 되므로 다루기가 쉽습니다. 하지만 일반적으로는 매우 복잡한 컴파운드 패스가 만들어지고 이를 수정하여 새로운 컬러를 지정하기가 쉽지는 않습니다.

구체적으로 어떻게 하는지 예를 들어 설명하겠습니다. 이 방법은 SVG 폰트의 패스가 어떻게 구성되어 있는가에 따라 작업의 난이도가 크게 달라집니다.

❶ SVG 폰트(40쪽 ColorTube 폰트)가 적용된 글자가 들어 있는 텍스트 프레임을 선택합니다.

❷ 메뉴에서 [문자〉윤곽선 만들기]를 선택하면 텍스트 프레임이 사라지고 패스들의 그룹으로 바뀝니다. SVG 폰트에 사용된 컬러들이(7개 컬러가 사용됨) 인디자인 문서에 색상 견본으로 등록되는데, 이것들은 RGB 컬러이므로 CMYK 컬러로 변경해야 합니다. 해당 컬러의 [색상 견본 옵션] 대화상자에서 색상 모드를 'RGB'에서 'CMYK'로 수정하면 됩니다.

❸ 메뉴에서 [개체〉그룹 해제]를 선택하여 그룹을 해제합니다.

❹ 패스를 하나씩 선택한 뒤에 컬러를 수정합니다. 지정할 색상 견본을 미리 만들어 놓은 뒤에 작업하는 것이 좋습니다.

ColorTube 폰트의 A

개별 패스로 해체한 모습
이해하기 쉽게 위치를 변경

패스의 컬러를 수정한 예

Carve 폰트의 A

개별 패스로 해체한 모습
이해하기 쉽게 위치를 변경

패스의 컬러를 수정한 예

내부 광선 효과로 SVG 폰트의 컬러 지정하기 (인디자인)

비트맵 이미지가 포함된 SVG 폰트는 윤곽선(패스)으로 바꿀 수 없습니다. 그래서 컬러를 바꾸려면 다른 방법을 사용해야 합니다. 그 방법이란 텍스트 프레임에 적용할 수 있는 '효과' 중에서 '내부 광선' 기능을 사용하는 것입니다. 이 방법은 포토샵과 일러스트레이터에서도 가능합니다.

❶ SVG 폰트가 적용된 글자가 들어 있는 텍스트 프레임을 선택합니다.

❷ 메뉴에서 [개체〉효과〉내부 광선]을 선택하여 [효과] 대화상자를 불러냅니다.

❸ '표준' 모드를 선택하고 원하는 컬러를 선택하고 불투명도는 100%를 지정합니다. 미리 색상 견본을 만들어 두는 것이 편리합니다.

❹ [기교]는 '약하게', [소스]는 '가장자리'를 선택합니다. [크기]와 [경계감소]는 상황에 따라 적절한 값을 입력해야 합니다. 이 숫자가 너무 작으면 효과가 잘 보이지 않으며, 너무 크면 SVG 폰트의 질감이 사라져 버립니다. 여기에서는 2㎜와 20%를 입력합니다. [노이즈]는 3%로 하였습니다. 포토샵과 일러스트레이터는 인디자인보다 훨씬 더 많은 옵션이 있고 그 효과도 약간 다릅니다.

Ivory Heart 폰트를 적용한 단어

내부 광선 효과를 적용한 예

Dream Chaser 폰트를 적용한 단어

내부 광선 효과를 적용한 예

내부 광선 효과로 SVG 폰트의 컬러 지정하기 (포토샵)

포토샵에서도 비트맵 이미지로 구성된 SVG 폰트의 컬러를 바꿀 수 있습니다. '내부 광선' 기능을 사용하는 것은 같으나 사용자 인터페이스가 다르며, 세부 옵션들이 더 많아 복잡합니다. 여기에서는 포토샵 영문 버전으로 설명합니다.

❶ SVG 폰트를 적용한 단어를 입력하여 텍스트 레이어를 만듭니다.

❷ 텍스트 레이어를 선택한 상태에서 [fx] 단추를 클릭하고 [Inner Glow]를 선택합니다.

❸ [Layer Style] 대화상자가 나타나고 Inner Glow 섹션이 표시됩니다. [Blend Mode]는 Normal, [Opacity]는 100%를 선택하고 [Set color of glow] 단추를 클릭합니다.

20

❹ [Color Picker] 대화상자가 나타나면 컬러를 선택합니다. 오른쪽 아래에 CMYK 값을 입력하는 4개의 칸이 있으므로 0, 100, 100, 0을 입력하고 [OK] 단추를 클릭합니다.

❺ 이제 나머지 항목들을 선택합니다. [Technique]는 Softer(부드럽게), [Source]는 Edge(가장자리)를 선택하고 [OK] 단추를 클릭합니다.

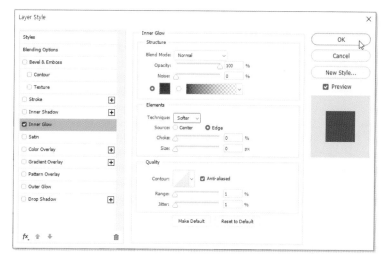

❻ 내부 광선 효과가 적용되어 지정한 컬러로 바뀌어 표시됩니다. [Layers] 패널을 보면 텍스트 레이어 아래에 Inner Glow 효과가 적용된 표시가 나타납니다.

내부 광선 효과로 SVG 폰트의 컬러 지정하기 (일러스트레이터)

일러스트레이터에서도 비트맵 이미지로 구성된 SVG 폰트의 컬러를 바꿀 수 있습니다. '내부 광선' 기능을 사용하는 것은 같으나 사용자 인터페이스가 다르며, 다른 옵션들을 추가할 수도 있습니다. 여기에서는 영문 버전으로 설명합니다.

❶ Type tool을 선택하고 SVG 폰트를 적용하여 단어를 입력합니다.

❷ 텍스트 오브젝트를 선택한 상태에서 메뉴에서 [Type〉 Create Outlines]를 선택합니다.

❸ 비트맵 이미지가 있는 폰트이므로 윤곽선(패스)이 아니라 이미지들이 추출됩니다. 이들은 그룹으로 묶여 있습니다.

❹ 그룹 전체가 선택되어 있는 상태에서 메뉴에서 [Effect〉 Stylize〉Inner Glow]를 선택하면 [Inner Glow] 대화상자가 나타납니다. [Mode]를 Normal로 선택한 뒤에 그 오른쪽에 있는 정사각형을 클릭합니다.

❺ [Color Picker] 대화상자가 나타나면 새로운 컬러를 지 정합니다. 대화상자의 오른 쪽 아래에 CMYK 값을 입력 하는 4개의 칸이 있으므로 0, 100, 100, 0을 입력하고 [OK] 단추를 클릭합니다.

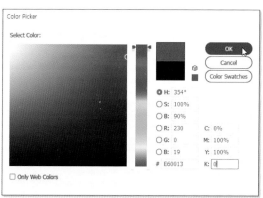

❻ [Inner Glow] 대화상자로 돌아오면 [Opacity] 값을 지정합니다. 100%로 하면 비트맵 이미지의 질감이 덮여서 보이지 않게 되고, 너무 낮은 값으로 하면 컬 러가 약하게 표시됩니다. 여기에서는 60%를 입력합 니다. [Blur] 값은 4mm 정도로 합니다. 컬러 적용을 가 장자리*Edge*에서부터 할 것이므로 컬러가 글자의 대 부분을 덮을 수 있도록 충분히 큰 값을 입력해야 합니 다. 이제 [OK] 단추를 클릭합니다.

❼ 그 결과 SVG 폰트에서 추출한 이 미지에 새로운 컬러가 적용되어 표시됩니다. 이때 [Appearance]

패널을 보면 오른쪽 그림에서 보듯이 [Inner Glow] 효과가 추가된 것을 알 수 있습니다. 이 부분을 클릭 하면 바로 [Inner Glow] 대화상자를 불러내서 컬러 를 바꾸거나 다른 옵션을 변경할 수 있습니다.

❽ 이외에도 Effect 메뉴에 있는 다양한 포토샵 효과들을 적 용할 수 있습니다. 예를 들면, Brush Strokes의 Sprayed Strokes를 선택하면 오른쪽 그림과 같이 됩니다.

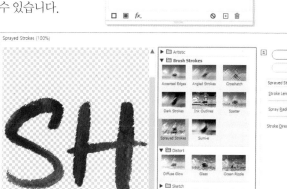

Fiesta Color Decorative 30p, 0

쓸만한 무료 SVG 폰트는 어디에 있나?

SVG 폰트는 새로 등장한 형식의 폰트이며 이를 지원하는 소프트웨어는 많지 않습니다. 그래서 무료 SVG 폰트를 찾기가 힘듭니다. 위에 표시된 Fiesta Color 폰트는 괜찮은 SVG 폰트인데, 2017년에 무료로 받은 것입니다. 하지만 지금은 유료로 전환되어 판매되고 있습니다. SVG 폰트를 만드는 소프트웨어 Fontself 사이트 *www.fontself.com/colorfontweek/2018* 를 보면 5개의 SVG 폰트가 소개되어 있는데 처음에는 5개 모두 무료였으나 현재는 2개만 무료입니다.

무료 SVG 폰트를 많이 소개할 수가 없었습니다. 추천하기에는 폰트의 품질이 좋지 않거나 개인용으로만 사용할 수 있는 것들이 많았습니다.

템플릿 파일을 판매하는 AUGETYPE 사이트는 사람들을 모으기 위해 꽤 많은 무료 SVG 폰트들을 제공하는데 품질이 만족스럽지는 않습니다. *www.augetype.com/warehouse/svgfonts/colorfont-01-en.html* 그중에서 괜찮아 보이는 14개 폰트를 골라 한 페이지씩 할당하여 간단하게 소개하였습니다. (32, 33, 34, 35, 38, 39, 42, 43, 46, 47, 54, 55, 60, 61쪽) 저작권에 대한 설명은 따로 없지만 아무런 조건 없이 폰트 파일을 내려받을 수 있고 Free라고 명시하고 있습니다.

Elements.envato.com(회원제 유료)에서 SVG 폰트 찾아 내려받기

엘레먼츠엔바토닷컴은 여러 가지 디자인 소스들을 월회비 방식으로 제공하는 사이트입니다. 월회비는 19달러이며, 연회비는 일시불 198달러(월 16.5달러)입니다. 회비를 내는 동안에는 이 사이트에 있는 모든 자료를 내려받아(다운로드할 때 사용할 프로젝트 이름을 지정해야 합니다) 사용해볼 수 있으며 상업적으로 사용할 수도 있습니다. 단, 회원 자격이 종료되면 사용할 수 없게 됩니다. 회원 자격이 있는 동안에 제작한 책이나 디자인 상품은 계속해서 판매할 수 있습니다. 따라서 이 사이트는 지속적으로 디자인 작업을 하는 디자이너에게 적합합니다.

이 사이트에서 얻을 수 있는 자료는 폰트뿐 아니라 그래픽, 그래픽 템블릿, 그래픽 소프트웨어 애드온, 프리젠테이션 템블릿, 웹 템플릿, 사진, 동영상, 음악 등 다양합니다.

Fonts 섹션에서 'color font'를 검색하면 아래와 같이 7천개가 넘는 SVG 폰트들이 나열됩니다. 이때 정렬방법을 'Sort by Relevant' 대신에 'Sort by Popular'로 바꾸면 인기가 높은 것들이 앞쪽에 표시됩니다. 관심 있는 폰트를 클릭하고 살펴본 뒤에 마음에 들면 Download 단추를 클릭하고 사용할 프로젝트 이름을 선택하고 다운로드받으면 됩니다.

검색어

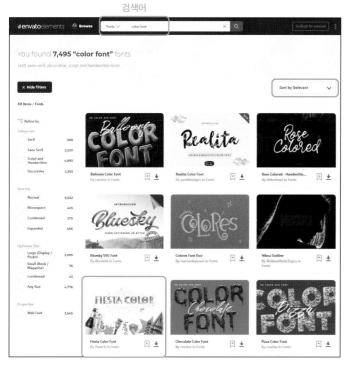

정렬 기준

다운로드 단추

MARQUEE BUL

MARQUEE BUL

Creativemarket.com에서 SVG 폰트 찾아 구입하기

크리에이티브마켓닷컴은 디자이너들이 입점하는 오픈마켓입니다. 다른 사이트에 비해 가격은 비싸지만 이곳에서만 구할 수 있는 것들이 많고, 품질이 더 높은 편입니다. 같은 디자인 샵이 여러 사이트에 있다면 크리에이티브마켓닷컴에서 파는 가격이 더 비쌉니다. 하지만 다른 곳에는 없는 것이 있을 수 있습니다. 얻을 수 있는 자료는 폰트뿐 아니라 사진, 그래픽, 템플릿, 웹 테마, 그래픽 소프트웨어 애드온, 3D 이미지 등 다양합니다.

SVG 컬러 폰트들을 모아서 볼 수 있는 페이지 creativemarket.com/tags/colour-font 가 있습니다. 제작자가 붙인 태그로 분류되기 때문에 검색해서 찾는 것보다 정확합니다. 이곳에서만 구입할 수 있는 폰트들이 있습니다.

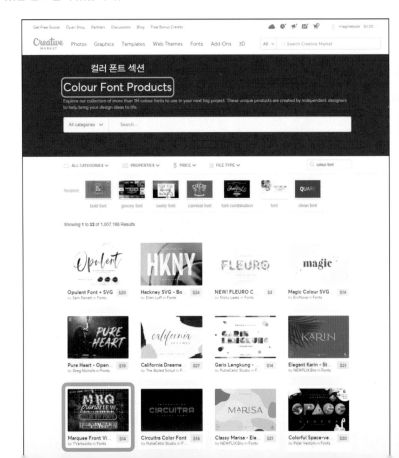

MarqueeFrontWithBulb Regular 180p, -30

　　관심 있는 아이템(SVG 폰트)을 클릭하면 자세한 정보가 표시됩니다. 마음에 들면 라이선스 종류를 선택한 뒤에 구입합니다. 라이선스 종류는 디자인 소스에 따라 다른데, 폰트의 경우 Desktop(컴퓨터에서 사용 가능), E-pub(전자책에도 사용 가능), App(개발하는 소프트웨어에도 사용 가능) 중에서 선택하게 됩니다. 폰트를 한번 구입하면 기간 제한 없이 계속 사용할 수 있습니다. 아래의 폰트는 엘레먼츠엔바토닷컴에서도 다운로드할 수 있는데*elements.envato.com/marquee-front-view-color-fonts-4ACXET* 기간 제한 없이 사용하고 싶다면 크리에이티브마켓닷컴에서 구입하는 것이 유리하겠지요. 이 폰트는 매우 큰 비트맵 이미지를 포함하고 있기 때문에 파일 용량이 매우 큽니다. 폰트 파일 크기가 40MB 이상입니다.

라이선스 종류

ABELONE

Abelone Regular 70p, 0

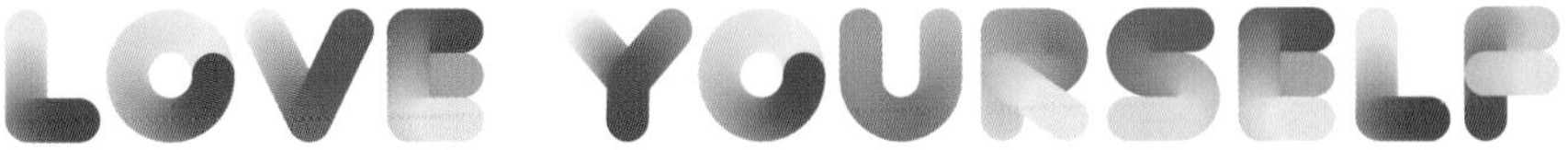

LOVE YOURSELF

39p, 0

ABCDEFFGHI
JKLMNOPQR
STUVWXYZ
1234567890
+ - * ÷ = ' " ..
# $ % & ! ? \/ . |
<> () () [] {}

50/55p, 0

License	free for commercial projects
Font tag	Color, Sans Serif, Round, Gradient, Heading

Link	www.fontself.com/colorfontweek/2018
Note	그라디언트 효과로 SVG 폰트의 장점을 살린 폰트

122p, 0

523p, 0

Agreloyc Almond/Asparagus/Azure/Turquoise Medium 68p, 0

AGRELOY REGULAR
AGRELOYC ALMOND
AGRELOYC ASPARAGUS
AGRELOYC AZURE
AGRELOYC TURQUOISE

28/26p, 0

ABCDEFGHIJKLMNOPQRSTUVWXYZ
1234567890 +-×÷=#%& ,.:;~!?§/|\---
‹›«»()[]{}'‚""„ $¢£¥€& _•‣ ←↑→↓

ABCDEFGHIJKLMNOPQRSTUVWXYZ
1234567890 +-×÷=#%& ,.:;~!?§/|\---
‹›«»()[]{}'‚""„ $¢£¥€& _•‣ ←↑→↓

ABCDEFGHIJKLMNOPQRSTUVWXYZ
1234567890 +-×÷=#%& ,.:;~!?§/|\---
‹›«»()[]{}'‚""„ $¢£¥€& _•‣ ←↑→↓

ABCDEFGHIJKLMNOPQRSTUVWXYZ
1234567890 +-×÷=#%& ,.:;~!?§/|\---
‹›«»()[]{}'‚""„ $¢£¥€& _•‣ ←↑→↓

ABCDEFGHIJKLMNOPQRSTUVWXYZ
1234567890 +-×÷=#%& ,.:;~!?§/|\---
‹›«»()[]{}'‚""„ $¢£¥€& _•‣ ←↑→↓

20/21, 0

| License | Open Font License |
| Font tag | Color, Serif, Decorative, Heading |

| Link | www.glukfonts.pl/font.php?font=Agreloyc |
| Note | 투톤 효과로 SVG 폰트의 장점을 살린 폰트 |

AT ANY RATE, THAT IS HAPPINESS;
TO BE DISSOLVED INTO SOMETHING
COMPLETE AND GREAT.

21.5, 20.7, 32.8p, -25

HAPPINESS
IS A CHOICE

40/35, 0

VINTAGE
DESIGN

80/70, 0

260p, 0

License	free
Font tag	Color, Shadow

Link www.augetype.com/warehouse/svgfonts/pg01/svg_babershop/babershop.zip

Note 투톤 효과로 SVG 폰트의 장점을 살린 폰트

BARBERSHOP

Barbershop Regular 73p, 0

ABCDEFGHIJKLM
NOPQRSTUVWXYZ

52/44p, 0

PLASTIC
BASKET

70/65p, Optical -25

OLD DO

160p, Optical -50

License	free
Font tag	Color, Ribon, Gradation

Link	www.augetype.com/warehouse/svgfonts/pg01/svg_benda/benda.zip
Note	그라데이션 효과로 SVG 폰트의 장점을 살린 폰트

Benda Regular 96p, 0

32/32p, 0

60/60p, Optical -25

140p, Optical -50

License	free	Link	www.augetype.com/warehouse/svgfonts/pg02/svg_bluecurves/bluecurves.zip
Font tag	Color, Blue	Note	투톤 효과로 SVG 폰트의 장점을 살린 폰트

Blue Curves

Blue Curves Regular 55p, 0

ABCDEFGHIJKLM
NOPQRSTUVWXYZ
abcdefghijklmn
opqrstuvwxyz

35/35p, 0

undersea
Blue Water

60/60p, Optical 0

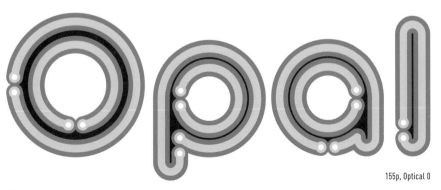

155p, Optical 0

License	free	Link	www.augetype.com/warehouse/svgfonts/pg04/svg_brigity/brigity.zip
Font tag	Color, Lines, Stripe	Note	글자마다 다른 효과로 SVG 폰트의 장점을 살린 폰트

Brighty Regular 94p, 0

A 6 C D E F G H I J K L M N
O P Q R S T U V W X Y Z

40/40p, 0

6EAUTIFUL
PATTERN

62/60p, Optical 0

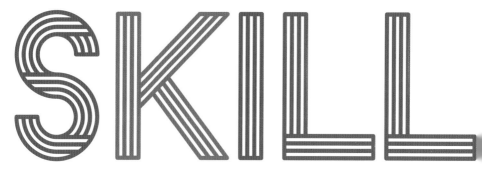

160p, Optical 0

BROSHK-FRUITS

BroshK Lime/Oragne/Plum 68p, 0

BROSHK LIME

BROSHK ORANGE

BROSHK PLUM

50/50p, 0

ABCDEFGHIJKLMNOPQRSTUVWXYZ
1234567890 + – * / = ! # % ~ ? @
‹ › « » ( ) [ ] { } $ ¢ € & , . : ; _ | \

ABCDEFGHIJKLMNOPQRSTUVWXYZ
1234567890 + – * / = ! # % ~ ? @
‹ › « » ( ) [ ] { } $ ¢ € & , . : ; _ | \

ABCDEFGHIJKLMNOPQRSTUVWXYZ
1234567890 + – * / = ! # % ~ ? @
‹ › « » ( ) [ ] { } $ ¢ € & , . : ; _ | \

28/25, 0

| License | Open Font License |
| Font tag | Color, Sans Serif, Gradient, Heading |

| Link | www.glukfonts.pl/font.php?font=BroshK-fruits |
| Note | 겹친 그림자 효과로 컬러 폰트의 장점을 살린 SVG 폰트 |

AT ANY RATE, THAT IS HAPPINESS; TO BE DISSOLVED INTO SOMETHING COMPLETE AND GREAT.

31.1, 30.6, 46.7p, -25

LIME is GREEN
ORANGE is ORANGE
PLUM is PURPLE

40/35, 0

FRESH FRUITS

108p, 20 | 103/70, 0

260p, 0

BEAI

License	free
Font tag	Color, Grey

Link www.augetype.com/warehouse/svgfonts/pg01/svg_carve/carve.zip
Note 회색과 흰색 투톤 효과로 부드럽고 우아한 분위기를 내는 SVG 폰트

CARVE

Carve Regular 93p, 0

ABCDEFGHIJKLMN
OPQRSTUVWXYZ

35/35p, 0

ELEGANT
BEHAVIOR

60/60p, Optical 0

FLAT

150p, Optical -50

| License | free |
| Font tag | Color, Lines, Stripe |

| Link | www.augetype.com/warehouse/svgfonts/pg02/svg_colortape/colortape.zip |
| Note | 글자마다 다른 원색 컬러로 화려한 분위기를 조성하는 SVG 폰트 |

Colortape Regular 57p, 0

ABCDEFGHIJKLMN
OPQRSTUVWXYZ
1234567890

37/37p, 0

COLORFUL
WARDROBE

60/60p, Optical 0

134p, Optical 0

ColorTube

ColorTube Regular 42p, 0

ABCDEFFGHIJKLMNOPQRSTUVWX
abcdefghijjklmnooooopqrstuuvvwxy
1234567890 !&?. $£€ ÄËÖÜ

12/23p, 0

ABCDFF
VWXYZ

50/70p, 0

COLOR
STORY

60/80p, -50

License	CC BY 4.0	Link	www.neogrey.com/portfolio/colortube-font
Font tag	Color, Sans Serif, Round, Colorful, Heading	Note	글자마다 다른 원색 컬러로 화려한 SVG 폰트

At any rate That is Happiness
To be dissolved into something
COMPLETE AND GREAT.

14.2, 13.7, 18.2p, -25

Love Yourself

32p, 0

Happiness
is a choice

42/60, 0

50p, 0

| License | free |
| Font tag | Color, Shadow, Curve |

| Link | www.augetype.com/warehouse/svgfonts/pg02/svg_curls/curls.zip |
| Note | 투톤 컬러 커브에 그림자 효과를 적용한 디스플레이용 SVG 폰트 |

CURLS

Curls Regular 127p, 0

ABCDEFGhIJKLM
NOPQRSTUVWXYZ
1234567890

44/44p, 0

DOLL hOUSE

60p, 0

CRAZY

140p, 0

License	free
Font tag	Color, Stripe, Three
Link	www.augetype.com/warehouse/svgfonts/pg01/svg_electricline/electricline.zip
Note	세 가지 컬러 라인과 원으로 화려한 분위기를 만드는 SVG 폰트

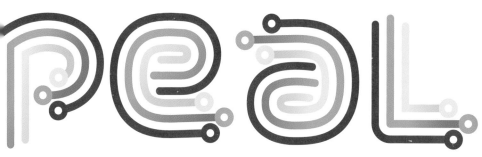

ELECTRICLINE

Electricline Regular 45p, Optical -50

ABCDEFGHIJKLM
NOPQRSTUVWXYZ

34/34p, 0

SEVEN
RAINBOW
COLORS

50p | 60/54p | 88/74p, Optical -50

PEAL

150p, Optical -50

Gilbert Color

Gilbert Color Bold Peview5 68p, 0

Gilbert Bold

Gilbert Color Bold

20/24p, 0

ABCDEFGHIJKLMNOPQRSTUVWXYZ

abcefghijklmnopqrstuvwxyz abc@gmail.com

1234567890 $¢£¥€%& , . : ; +-×= · · · ‹ › « » #§!?/|\

( ) [ ] { } * † ' " ' ' " " – – — — ®©@ ª 1 2 3 º ß ■ ◢

AAA BBB CCC DDD EEE FFF GGG HHH III JJJ KKKKK

LLL MMM NNN OOO PPP QQQ RRR SSS TTT UUU VVV

WWW XXX YYY ZZZ

aaa bbb ccc ddd eee fff ggg hhh iii jjj kkk lllll mmm

nnn ooo ppp qqq rrr sss ttt uuu vvv www xxx yyy zzz

ABCDEFGHIJKLMNOPQRSTUVWXYZ

abcdefghijklmnopqrstuvwxyz abc@gmail.com

111 222 333 444 555 666 777 888 999 000/

1234567890 1234567890 1234567890 1234567890

$$ ¢¢ ££ ¥¥ €€ %% && ,,, ... ::: ;;; +-×= · · · ‹ › « » #§!?/|\

( ) [ ] { } * † ' " ' ' " " – – — — ®©@ ªª 11 22 33 ºº ß ▬ ◰

14/20p, 0

"I loved her against reason, against promise, against peace, against
hope, against happiness, against all discouragement that could be."

— Charles Dickens, Great Expectations

10/14p, 0

| License | CC BY 4.0 |
| Font tag | Color, Sans Serif, Transparent, Colorful |

| Link | www.typewithpride.com |
| Note | 글자마다 다른 컬러로 화려한 분위기를 내는 SVG 폰트 |

Quick brown fox jumps over the lazy dog.
Quick brown fox jumps over the lazy dog.

20/26p, 0

Happiness is a choice.
Happiness is a choice.

38/40p, 0

At any rate, That is Happiness;
To be dissolved into something
COMPLETE AND GREAT.

27.6p-27p-35.4p, 10p

— Willa Cather, My Ántonia

10/14p, 0

250p, -20

| License | free |
| Font tag | Color, Colorful, Line |

| Link | www.augetype.com/warehouse/svgfonts/pg01/svg_koloreen/koloreen.zip |
| Note | 글자마다 다른 다양한 컬러로 화사한 분위기를 내는 SVG 폰트 |

KOLOREEN

Koloreen Regular 82p, 0

ABCDEFGHIJKLMN
OPQRSTUVWXYZ

44/44p, 0

RAINBOW
GEUSTHOUSE

60/60p, 0

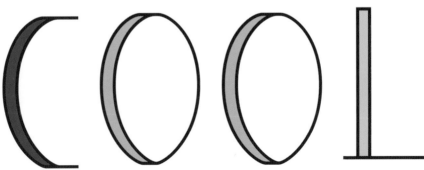

168p, 0

License	free
Font tag	Color, Stripe, Duo
Link	www.augetype.com/warehouse/svgfonts/pg04/svg_modernduo/modernduo.zip
Note	대조적인 두 컬러를 대비시켜 멋진 분위기를 조성할 수 있는 SVG 폰트

MODERN DUO

Modern Duo Regular 54p, 0

ABCDEFGHIJKLM NOPQRSTUVWXYZ

38/38p, 0

ROMANTIC OPERA

50p | 82/70p, 0

140p, Optical 0

MULTICOLORE

Multicolore Pro V2 Regular 36p, 0

ABCDEFFGHIJKLMNOPQRSTUVWXYZ
1234567890 !&? .,-_ $£€ ÀÁÂÄÆÇ

14/25p, 0

ABCDEF
GHIJKLM

50/60p, 0

NOPQR
STUVW
XYZ

60/70p, 0

| License | CC BY 4.0 |
| Font tag | Color, Sans Serif, Round, Colorful |

| Link | www.neogrey.com/portfolio/multicolore-vector-typeface |
| Note | 글자마다 다른 컬러로 화려한 분위기를 내는 SVG 폰트 |

1234567

890!&?$

60/70p, -50

GOOD

MUSIC

80/90P, -50

160P, -50

SING

49

NAMSKOW

Namskow Blue/Green/Orange/White Medium 97p, 0

NAMSKOW-BLUE
NAMSKOW-GREEN
NAMSKOW-ORANGE
NAMSKOW-WHITE

54/42p, 0

ABCDEFGHHIJKKLMMNNO
PQRSTUVWXYYZ!#%~?@$¢
1234567890+-=<>(){}[],.:;

ABCDEFGHHIJKKLMMNNO
PQRSTUVWXYYZ!#%~?@$¢
1234567890+-=<>(){}[],.:;

ABCDEFGHHIJKKLMMNNO
PQRSTUVWXYYZ!#%~?@$¢
1234567890+-=<>(){}[],.:;

ABCDEFGHHIJKKLMMNNO
PQRSTUVWXYYZ!#%~?@$¢
1234567890+-=<>(){}[],.:;

27/21, 220

License	Open Font License	Link	www.glukfonts.pl/font.php?font=Namskow
Font tag	Color, Sans Serif, Overlap, Heading	Note	겹친 효과를 내는 그라데이션 컬러가 적용된 SVG 폰트

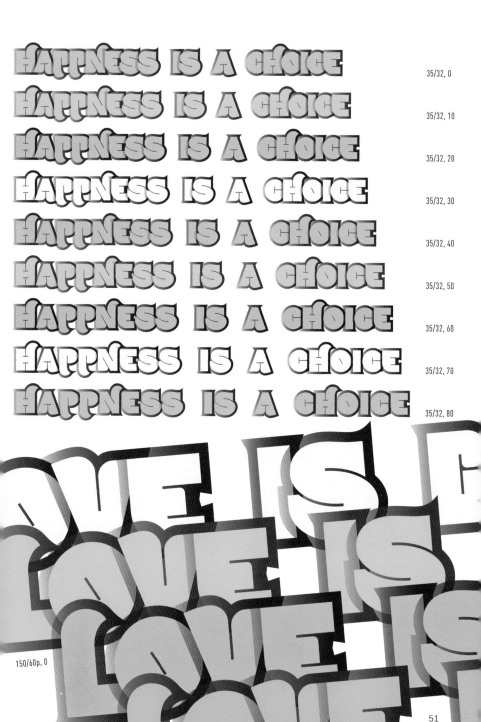

HAPPNESS IS A CHOICE
35/32, 0

HAPPNESS IS A CHOICE
35/32, 10

HAPPNESS IS A CHOICE
35/32, 20

HAPPNESS IS A CHOICE
35/32, 30

HAPPNESS IS A CHOICE
35/32, 40

HAPPNESS IS A CHOICE
35/32, 50

HAPPNESS IS A CHOICE
35/32, 60

HAPPNESS IS A CHOICE
35/32, 70

HAPPNESS IS A CHOICE
35/32, 80

150/60p, 0

NEWPORT

Newport Tracks Colour 61p, 0

NEWPORT TRACKS COLOR
NEWPORT TRACKS GREY DARK
NEWPORT TRACKS GREY LIGHT

20/24p, 0

ABCDEFGHIJKLMN
OPQRSTUVWXYZ
1234567890 +-*/=
!#$%&<>()[]{} ,.'"@

ABCDEFGHIJKLMN
OPQRSTUVWXYZ
1234567890 +-*/=
!#$%&<>()[]{} ,.'"@

ABCDEFGHIJKLMN
OPQRSTUVWXYZ
1234567890 +-*/=
!#$%&<>()[]{} ,.'"@

32/32p, 0

| License | 100% free | Link | www.huebert-world.co/products/newport-tracks-colour-font |
| Font tag | Color, Sans Serif, Pastel, Grey | Note | 파스텔 컬러의 그라데이션 효과를 적용한 SVG 폰트 |

QUICK BROWN FOX JUMPS OVER THE LAZY DOG.

QUICK BROWN FOX JUMPS OVER THE LAZY DOG.

QUICK BROWN FOX JUMPS OVER THE LAZY DOG.

12/18p, 0

DREAM
COME TRUE

DREAM
COME TRUE

DREAM
COME TRUE

DREAM
COME TRUE

DREAM
COME TRUE

DREAM
COME TRUE

38p, 23/27p, 0

250p, Optical -75

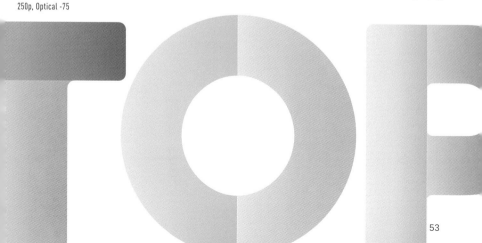

53

License	free
Font tag	Color, Gradiant

Link	www.augetype.com/warehouse/svgfonts/pg06/svg_orthodox/orthodox.zip
Note	부드러운 그라디언트 효과를 적용하여 우아한 느낌의 SVG 폰트

Orthodox Regular 78p, 0

ABCDEFFGHJKLM
NOPQRSTUVWXYZ

46/42p, 0

ARTIFICIAL
INTELLIGENCE

58/50p, 0

162p, 0

License	free
Font tag	Color, Dot, Circle
Link	www.augetype.com/warehouse/svgfonts/pg03/svg_pixel/pixel.zip
Note	작은 원들이 모여서 글자가 이루어진 독특한 모양의 SVG 폰트

Pixel Blue/Green/Red Regular 84p, 0

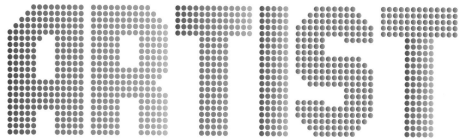

38/38p, 0

SVG 폰트를 윤곽선으로 바꾸고 다른 컬러를 지정할 수 있습니다. 자세한 내용은 17쪽을 참고하기 바랍니다. 아래에서 왼쪽의 예는 'AR'이 하나의 컴파운드 패스에 그라디언트 색상을 적용한 것입니다. 가운데는 'T'와 'I'가 각각 독립적인 컴파운드 패스입니다. 반면에 'S'는 모든 원들이 독립적인 패스로 존재하는 예이며, 'T'는 기둥 부분은 하나의 컴파운드 패스이고 위쪽의 원들은 독립적인 패스들인 예입니다.

140p, 0

Playbox

Playbox Regular 80p, 0

ABCDEFGH!
JKLMNOPQRS
TUVWXYZ
abcdefghijklm
nopqrstuvwxyz
1234567890/\

' " ' " " "

+ - × ÷ = - ; :

! # & ? * ❋ ▽ ◇ ⬦ ( ) [ ]

50/55p, 0

License	free for commercial projects
Font tag	Color, Serif, Decorative, Children, Colorful
Link	www.fontself.com/colorfontweek/2018
Note	아이들의 그림 같이 화려한 컬러의 SVG 폰트

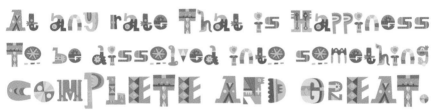

22.3p·21.6p·28.7p, Optical 0

49p, 0

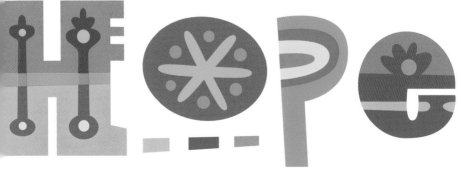

70p, 0

160p, 0

PROSH3 FRUITS

Prosh3-Lime/Orange/Plum/Rubus 89p, 0

PROSH3-COCONUT

PROSH3-LIME

PROSH3-ORANGE

PROSH3-PLUM

PROSH3-RUBUS

40/40p, 0

ABCDEFGHIJKLMNOPQRSTUVWXYZ 1234567890
+ − * / = ! # % & ~ ? @ < > ( ) [ ] { } $ € , . : ; _ | \

ABCDEFGHIJKLMNOPQRSTUVWXYZ 1234567890
+ − * / = ! # % & ~ ? @ < > ( ) [ ] { } $ € , . : ; _ | \

ABCDEFGHIJKLMNOPQRSTUVWXYZ 1234567890
+ − * / = ! # % & ~ ? @ < > ( ) [ ] { } $ € , . : ; _ | \

ABCDEFGHIJKLMNOPQRSTUVWXYZ 1234567890
+ − * / = ! # % & ~ ? @ < > ( ) [ ] { } $ € , . : ; _ | \

ABCDEFGHIJKLMNOPQRSTUVWXYZ 1234567890
+ − * / = ! # % & ~ ? @ < > ( ) [ ] { } $ € , . : ; _ | \

30/28

License	Open Font License
Font tag	Color, Sans Serif, Gradient, Heading

Link	www.glukfonts.pl/font.php?font=Prosh3-fruits
Note	그라데이션 효과를 사용한 특이한 SVG 폰트

AT ANY RATE, THAT IS HAPPINESS;
TO BE DISSOLVED INTO SOMETHING
COMPLETE AND GREAT.

45.8, 43.8, 67.1p, -25

LIME is GREEN

ORANGE is ORANGE

PLUM is PURPLE

40/35p, 0

FRESH

FRUITS

100/50p, 20

280p, 0

KOREA

License free
Font tag Color, Neon, Red
Link www.augetype.com/warehouse/svgfonts/pg01/svg_redneon/redneon.zip
Note 네온 컬러 효과를 구현한 멋진 SVG 폰트

RED NEON

Red Neon Regular 58p, 0

ABCDEFGHIJKLM
NOPQRSTUVWXYZ
1234567890.!&

32/32p, 0

BLOODY
COLOR
CRIMSON

60/55p, Optical 0

KARM

100p, Optical 0

License	free
Font tag	Color, Lines

Link	www.augetype.com/warehouse/svgfonts/pg04/svg_threelinear/threelinear.zip
Note	한 글자에 세 가지 컬러를 사용하여 SVG 폰트의 장점을 살린 폰트

THREE LINEAR

Three Linear Regular 42p, 0

ABCDEFGHIJKLM
NOPQRSTUVWXYZ
1234567890

32/32p, 0

VEGA
SIRIUS
CANOPUS

62/60p, Optical 0

STAR

130p, Optical 0

USE YOUR IMAGINATION

UseYourImagination B/G/R Medium 57p, 0

USE YOUR IMAGINATION B
USE YOUR IMAGINATION G
USE YOUR IMAGINATION R

56/46p, 0

ABCDEFGHIJKLMNOPQRST
UVWXYZ1234567890+-*=!
#%~?Q◄►()[]{}$¢£,.:;_|\/

ABCDEFGHIJKLMNOPQRST
UVWXYZ1234567890+-*=!
#%~?Q◄►()[]{}$¢£,.:;_|\/

ABCDEFGHIJKLMNOPQRST
UVWXYZ1234567890+-*=!
#%~?Q◄►()[]{}$¢£,.:;_|\/

31/26, 0
글자 사이에 빈칸 입력

License Open Font License
Font tag Color, Sans Serif, Overlap, Heading

Link www.glukfonts.pl/font.php?font=UseYourImagination
Note 단어를 입력할 때 3가지 종류 글자가 교대로 입력됩니다.

HAPPYNESS IS A CHOICE

44/35, 0

HAPPYNESS IS A CHOICE

44/35, 10

HAPPYNESS IS A CHOICE

44/35, 20

HAPPYNESS IS A CHOICE

44/35, 30

HAPPYNESS IS A CHOICE

44/35, 40

HAPPYNESS IS A CHOICE

44/35, 50

HAPPYNESS IS A CHOICE

44/35, 60

HAPPYNESS IS A CHOICE

44/35, 70

HAPPYNESS IS A CHOICE

44/35, 80

130/60p, 0

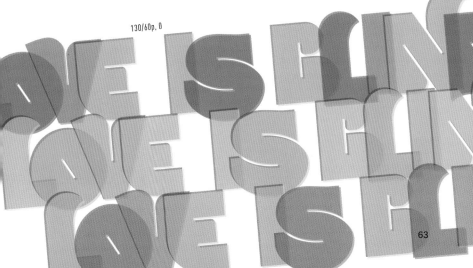

DREAM CHASER

Dream Chaser SVG Regular 78p, 0

ABCDEFGHIJKLMN

OPQRSTUVWXYZ

1234567890

~+-=_,.:;'""*\|/

!#@$%&<>()[]{}

60/60p, 0

SHADE

200p, 0

| **License** | Free for commercial project | **Link** | setsailstudios.com/downloads/dream-chaser-svg-font |
| **Font tag** | SVG, Sans serif, Texture, Watercolor | **Note** | 수묵화처럼 농담이 섬세하게 표현되는 SVG 폰트입니다 |

50p, 0 | 투명도 70%, 내부 광선: 표준 C100 80%, 약하게, 가장자리, 크기 2.5㎜, 경계감소 20%, 노이즈 3%

40p, 50 | 100/80p, 0 | 내부 광선: 표준 C100Y100 80%, 약하게, 가장자리, 크기 3㎜, 경계감소 10%, 노이즈 3%

IVORY HEART

Ivory Heart SVG Regular 68p, 0

ABCDEFGHIJKLMN
OPQRSTUVWXYZ
1234567890
+-=_,.;:'"©\|/
!#Ⓐ$%&<>()[]{}

50/50p, 0

SHADE
SHADE

150p, 0   내부 광선: 표준 M100Y100 80%, 약하게, 가장자리, 크기 3㎜, 경계감소 10%, 노이즈 3%

License	Free for commercial project	Link	setsailstudios.com/ivory-heart-··free-svg-font
Font tag	SVG, Texture, Watercolor	Note	수묵화처럼 농담이 섬세하게 표현되는 SVG 폰트

60p, 0   투명도: 오버레이 100%, 내부 광선: 표준 C20 100%, 약하게, 가장자리, 크기 2㎜, 경계감소 20%, 노이즈 3%

40p, 0   내부 광선: 표준 Y100 100%, 약하게, 가장자리, 크기 1㎜, 경계감소 20%, 노이즈 3%

Macbeth

Macbeth Regular 196p, 0

ABCDEFGHIJKLMNOPQRSTUVWXYZ

abcdefghijklmnopqrstuvwxyz ™ © ®

1234567890 ~ + - × = _ , . : : ' " \ | /

@ ! # $ % & ‹ › ( ) [ ] { } ☠ ✚ • ♥

① ② ③ ④ ⑤ ⑥

46/46p, 0

Soundwave

140p, 0 | ① 18°

License	Free for commercial project
Font tag	SVG, Texture, Brush

Link	www.behance.net/gallery/60517957/MACBETH-FREE-SVG-FONT
Note	거칠고 강한 질감이 생생하게 느껴지는 SVG 폰트

80p, 0 | 60p, 0 | 60p ④   투명도 60%, 내부 광선: 표준 C100Y100K20 80%, 약하게, 가장자리, 크기 2㎜, 경계감소 20%, 노이즈 3%

100p, 50   내부 광선: 표준 용지색 100%, 약하게, 가장자리, 크기 3㎜, 경계감소 20%, 노이즈 3%

Marker-Mark

Text07 Regular 82p, 0

ABCDEFGHIJKLM
NOPQRSTUVWXYZ
abcdefghijklmnopqrstuvwxyz
1234567890+-=,.;:
@!#$%&<>()[]{}\|/*

40/42p, 0

Marker Mark SVG font

Marker Mark is my first SVG font. Now I think you are wondering what a SVG font is. It's that kind of font that preserves color and transparency. Marker Mark is made by using a marker and a tone of paper, than scaned everything and exported to photoshop. There everything is cleaned and with the help of Fontself the SVG font is created.

40p, 0 | 20/22p, 0

License	Free for commercial project	Link	www.graphicdelivery.com/marker-mark-svg-font
Font tag	SVG, Texture, Brush, Handwritten	Note	파일명은 Marker-Mark.otf이지만 앱에서 폰트명은 Text07

30p, 0   투명도 80%

60p, 0   내부 광선: 표준 C100 80%, 약하게, 가장자리, 크기 2㎜, 경계감소 20%, 노이즈 3%

Surging

Surging Regular 180p, 0

ABCDEFGHIJKLMNOPQRSTUVWXYZ

abcdefghijklmnopqrstuvwxyz 1234567890

! # $ % & ( ) [ ] { } \ | / @ + - x ÷ = * © ® , . ; :

32/40p, 0

Strive for greatness.

What we think, we become.

Die with memories, not dreams.

Yesterday you said Tomorrow. Just

45/45p, 0

Yesterday you said Tomorrow. Just

45/45p, 0   내부 광선: 표준 M100Y100 100%, 약하게, 가장자리, 2mm, 경계감소 20%, 노이즈 3%

| License | Free for commercial use | Link | www.pixelsurplus.com/freebies/surging-svg-free-hand-drawn-font |
| Font tag | SVG, Texture, Handwritten | Note | 질감이 섬세한 필기체 SVG 폰트. 가독성이 낮은 것이 단점 |

40p, 0 내부 광선: 표준 용지색 100%, 정밀하게, 가장자리, 크기 2㎜, 경계감소 10%, 노이즈 3%
외부 광선: 표준 용지색 50%, 정밀하게, 크기 0.3㎜, 경계감소 0%, 노이즈 0%

45p, 0 내부 광선: 표준 Y100 100%, 정밀하게, 가장자리, 크기 2㎜, 경계감소 10%, 노이즈 3%
외부 광선: 표준 용지색 50%, 정밀하게, 크기 0.3㎜, 경계감소 0%, 노이즈 0%

THRONE

THRONE Regular 70p, -10

ABCDEFGHIJKLM
NOPQRSTUVWXYZ
1234567890-=.,,.
!?$%()[]{}/@&®©TM*'

30/35p, 0

OLIMPICS 2020

39p, -25

ROAD TO THE THRONE

25p, -50   내부 광선: 표준 M10Y100 100%, 약하게, 가장자리,크기 2mm, 경계감소 20%, 노이즈 3%

License	Free for commercial use	Link	pinspiry.com/throne-free-font
Font tag	SVG, Texture, Brush, Handwritten	Note	큰 붓으로 굵고 짧게 쓴 것 같은, 텍스쳐가 확실한 SVG 폰트

45/45내부광선: 표준 용지색 100%, 약하게, 가장자리, 크기 2㎜, 경계감소 20%, 노이즈 3%

45p. -10   내부 광선: 표준 M80Y50 100%, 약하게, 가장자리, 크기 2㎜, 경계감소 20%, 노이즈 3%

White Christmas

White Christmas Regular 51p, 0

ABCDEFGHIJKLM
NOPQRSTUVWXYZ
abcdefghijklm
nopqrstuvwxyz
1234567890+-,.;'
!$%&<>()[]/@©®™

38/38p, 0

Decorate your Christmas with joy!
Wishing you a very Merry Christmas.
Merry Christmas and a Happy New Year!
Wishing you a magical and blissful holiday!
Warmest wishes for a happy holiday season.
Merry up and have your best Christmas ever
May your days be filled with magic and chee
Thinking of you with lots of love at Christm

20/25p, -10

License	Free for commercial use	Link	www.behance.net/gallery/76849043/Free-White-Christmas-SVG-font
Font tag	SVG, Serif, Brush, Handpainting	Note	SVG 폰트의 특성을 활용하여 만든 크리스마스용 폰트

40p, 0　　투명도: 10%, 그림자: 표준 검정 100%, 거리 0.7㎜, 135°, 크기 1㎜, 스프레드 10%, 노이즈 3%

40p, 0　　내부 광선: 표준 C40Y40 100%, 약하게, 가장자리, 크기 2㎜, 경계감소 40%, 노이즈 3%

AEMSTEL

Aemstel Regular 67p, 0

Regular 35p, 0 Line Inside 35p, 0 Line Outside 35p, 0 Line Horizontal 35p, 0 Shadow 35p, 0

| License | Free for commercial use |
| Font tag | Sans serif, Layered, Sign, Retro |

| Link | befonts.com/aemstel-font-family.html |
| Note | 5개 폰트로 복구풍 분위기를 낼 수 있는 레이어드 폰트 |

ABCDEFGHIJKLM
NOPRSTUVWXYZ
1234567890!?$&(),.

36/36p, 0

Line Inside + Line Outside + Regular 40p, 0
Y=+0.4mm   Y=+0.4mm

LAYERED FONT

Line Outside + Regular + Shadow 40p, 0
Y=+0.4mm

FREE FONT

Regular + Line Outside + Regular 55p, 0
Y=+0.6mm   X=+1.2mm
                  Y=+1.7mm

FREE FONT

텍스트 프레임을 윤곽선으로 변환하여 컴파운드 패스를 만들고 그것을
선택한 상태에서 이미지를 가져오면 글자 내부에 이미지가 놓입니다.

Regular(image) + Line Outside + Regular 55p, 0
Y=+0.6mm   X=+1.2mm
                  Y=+1.7mm

BERG WESTERN

Berg Western Regular 44p, 0

BERG WESTERN ROUGH

Berg Western Rough Regular 44/48p, 0

BERG REUGLAR

Berg Regular 44p, 0

Berg Regular 35p, -50   Berg Inline 35p, -50   Berg Shadow 35p, -50   Berg Extrude 35p, -50   Berg Inner Ornament 35p,

BERG + BERG = BERG

BERG + BERG = BERG

BERG + BERG = BERG

BERG + BERG = BERG

BERG + BERG + = BERG

BERG + + BERG = BERG

| License | Free for commercial use |
| Font tag | Sans serif, Layered, Vintage, Sign |

| Link | www.dafontfree.io/berg-font-family-free |
| Note | 4개 폰트로 빈티지 분위기를 낼 수 있는 레이어드 폰트 |

AaBbCcDdEeFfGgHhIiJjKk
LlMmNnOoPpQqRrSsTtUu
VvWwXxYyZz 1234567890
+−×÷= _,.;:°✝ \|/ ©®™¶^
!#@$%&<>《》()[]{} ‴″''""

Berg Western Regular 32/32p, 0

AaBbCcDdEeFfGgHhIiJjKk
LlMmNnOoPpQqRrSsTtUu
VvWwXxYyZz 1234567890
+−×÷= _,.;:°✝ \|/ ©®™¶^
!#@$%&<>《》()[]{} ‴″''""

Berg Western Rough Regular 32/32p, 0

AaBbCcDdEeFfGgHhIiJjKk
LlMmNnOoPpQqRrSsTtUu
VvWwXxYyZz 1234567890
+−×÷= _,.;:°✝ \|/ ©®™¶^
!#@$%&<>《》()[]{} ‴″''""

Berg Regular 32/32p, 0

81

BUNGEE REGULAR
BUNGEE HAIRLINE
BUNGEE INLINE
BUNGEE OUTLINE
BUNGEE SHADE

겹치지 않고 사용하는 Bungee 폰트 5종

Bungee Regular/Hairline/Inline/Outline/Shade 34/34p, 0

LAYERED FONT

Bungee Hairline 42p, 0

LAYERED FONT

Bungee Regular 42p, 0

THE GOOD FONT

Bungee Inline 40p, 0

FREE FONT

Bungee Outline 59p, 0

FONT

Bungee Shade 106p, 0

| License | Open Font License |
| Font tag | Sans serif, Layered, Bold, Sign |

| Link | https://djr.com/bungee |
| Note | 세로쓰기 폰트가 포함된 대규모 레이어드 폰트 |

Bungee Hairline 17/20p, 0

ABCDEFGHIJKLMNOPQRSTUVWXYZ
AAEEIILLMMNNXXKYY1234567890
!?#$%&<>()[]{}@©®™\||/+-=''''""||||

Bungee Regular 17/20p, 0

ABCDEFGHIJKLMNOPQRSTUVWXYZ
AAEEIILLMMNNXXKYY1234567890
!?#$%&<>()[]{}@©®™\||/+-=''''""||||

Bungee Inline 17/20p, 0

ABCDEFGHIJKLMNOPQRSTUVWXYZ
AAEEIILLMMNNXXKYY1234567890
!?#$%&<>()[]{}@©®™\||/+-=''''""||||

Bungee Outline 17/20p, 0

Bungee Shade 17/20p, 0

BUNGEE REGULAR
BUNGEE INLINE
BUNGEE OUTLINE
BUNGEE SHADE

겹쳐서 사용하는 Bungee Layers 폰트 4종

LAYERED FONT

LAYERED FONT

텍스트 프레임을 윤곽선으로 변환하여 컴파운드 패스를 만들고 그것을
선택한 상태에서 이미지를 가져오면 글자 내부에 이미지가 놓입니다.

FREE FONT

다양한 기호를 사용하면 재미 있는 효과를 얻을 수 있습니다.

FONT

License	Open Font License
Font tag	Sans serif, Layered, Bold, Sign

Link	https://djr.com/bungee
Note	세로쓰기 폰트가 포함된 대규모 레이어드 폰트

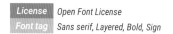

ABCDEFGHIJKLMNOPQRSTUVWXYZ
AAEEIILLMMNNXXXYY1234567890
!?#$%&<>(){}[]{}@©®™\||/+-=''""''''IIII

Bungee Layers Regular 17/20p, 0

ABCDEFGHIJKLMNOPQRSTUVWXYZ
AAEEIILLMMNNXXXYY1234567890
!?#$%&<>(){}[]{}@©®™\||/+-=''""''''IIII

Bungee Layers Inline 17/20p, 0

ABCDEFGHIJKLMNOPQRSTUVWXYZ
AAEEIILLMMNNXXXYY1234567890
!?#$%&<>(){}[]{}@©®™\||/+-=''""''''IIII

Bungee layers Outline 17/20p, 0

ABCDEFGHIJKLMNOPQRSTUVWXYZ
AAEEIILLMMNNXXXYY1234567890
!?#$%&<>(){}[]{}@©®™\||/+-=''''''''''

Bungee Layers Shade 17/20p, 0

Bungee Layers Rotated
Outline 22/27p, 0

Bungee Layers Rotated
Inline 22/27p, 0

Bungee Layers Rotated
Regular 22/27p, 0

겹쳐서 사용할 수 있도록 만든 4개의 세로 방향 Bungee Layers 폰트

| License | Open Font License |
| Font tag | Sans serif, Layered, Bold, Sign |

| Link | https://djr.com/bungee |
| Note | 세로쓰기 폰트가 포함된 대규모 레이어드 폰트 |

Bungee Layers Roatated
Inline + Outline + Regular 40p, 0
X=-3mm
Y=-9.6mm

텍스트 프레임을 윤곽선으로 변환하
여 컴파운드 패스를 만들고 그것을
선택한 상태에서 이미지를 가져오면
글자 내부에 이미지가 놓입니다.

Bungee Layers Roatated
Inline + Regular + Shade + Regular 40p, 0
50%   X=-0.8mm
       Y=-6mm

Bungee Layers Roatated
Regular 36p + Regular 34p + Regular 39p, -75
X=-0.7mm
Y=-0.3mm   Y=-5.5mm

FIXER REGULAR

FIXER DISPLAY

FIXER DISPLAY FILL

FIXER INLINE

FIXER LINE

FIXER OUTLINE

FIXER 3D

Fixer 70/40p, 0

FREE LAYERED FONT

Line + Regular 80p, -50

LAYERED FONT

Inline + Outline + Regular + 3D 111p, -50
Y=+0.8mm

FREE FONT

Display Fill + Regular 158p, -50
Y=+0.5mm

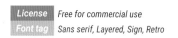 **License** Free for commercial use
Font tag Sans serif, Layered, Sign, Retro

 Link www.pixelsurplus.com/freebies/fixer-free-layered-type-system
Note 7개 폰트로 다양한 분위기를 조성할 수 있는 레이어드 폰트

ABCDEFGHIJKLMNOPQRSTUVWXYZ
1234567890!#$%&?+-×÷=,.:""\/()[]

Fixer Regular 41/26p, 0

ABCDEFGHIJKLMNOPQRSTUVWXYZ
1234567890!#$%&?+-×÷=,.:""\/()[]

Fixer Display 41/26p, 0

ABCDEFGHIJKLMNOPQRSTUVWXYZ
1234567890!#$%&?+-×÷=,.:""\/()[]

Fixer Display Fill 41/26p, 0

ABCDEFGHIJKLMNOPQRSTUVWXYZ
1234567890!#$%&?+-×÷=,.:""\/()[]

Fixer Inline 41/26p, 0

ABCDEFGHIJKLMNOPQRSTUVWXYZ
1234567890!#$%&?+-×÷=,.:""\/()[]

Fixer Line 41/26p, 0

ABCDEFGHIJKLMNOPQRSTUVWXYZ
1234567890!#$%&?+-×÷=,.:""\/()[]

Fixer Outline 41/26p, 0

ABCDEFGHIJKLMNOPQRSTUVWXYZ
1234567890!#$%&?+-×÷=,.:""\/()[]

Fixer 3D 41/26p, 0

A first complete display
of the

GARAMOND
Series

after the beautiful XVIth century types
of Claude Garamond,
together with

Garamond Italic

1540-1923

Embellished with the

CLELAND BORDERS AND ORNAMENTS
especially designed for these letters
by T. M. CLELAND

역사적으로 유명한 폰트 20종의 대안 폰트들

타이포그래피의 역사에서 중요한 역할을 맡았거나 한때 널리 사용되었던 영문 폰트 20종을 소개합니다. 디자이너로 활동한다면 언젠가 이 폰트들을 만날 기회가 있을 것입니다. 이들은 워낙 유명한 폰트들이어서 많은 수의 패밀리 폰트로 구성되며 가격도 비쌉니다. 다행스럽게도 이들과 유사한 폰트들이 있고 그 중에는 무료 폰트도 있습니다. 유명한 폰트의 유래와 특징을 간단하게 소개하고 그와 유사한 느낌을 표현할 수 있는 무료 폰트를 소개합니다. 다만, 무료 폰트는 유료 폰트보다 패밀리 폰트의 수가 부족합니다.

1. Garamond (Claude Garamond, 1530)
2. Baskerville (John Baskerville, 1757)
3. Didot (Firmin Didot, 1784-1811)
4. Bodoni (Giambattista Bodoni, 1790)
5. Akzidenz Grotesk (Brethold Type Foundry, 1898)
6. Franklin Gothic (Morris Fuller Benton, 1902-1967)
7. News Gothic (Morris Fuller Benton, 1908)
8. Futura (Paul Renner, 1927)
9. Gill Sans (Eric Gill, 1928)
10. Bembo (Aldus Manutius, Francesco Griffo, 1929)
11. Times New Roman (Stanley Morison, 1931)
12. Rockwell (Monotype Foundry, 1934)
13. Helvetica (Max Miedinger, 1957)
14. Sabon (Jan Tschichold, 1967)
15. Frutiger (Adrian Frutiger, 1977)
16. Minion (Rober Slimbach, 1990)
17. Myriad (Robert Slimbach, Carol Twombly, 1992)
18. Georgia (Matthew Carter, 1993)
19. Mrs Eaves (Zuzana Licko, 1996)
20. Gotham (Hoefler and Frere-Jones, 2000)

Garamond

Adobe Garamond Pro Bold 76p, 0

Garamond

EB Garamond Bold 76p, 0

1530년: 고전적인 올드 스타일의 아름다운 폰트, 가라몬드

가라몬드는 16세기의 활자 조각가 클로드 가라몬드*Claude Garamond, 1480-1561*가 만든 고전적 스타일의 세리프 폰트입니다. 폰트의 이름을 제작자의 이름으로 한 최초의 폰트이기도 합니다. 가라몬드 폰트는 펜으로 쓴 글씨를 기본으로 하되 일관성과 가독성을 높이고 새로 등장한 인쇄 기술에 적합한 형태로 디자인되었습니다. 가라몬드 폰트는 유럽에서 한동안 아름답고 편안한 본문용 폰트로, 품격 있는 제목용 폰트로 인기가 높았습니다.

1984년 애플이 자사의 새로운 기업 폰트로 애플 가라몬드(폭을 좁히고 x 높이는 늘려서 날씬하게 변형)를 사용하면서 가라몬드 폰트는 더욱 유명해졌습니다. 애플 로고 옆에는 항상 애플 가라몬드 폰트로 글자를 표기했으며 'Think different' 같은 유명 광고, 매뉴얼, 상품 라벨 등에도 사용되어 거의 20년 동안 애플을 상

징하며 현대적이면서도 친숙한 브랜드 이미지를 만드는데 도움을 주었습니다.

마이폰츠닷컴*myfonts.com*을 보면 ITC Garamond 폰트는 1개당 35달러, 26개 폰트로 구성되어 있으며 Linotype의 Stempel Garamond 폰트는 1개당 35달러, 8개 폰트로 구성되어 있습니다. 어도비 폰트 서비스를 이용하고 있다면 Adobe Garamond *fonts.adobe.com/fonts/adobe-garamond* 폰트(6개 폰트 패밀리)를 무료로 사용할 수 있습니다. 가라몬드를 대체할 수 있는 무료 폰트로는 EB Garamond 폰트가 있습니다. EB Garamond 폰트는 구글 폰트에 있으며 10개의 폰트 파일로 구성됩니다.

Baskerville

Baskerville Display PT Bold 69p, 0

Baskerville

Libre Baskerville Bold 57p, 0

1757년: 올드 스타일에서 모던 스타일로, 바스커빌 폰트

바스커빌은 1757년에 영국의 존 바스커빌*John Baskerville, 1706-1775*이 디자인한 세리프 폰트입니다. 올드 스타일에서 모던 스타일로 넘어가는 대표적인 과도기 스타일이라고 합니다. 당시 영국에서 유행하던 올드 스타일보다 세리프는 얇고 날카롭게, 곡선은 원형으로 바뀌며 일관성이 증가하는 등 여러 가지 변화가 일어났습니다. 바스커빌 폰트의 주요한 특징은 '원형'과 '날카로운 절단'입니다.

고전적인 아름다움에 통일성이 더해진 바스커빌 폰트이지만 당시 영국에서는 인기가 높지는 않았다고 합니다. 하지만 우아한 모양, 적절한 굵기, 대문자와 소문자 높이의 적절한 비율 등으로 가독성이 좋은 폰트였으며 20세기에 들어와 리바이벌되면서 인기가 더욱 높아졌습니다. 본문과 제목 모두에 잘 어울리는 폰트입니다.

마이폰츠닷컴*myfonts.com*을 보면 Bitstream의 Baskerville 폰트는 1개당 29달러, 4개 폰트로 구성되어 있으며 URW Type Foundry의 Baskerville 폰트는 1개당 19.95달러, 5개 폰트로 구성되어 있습니다. 어도비 폰트 서비스를 이용하고 있다면 Baskerville PT *fonts.adobe.com/fonts/baskerville-pt* 폰트(6개 폰트 패밀리)를 무료로 사용할 수 있습니다. 가라몬드를 대체할 수 있는 무료 폰트로는 Libre Baskerville 폰트가 있습니다. Libre Baskerville 폰트는 구글 폰트에 있으며 3개의 폰트 파일로 구성됩니다.

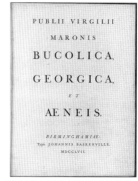

바커스빌 폰트가 처음 사용된 출판물

Didot

Didot LT Pro Roman 76p, 0

Didot

Prata Regular 72p, 0

1784-1811년: 모던 스타일의 고급스러운 디도 세리프 폰트

디도는 인쇄기 제조사로 유명한 프랑스 가문의 이름에서 유래한 이름의 폰트입니다. 손으로 쓴 것이 아니라 부품을 조립한 느낌이라서 모던 스타일의 네오클라식 세리프 폰트 혹은 디돈didone으로 분류됩니다. 가장 유명한 디돈 폰트들은 1784년과 1811년 사이에 개발되었습니다.

바스커빌 폰트의 영향을 받은 디도 폰트는 굵은 획과 가는 획의 두께가 차이가 많이 나고, 기둥의 폭이 좁아지고, 동그라미의 중심축이 수직 방향으로 설정되며, 세리프가 납작한 직각 모양이 되는 특징을 보입니다. 이것은 보도니와 유사한 스타일입니다.

현재에 이르러 디도 폰트는 전통과 품위를 표현하는 느낌을 풍깁니다. 그 독특한 구조와 스트로크 때문에 주로 로고와 제목에 많이 사용됩니다. 가장 대표적인 사례로는 1955년부터 잡지의 제호로 커스텀 디도 폰트를 사용한 보그Vogue 잡지, 2019년에 자간을 좁혀 글자가 겹쳐지게 만든 로고를 사용한 자라Zara 브랜드를 들 수 있습니다.

마이폰츠닷컴myfonts.com을 보면 Linotype Didot 폰트는 1개당 35달러, 10개 폰트로 구성되어 있으며 DietDidot 폰트는 1개당 30달러, 9개 폰트로 구성되어 있습니다. 어도비 폰트 서비스를 이용하고 있다면 Linotype Didot fonts.adobe.com/fonts/linotype-didot 폰트(5개 폰트 패밀리)를 무료로 사용할 수 있습니다. 디도 폰트를 대체할 수 있는 무료 폰트로는 Prata 폰트가 있습니다. Prata 폰트는 구글 폰트에 있으며 아쉽게도 1개의 폰트 파일로 구성됩니다.

Bodoni

Bodoni

1790년: 우아한 카리스마로 고급 브랜드를 접수한 보도니 폰트

보도니는 이탈리아의 잠바티스타 보도니*Giambattista Bodoni 1740–1813*가 18세기 후반에 디자인한 폰트입니다. 보도니 폰트는 당시 향상된 인쇄기술을 고려하여 과거에는 표현하기 어렵던 가는 획을 도입해서 대비를 높였는데 그 덕분에 기하학적인 느낌이 강해졌습니다. 보도니는 로마나 르네상스 문자 스타일을 개선한 것이 아니라 새로운 디자인이었습니다. 그래서 디도 폰트와 함께 대표적인 모던 세리프 폰트로 분류됩니다. 여기에서 모던하다는 것은 17세기를 기준으로 새롭다는 표현입니다.

우아한 느낌의 보도니 폰트는 본문용으로는 적합하지 않지만 제목과 로고에 많이 사용됩니다. 엘르, 엘리자베스 아덴, 조르지오 아르마니, 캘빈 클라인과 같은 럭셔리 브랜드의 로고에, 하퍼 바자르와 메트로폴리스 같은 잡지의 기본 폰트로 사용되고 있습니다. 특히 패션 잡지에 많이 사용되는데 그들은 얇고 미세한 획을 멋지게 인쇄할 수 있는 고광택 용지를 사용하기 때문입니다.

마이폰츠닷컴*myfonts.com*을 보면 Linotype의 Bodoni 폰트는 1개당 35달러, 14개 폰트로 구성되어 있으며 Bitstream의 Bodoni 폰트는 1개당 29달러, 7개 폰트로 구성되어 있습니다. 어도비 폰트 서비스를 이용하고 있다면 Bodoni URW *fonts.adobe.com/fonts/bodoni-urw* 폰트(10개 폰트 패밀리)를 무료로 사용할 수 있습니다. 보도니를 대체할 수 있는 무료 폰트로는 Libre Bodoni 폰트가 있습니다. Libre Bodoni 폰트는 4개의 폰트 파일로 구성됩니다.

Akzidenz

Aktiv Grotesk Regular 76p, 0

Akzidenz

Manrope Regular 74p, -20

1898년: 신 타이포그래피의 대표적 폰트, 악치덴츠 그로테스크

악치덴츠 그로테스크*Akzidenz Grotesk*는 19세기 후반에 독일에서 널리 사용되던 단순하고 간결한 산세리프 폰트입니다. 단어의 의미도 밋밋해서 상업인쇄용 산세리프 폰트라는 뜻 입니다. 악치덴츠 그로테스크 폰트의 탄생 역사는 좀 복잡합니다. 간단하게 줄이면 베르 톨트*Berthold* 가문이 1898년에 해당 폰트의 특허를 취득했다고 합니다.

악치덴츠 그로테스크 폰트는 장식을 모두 덜어내 알파벳의 기본 형태를 드러내고 획의 굵기와 글자 폭을 일정하게 고른 것이 특징입니다. 초창기 시절에는 이탤릭 폰트도 없었 다고 합니다.

1950년대부터 많은 그래픽 디자이너들이 악치덴츠 그로테스크 폰트를 심플하고 읽기 쉬운 폰트로 선호하게 되었고, 그 단순하고 중립적인 디자인은 후대에 많은 영향을 미쳤 습니다. 디자이너 개인의 성향이 드러나지 않는 보편적인 형태이면서 우수한 조형성을 가 진 산세리프 서체인 악치덴츠 그로테스크는 20세기 모더니즘 운동의 하나였던 신 타이포 그래피의 대표격인 폰트가 되었습니다. 또한, 나중에 아이폰의 전용 서체가 된 헬베티카 *Helvetica* 폰트의 전신이기도 합니다.

Akzidenz-Grotesk www.bertholdtypes.com 폰트는 Normal, Condensed, Extended 각 10 개씩 30개의 폰트로 구성되어 있으며 있습니다. 어도비 폰트 서비스를 이용하고 있다면 Aktiv Grotesk fonts.adobe.com/fonts/aktiv-grotesk 폰트(48개 폰트 패밀리)를 무료로 사용할 수 있 습니다. 대체할 수 있는 무료 폰트로는 Manrope 폰트(7개 폰트 패밀리)가 있습니다.

Franklin

Franklin Gothic URW Book 76p, 0

Franklin

Libre Franklin Regular 69p, 0

1902-1967년: 산세리프 폰트의 대중화를 이끈 프랭클린 고딕 폰트

프랭클린 고딕*Franklin Gothic*은 1903년에 미국의 ATF*American Type Founders Company*사의 수석 디자이너 모리스 풀러 벤튼*Morris Fuller Benton 1878-1956*이 디자인한 산세리프 폰트입니다. 기존의 신세리프 폰트들은 굵기와 모양에 일관성이 부족하다는 단점이 있었는데 프랭클린 고딕 폰트의 일관성과 균형이 좋아졌습니다. 그 덕분에 광고와 신문 기사의 헤드라인은 물론이고 책에서부터 광고판까지 다양한 곳에 사용되었고, 미국에서 산세리프 폰트가 널리 사용되는 계기를 만들었습니다.

1930년대에 잠시 인기가 식었지만 1940년대에 다시 관심이 높아진 이후 계속하여 높은 인기를 유지하고 있습니다. 또한 여러 회사에서 새로운 버전을 디자인하여 다양한 프랭클린 고딕이 만들어졌습니다. 그 중에서 가장 많이 알려진 것은 빅터 카루소*Victor Caruso*가 만든 ITC 프랭클린 고딕 폰트입니다. 이 폰트의 일부는 마이크로소프트 윈도우에 번들되기도 했습니다.

마이폰츠닷컴*myfonts.com*을 보면 URW Type Foundry의 Franklin Gothic 폰트는 1개당 19.95달러, 23개 폰트로 구성되어 있으며 Bitstream의 Franklin Gothic 폰트는 1개당 29달러, 4개 폰트로 구성되어 있습니다. 어도비 폰트 서비스를 이용하고 있다면 Franklin Gothic URW *fonts.adobe.com/fonts/franklin-gothic-urw* 폰트(22개 폰트 패밀리)를 무료로 사용할 수 있습니다. 프래클린 고딕 폰트를 대체할 수 있는 무료 폰트로는 Libre Franklin 폰트가 있습니다. Libre Franklin 폰트는 구글 폰트에 있으며 18개의 폰트 파일로 구성됩니다.

News Gothic

News Gothic Std Medium 58p, 0

News Gothic

News Cycle Bold 62.5p, 0

1908년: 20세기의 뉴스를 전달한 가벼운 폰트, 뉴스 고딕

뉴스 고딕은 모리스 풀러 벤튼(앞 페이지 프랭클린 고딕 폰트 참조)이 1908년에 디자인한 산세리프 폰트이며 ATF가 판매하였습니다. 뉴스 고딕은 프랭클린 고딕과 구조와 비례가 비슷하지만 더 가벼운 모양입니다.

20세기 초반 북미에서는 산세리프 폰트를 '고딕'이라고 불렀으며, 독일에서는 '그로테스크'라고 불렀습니다. 모리스 벤튼이 만든 다른 폰트들처럼, 뉴스 고딕도 세리프 폰트를 흉내낸 그로테스크 스타일을 따르고 있습니다. 예를 들면 글자 모양은 간결하고 디센더는 길지 않고 짧습니다. 뉴스 고딕 폰트는 20세기 내내 신문과 잡지에서 사용되었고, 헤드라인을 위해 글자 폭이 좁은 스타일(condensed, extra-condensed)들이 추가되었습니다.

ATF가 디지털 폰트를 만들지 않기 때문에 여러 회사들이 다양한 뉴스 고딕 폰트들을 만들었습니다. 그중에서도 뉴스 고딕에 다양한 스타일(폭이 넓거나 매우 굵은)을 추가하여 거대한 패밀리를 구성하여 널리 사용되었던 폰트가 벤튼 샌스(1995년)입니다. 벤튼 샌스 폰트는 뉴스위크, 포춘, 보스톤 글로브 등 다양한 매체에서 사용하였습니다.

마이폰츠닷컴*myfonts.com*을 보면 URW Type Foundry의 News Gothic 폰트는 1개당 19.95달러, 14개 폰트로 구성되어 있습니다. 어도비 폰트 서비스를 이용하고 있다면 News Gothic *fonts.adobe.com/fonts/news-gothic* 폰트(4개 폰트 패밀리)를 무료로 사용할 수 있습니다. 대체 무료 폰트로는 News Cycle 폰트가 있습니다. News Cycle 폰트는 1908년 디자인을 바탕으로 만들어졌으며 구글 폰트에 2개의 폰트 파일로 구성되어 있습니다.

Futura

Futura PT Book 70p, 0

Futura

Spartan Medium 52p, 0

1927년: 기하학적 산세리프 폰트의 대명사 푸투라

푸투라는 독일의 파울 레너*Paul Renner 1878-1956*가 뉴 프랑크푸르트 프로젝트를 위해 디자인한 산세리프 폰트입니다. 그는 이전 세대의 산세리프 폰트 스타일(그로테스크)을 거부하고 기하학적인 모양(원, 삼각형, 사각형)을 모티브로 삼고 시각적인 대비를 낮추기 위해 획의 두께를 균일하게 만들었습니다. 당시 유행하던 바우하우스 디자인 스타일을 따른 것입니다.

매력적인 기하학적 산세리프 폰트인 푸투라의 특징은 효율과 진보성입니다. 장식을 모두 제거한 기하학적 아름다움을 추구합니다. 푸투라는 독일에서 태어났지만 미국의 디자이너와 광고주들을 매혹시켰습니다. 푸투라 폰트가 사용된 가장 유명한 광고는 나이키의 JUST DO IT 광고입니다. 푸투라 Extra Bold Condensed 폰트는 나이키를 떠올리게 하는 상징이 되었습니다. 보그, 루이비통, 스위스항공, 폭스뉴스, 앱솔루트보드카, 이케아, 폭스바겐, 휴렛팩커드, NASA 등 많은 기업이 푸투라 폰트를 사용하였습니다.

마이폰츠닷컴*myfonts.com*을 보면 Linotype의 Futura 폰트는 1개당 35달러, 43개 폰트로 구성되어 있으며 Bitstream의 Futura 폰트는 1개당 29달러, 20개 폰트로 구성되어 있습니다. 어도비 폰트 서비스를 이용하고 있다면 Futura PT *fonts.adobe.com/fonts/futura-pt* 폰트(22개 폰트 패밀리)를 무료로 사용할 수 있습니다. 푸투라 폰트를 대체할 수 있는 무료 폰트로는 **Spartan** 폰트가 있습니다. Spartan 폰트는 구글 폰트에 있으며 9개의 폰트 파일로 구성됩니다.

Gill Sans

Gill Sans Nova Book 76p, 0

Gill Sans

Gillius ADF No2 Regular 76p, 0

1928년: 영국의 헬베티카, 길 산스 폰트

독일에서 전통과 단절한 산세리프 폰트 푸투라가 나타났을 때 영국에서는 전통과 소통한 산세리프 폰트 길 산스가 등장했습니다. 길 산스는 에릭 길*Eric Gill 1882–1940*이 디자인하고 모노타입사가 발표한 폰트이며, 당시 유럽에서 유행하던 기하학적 산세리프이면서도 고전적인 세리프 폰트의 속성을 계승한 것이 특징입니다. 길 산스 폰트는 현대의 본문용 폰트와 비교할 때 약간 두꺼운 편입니다.

　'고전적인 단순함과 진정한 아름다움'이라고 홍보된 길 산스 폰트는 포스터와 광고뿐 아니라 시간표나 가격표 등에도 사용할 수 있도록 작은 크기에도 잘 보이도록 설계되었습니다. 길 산스는 영국의 헬베티카로 불리울 정도로 인기가 높았습니다. 영국의 철도청은 길 산스를 표준 폰트로 선택했고 영국다움의 상징으로 국영방송국 BBC의 로고에도 사용되었습니다.

　마이폰츠닷컴*myfonts.com*을 보면 Monotype의 Gill Sans 폰트는 1개당 35달러, 21개 폰트로 구성되어 있습니다. 어도비 폰트 서비스를 이용하고 있다면 Gill Sans Nova *fonts. adobe.com/fonts/gill-sans-nova* 폰트(43개 폰트 패밀리)를 무료로 사용할 수 있습니다. Gill Sans 와 거의 비슷한 대체 무료 폰트는 찾기가 정말 쉽지 않습니다. 검색해보면 구글 폰트에 있는 Cabin이나 Lato 폰트를 추천하는 사람들이 많은데 이들은 조금씩 다른 부분이 있어 아쉽습니다. 한참을 찾아보니 획이 조금 얇긴 하지만 Gillus ADF No2 폰트(8개 폰트 패밀리)가 추천할 만합니다. *www.1001fonts.com/gillius-adf-font.html*

Bembo

Cardo Regualr 76p, 0

Bembo

ETBembo Roman 81p, 0

1929년: 로만 스타일 세리프 폰트의 원조, 벰보

벰보는 1928~1929년에 모노타입의 영국 지사가 본문용으로 만든 세리프 폰트입니다. 벰보 폰트의 원형은 1495년 이탈리아에 있었습니다. 알도 마누치오*Aldo Manuzio*와 프란체스코 그리포*Prancesco Griffo*가 피에트로 벰보 주교의 논문을 출판하기 위해 디자인한 폰트였습니다. 이를 모노타입의 간부이자 인쇄학자 스탠리 모리슨*Stanley Morison*이 주도하여 재현한 것입니다.

벰보는 올드 스타일의 세리프 폰트인데 크고 넉넉한 모양에 크고 과장된 세리프가 붙어 있습니다. 글자의 속공간이 넓어서 본문이 밝아지는 효과가 있습니다. 매력적이고 읽기 쉬운 벰보는 특히 영국에서 책의 본문용 폰트로 오랜 세월동안 인기를 누려왔습니다. 예를 들면, 펭귄 북, 옥스포드 대학 출판부, 캠브리지 대학 출판부, 국립 갤러리, 예일 대학 출판부 등 유명한 출판사들이 벰보 폰트를 사용해 왔습니다.

마이폰츠닷컴*myfonts.com*을 보면 Monotype의 Bembo 폰트는 1개당 35달러, 18개 폰트로 구성되어 있으며 Adobe의 Bembo 폰트는 1개당 35달러, 8개 폰트로 구성되어 있습니다. 어도비 폰트 서비스를 이용하고 있다면 매우 유사한 Cardo *fonts.adobe.com/fonts/cardo* 폰트(3개 폰트 패밀리)를 무료로 사용할 수 있습니다. 벰보 폰트를 대체할 수 있다고 알려진 무료 폰트는 구글 폰트에 있는 EB Garamond 폰트(10개 폰트 패밀리)입니다. 하지만 그보다는 모노타입의 벰보 폰트에 만족하지 못해 드미트리 크라스니*Dmitry Krasny* 등이 만든 ET Book 폰트(5개 폰트 패밀리)가 더 나은 것 같습니다. *edwardtufte.github.io/et-book*

Times New

Times New Roman Regular 70p, 0

Times New

Jomohari Regular 62p, 0

1931년: 가장 인기 있고 널리 사용된 세리프 폰트, 타임스 뉴 로먼

타임스 뉴 로먼*Times New Roman*은 1931년에 모노타입 영국 지사의 스탠리 모리슨*Stanley Morison 1889-1967*이 영국 신문 더 타임스의 의뢰를 받아 레터링 아티스트 빅터 라덴트*Victor Lardent*와 함께 만든 본문용 세리프 폰트입니다. 타임스 뉴 로먼 폰트는 바로크 인쇄의 영향을 받았습니다. 그래서 타임스 뉴 로먼의 초기 명칭은 타임스 올드 스타일이었습니다. 획은 폭이 넓지 않고 어센더와 디센더는 짧으며 소문자 높이가 길어 선명도가 높습니다.

타임스 뉴 로먼 폰트는 신문용으로 만들어졌지만, 당시 더 타임스를 제외한 신문들을 인쇄하는 장비는 이 섬세한 폰트를 문제 없이 다룰 수 없었기에 오히려 출판업계에서 널리 사용되었습니다. 하여튼 타임스 뉴 로먼은 역사상 가장 인기 있고 영향력 있는 폰트 중 하나이며 개인용 컴퓨터의 표준 폰트이기도 합니다.

마이폰츠닷컴*myfonts.com*을 보면 Monotype의 Times New Roman 폰트는 1개당 65달러, 24개 폰트로 구성되어 있으며 Adobe의 Times New Roman 폰트는 1개당 35달러, 7개 폰트로 구성되어 있습니다. 어도비 폰트 서비스를 이용하고 있다면 Liberation Serif *fonts.adobe.com/fonts/liberation-serif* 폰트(4개 폰트 패밀리)를 사용할 수 있습니다. 그런데 Liberation Serif 폰트는 무료이며 *github.com/liberationfonts/liberation-fonts*에서 다운로드할 수 있습니다. Times New Roman의 대체 무료 폰트로는 Liberation Serif(4개 폰트 패밀리)와 구글 폰트에 있는 Lora 폰트(4개 폰트 패밀리)가 추천되지만 모양만 본다면 Jomohari 폰트(1개 폰트)가 더 비슷한 것 같습니다. Jomohari 폰트도 구글 폰트에 있습니다.

Rockwell

Rockwwell Std Regular 76p, 0

Rockwell

Sanchez Regular 75p, -35

1934년: 산세리프 같은 세리프 폰트, 슬래브 스타일의 록웰 폰트

록웰은 모노타입이 1934년에 다시 디자인하여 발표한 슬래브 스타일의 세리프 폰트입니다. 이 프로젝트를 감독한 사람은 모노타입의 엔지니어링 매니저 프랭크 힌만 피어폰트 *Frank Hinman Pierpont 1860-1937*였습니다. 슬래브 스타일은 두꺼운 블록 모양의 세리프와 기둥이 직각으로 연결되는 세리프 폰트입니다. 세리프의 끝은 록웰처럼 직각일 수도 있고 둥근 모양일 수도 있습니다.

록웰 폰트는 모든 획이 거의 같은 폭을 유지하고, O의 모양이 정원에 가까운 기하학적 슬라브 세리프 폰트입니다. 그래서 세리프 폰트임에도 마치 산세리프 폰트와 비슷한 느낌을 줍니다. 이런 특징 때문에 록웰 폰트는 두꺼운 제목용으로 적합하며, 본문에 사용된다면 작은 크기로 사용해야 합니다. 록웰 폰트는 독특한 개성 덕분에 활자판 시대를 지나 디지털 시대에서도 여전히 인기가 높습니다. 많은 디자이너들이 이 폰트를 기네스북 등 다양한 프로젝트에 사용해 왔습니다. 출력 해상도가 낮은 화면에 표시하기 좋은, 산세리프 폰트 같은 세리프 폰트라서 웹사이트에도 적합합니다.

마이폰츠닷컴*myfonts.com*을 보면 Monotype의 Rockwell 폰트는 1개당 35달러, 9개 폰트로 구성되어 있습니다. 어도비 폰트 서비스를 이용하고 있다면 같은 Monotype의 Rockwell *fonts.adobe.com/fonts/rockwell* 폰트(9개 폰트 패밀리)를 무료로 사용할 수 있습니다. 대체 무료 폰트로는 Sanchez 폰트가 있습니다. Sanchez 폰트는 구글 폰트에 2개의 폰트 파일로 구성됩니다.

Helvetica

Helvetica Neue LT Std 75 Bold 76p, 0

Helvetica Helvetica

NimbusSanL Bold 36p, 0   Arimo Bold 36p, 0

1957년: 20세기 모더니즘, 신 타이포그래피의 대표 헬베티카

1950년대에 스위스의 타입 디자이너 맥스 미딩거 *1910-1980*는 당시 널리 사용되고 있던 산세리프 폰트, 악치덴츠 그로테스크에 견줄 정도로 심플하며 읽기 쉬운 산세리프 서체를 만들고 싶었습니다. 악치덴츠 그로테스크는 20세기 모더니즘 운동의 하나였던 신 타이포그래피의 대표격인 폰트였습니다. 맥스 미딩거는 1957년에 하스*Haas* 타입 파운더리를 위해 Neue Haas Grotesk라는 폰트를 만들었는데, 이 회사가 나중에 라이노타입에 인수되면서 폰트의 이름을 Helvetica(스위스의 라틴어 이름인 *Helvetia*에서 유래)로 바꾸게 됩니다.

이렇게 등장한 헬베티카 폰트는 스위스 모던 타이포그래피의 영향을 받아 디자이너의 개성을 배제한 깔끔한 산세리프 서체로 큰 인기를 얻어 제록스, 어도비, 애플 컴퓨터 등 다국적 기업의 아이덴티티를 표현하는 디자인에 많이 사용되었습니다. 1983년에 발표된 Neue Helvetica는 아이폰과 매킨토시 운영체계의 전용 서체로 한동안 사용되었습니다. 헬베티카 폰트는 다양한 변형 폰트가 많은 것으로 유명합니다.

마이폰츠닷컴*myfonts.com*를 보면 Linotype의 Helvetica 폰트는 1개당 35달러, 34개 폰트로 Neue Helvetica 폰트는 1개당 35달러, 160개 폰트로 구성되어 있습니다. 어도비 폰트 서비스를 이용하고 있다면 Neue Haas Grotesk *fonts.adobe.com/fonts/neue-haas-grotesk* 폰트 (22개 폰트 패밀리)를 무료로 사용할 수 있습니다. 헬베티카를 대체할 수 있는 무료 폰트로는 Nimbus SansL(8개 폰트 패밀리)과 Arimo(4개 폰트 패밀리)가 있습니다. 두 폰트 모두 구글 폰트에 있습니다.

Sabon

Sabon LT Pro Bold 70p, 0

Sabon

Crimson Text SemiBold 76p, 0

1967년: 가라몬드 디자인을 계승한 실용적 폰트 사봉

독일 출신의 타입 디자이너 얀 치홀트*Jan Tschichold 1902–1974*는 1967년에 라이노타입, 모노타입, 스템펠*Stempel* 타입 파운더리와 함께 사봉 폰트를 발표했습니다. 사봉은 당시 사용되던 세 가지 금속 활자 조판 기술(수동 조판, 라이노타입과 모노타입의 기계 조판) 모두에서 동일하게 인쇄되고, 다양한 분야의 인쇄에 문제가 없을 정도로 가독성이 높고, 당시 널리 사용되던 본문용 서체인 가라몬드보다 문자 폭이 좁아서 경제적인 폰트였습니다. 사봉 폰트는 인쇄업계의 요구 사항들을 정확하게 만족시켜서 조판하기가 편리했기 때문에 상당히 오랫동안 본문 서체로 인기가 높았습니다.

사봉 서체의 로만*Roman* 문자는 클로드 가라몬드의 디자인을, 그 중에서도 프랑크푸르트 인쇄소에서 가져온 견본을 참고하고, 이탤릭 문자는 가라몬드의 제자 로베르 그랑정*Robert Granjon*의 새로운 가라몬드 디자인을 참고했습니다. 이렇게 사봉은 가라몬드를 계승한 폰트였으나 가라몬드라는 이름이 너무나 많이 사용되고 있어서, 일백 년 전에 프랑스에서 건너와 독일 인쇄업계에 가라몬드 폰트를 도입하는데 큰 역할을 했던 사람의 성을 이름으로 붙이게 되었다고 합니다.

마이폰츠닷컴*myfonts.com*을 보면 Linotype의 Sabon 폰트는 1개당 35달러, 4개 폰트로 구성되어 있습니다. 어도비 폰트 서비스를 이용하고 있다면 Sabon LT Pro *fonts.adobe.com/fonts/sabon* 폰트(4개 폰트 패밀리)를 무료로 사용할 수 있습니다. 사봉을 대체할 수 있는 무료 폰트로는 구글 폰트에 있는 Crimson Text(6개 폰트 패밀리)가 있습니다.

Frutiger

Frutiger 55 roman 76p, 0

Frutiger

Istok Web Regular 78p, 10

1977년: 헬베티카와는 다른 느낌의 모던한 폰트, 프루티거

프루티거 폰트는 프랑스에서 활동한 스위스 디자이너 아드리안 프루티거*Adrian Frutiger 1928-2015*가 만든 휴머니스트 산세리프 폰트입니다. 아드리안 프루티거는 샤를 드골 공항의 표지판 시스템을 위해 먼 거리에서 작은 크기로도 뚜렷하게 보이는 산세리프 폰트를 디자인한 것입니다. 프루티거는 로마 시대의 기념비에 새겨진 명각 글씨들로부터 영감을 받아 그가 50년대에 만들었던 유니버스 폰트의 골격에 접목시켜 헬베티카와는 또 다른 아름다운 산세리프 폰트를 만들었습니다.

현대적이면서도 헬베티카에 비해 개방적이고 부드러운 느낌이 강한 프루티거 폰트는 다양한 대학과 기업의 공식 폰트나 로고에 사용되었습니다. 그 목록에는 코넬 대학, 오하이오 대학, 마이아미 대학, 남가주 대학, 칼텍, 싱가폴 국립대학, 알카텔루슨트 주식회사, 암텍, 영국국립의료원, 폴라로이드, 로터리 인터내셔널, 세계보건기구 등 유명한 곳들이 한가드입니다.

마이폰츠닷컴*myfonts.com*을 보면 Linotype의 Frutiger 폰트는 1개당 35달러, 38개 폰트로 Neue Frutiger 폰트는 1개당 89달러, 40개 폰트로 구성되어 있습니다. 어도비 폰트 서비스를 이용하고 있다면 유사한 **Museo Sans** *fonts.adobe.com/fonts/museo-sans* 폰트(37개 폰트 패밀리)를 무료로 사용할 수 있습니다. Frutiger 폰트를 정확하게 대신할 수 있는 무료 폰트는 찾기가 쉽지 않습니다. 그나마 근접한 것으로 구글 폰트에 있는 Istok Web 폰트(4개 폰트 패밀리)가 있습니다.

Minion

Minion Pro Regular 76p, O

Minion

Cardo Regular 72p, O

1990년: 매우 효율적인 본문용 폰트, 어도비의 미니언 프로

미니언 폰트는 로버트 슬림바흐*Robert Slimbach 1956-*가 후기 르네상스 시대의 고전적인 활자체에서 영감을 받아 디자인하고 이를 어도비가 1990년에 발표한 올드 스타일의 세리프 폰트입니다. 미니언이란 이름은 활자 크기를 나타내는 옛 용어에서 유래하였습니다. 미니언은 7pt를 의미합니다. 미니언 폰트는 간결한 구조와 적절한 비율, 압축된 획과 여유 있는 내부 공간으로 장시간 읽을 수 있도록 만들어진 본문용 폰트입니다. 미니언 폰트는 2000년에 미니언 프로로 업데이트되었습니다. 브라운 대학과 스미소니언 박물관이 미니언 프로를 로고에 사용하고 있습니다.

미니언은 다양한 굵기와 크기, 폭의 글자를 표현할 수 있도록 매우 많은 패밀리 폰트를 거느리도록 설계되었습니다. 깨끗하고 과하지 않는 스타일의 다양한 패밀리 폰트를 제공하는 미니언은 매우 효율적인 폰트라는 평가를 받았습니다. 그리고 미니언의 기본 폰트들은 어도비가 판매하는 소프트웨어들에 기본으로 제공되었기 때문에 영어권에서 책을 편집하는데 가장 널리 사용되는 폰트가 되었습니다. 너무 많이 사용되었기 때문에 폰트는 좋지만 지루하다는 평가를 받기도 했습니다.

마이폰츠닷컴*myfonts.com*을 보면 Adobe의 Minion Pro 폰트는 1개당 35달러, 64개 폰트로 구성되어 있습니다. 어도비 폰트 서비스를 이용하고 있다면 Minion Pro *fonts.adobe.com/fonts/minion* 폰트(65개 폰트 패밀리)를 무료로 사용할 수 있습니다. 미니온 폰트를 대체할 수 있는 무료 폰트로는 구글 폰트에 있는 Cardo 폰트(3개 폰트 패밀리)가 있습니다.

Myriad

Myriad Pro Regular 76p, 0

Myriad

Aganè Regular 67p, 0

Myriad

Open Sans Regular 68p, 0

1992년: 애플의 기업 폰트로 유명한 미리아드 폰트

미리아드 폰트는 어도비를 위해 로버트 슬림바흐*Robert Slimbach 1956-*와 캐롤 텀블리*Carol Twombly 1959-*가 만든 휴머니스트 산세리프 폰트입니다. 폰트의 두께와 너비를 미세하게 조절할 수 있도록 하기 위하여 멀티플 마스터 폰트라는 기술을 도입한 것이 당시 큰 화제가 되었습니다. 미라아드 폰트는 위의 예에서 볼 수 있듯이 소문자 y의 휘어진 디센더로 다른 산세리프 폰트와 쉽게 구분이 됩니다. 미리아드 폰트는 2000년에 오픈타입의 미리아드 프로 폰트로 업데이트되었습니다.

미리아드 폰트를 사용한 가장 유명한 기업은 애플입니다. 애플은 2002년부터 2017년까지 변신을 하면서 기업 폰트를 애플 가라몬드에서 미리아드 폰트로 서서히 바꾸었습니다. 간결하면서 완성도 높은 폰트가 애플의 새로운 제품 이미지와 결합하면서 좋은 결과를 얻었습니다. 젊은 이미지를 원하는 대학들도 미리아드 폰트를 많이 사용합니다.

마이폰츠닷컴*myfonts.com*을 보면 Adobe의 **Myriad Pro** 폰트는 1개당 35달러, 40개 폰트로 구성되어 있습니다. 어도비 폰트 서비스를 이용하고 있다면 **Myriad Pro** *fonts.adobe.com/ fonts/myriad* 폰트(40개 폰트 패밀리)를 무료로 사용할 수 있습니다. 미리아드 폰트를 대체할 수 있는 무료 폰트로는 약간의 차이는 보이지만 **Aganè** 폰트(4개 폰트 패밀리)와 구글 폰트에 있는 **Open Sans** 폰트(11개 폰트 패밀리)가 있습니다.

Georgia

Georgia Regular 76p, 0

Georgia

Escrow Text Regular 77p, 0

Georgia

Neuton Regular 89p, 0

1993년: 종이 대신 화면을 위해 태어난 조지아 세리프 폰트

조지아 폰트는 매튜 카터*Matthew Carter 1937-*가 1993년에 디자인하고 마이크로소프트 사의 톰 릭너*Thomas Rickner 1966-*가 다듬은 세리프 폰트입니다. 마이크로소프트는 조지아 폰트를 1996년에 발표하였습니다. 익스플로러와 함께 설치되었기 때문에 대부분의 개인용 컴퓨터에 4개의 조지아 폰트들이*(Regular, Italic, Bold, Bold italic)* 설치되었습니다.

조지아 폰트는 저해상도 화면에 작은 크기로 표시되어도 잘 보이는(컴퓨터 화면에서 가독성 높은) 세리프 폰트가 필요했기 때문에 만들어졌습니다. 인쇄용 폰트에 비하여 획이 더 굵은 것이 특징입니다. 조지아 볼드는 다른 폰트의 블랙에 가깝게 두껍습니다. 이것은 1990년대의 저해상도 화면에 세리프 폰트를 표시하기 위한 노력이었습니다. 같은 목적으로 마이크로소프트는 버다나*Verdana* 산세리프 폰트도 제공하였습니다.

마이폰츠닷컴*myfonts.com*을 보면 Ascender의 Georgia 폰트는 1개당 49달러, 4개 폰트로 Georgia Pro 폰트는 1개당 40달러, 20개 폰트로 구성되어 있습니다. 어도비 폰트 서비스를 이용하고 있다면 상당히 유사한 Escrow Text *fonts.adobe.com/fonts/escrow-text* 폰트(8개 폰트 패밀리)를 무료로 사용할 수 있습니다. 조지아 폰트를 대체할 수 있는 무료 폰트로 정확하게 비슷한 것은 없지만 아쉬운 대로 구글 폰트에 있는 Neuton 폰트(6개 폰트 패밀리)를 추천합니다.

Mrs Eaves

Mrs Eaves OT Roman 78p, 0

Mrs Eaves

Libre Baskerville Regular 60p, 0

1996년: 원형 폰트와 관련된 여성의 이름을 붙인, 미시즈 이브 폰트

미시즈 이브는 디자이너 주잔나 릭코*Zuzana Licko*가 1996년에 디자인한 폰트로 1750년 대에 존 바스커빌이 만든 바스커빌 폰트를 변형한 것입니다. 위의 예에서 보듯이 미시즈 이브 폰트는 바스커빌 폰트와 상당히 비슷하지만 달라진 인쇄기술과 컴퓨터 화면에 표시되는 것도 고려하여 변형한 결과입니다. 상대적으로 폭이 넓어 시집처럼 분량이 적은 글이나 우아한 제목에 적합합니다. 세리프가 아름답고 여성적인 느낌이 있습니다. 주잔나 릭코는 미시즈 이브의 성공 뒤에 본문용 Mrs Eaves XL, 산세리프 폰트 미스터 이브*Mr. Eaves* 폰트도 만들었습니다.

이 폰트의 이름은 나중에 존 바스커빌의 아내가 된 사라 이브*Sarah Eaves*를 기려 붙여진 것입니다. 여기에는 사연이 있습니다. 존 바스커빌은 인쇄업을 시작하면서 사라 이브를 고용했습니다. 그런데 남편이 그녀와 다섯 아이들을 버리자 이브 부인은 베스커빌의 가정부가 되었고 업무 파트너가 되었으며 결혼에까지 이르렀습니다.

Emigre의 Mrs Eaves 폰트(8개 폰트 패밀리)는 자사의 홈페이지*www.emigre.com/Fonts/Mrs-Eaves*에서 구입할 수 있습니다. 8개 모두 산다면 358달러입니다. 어도비 폰트 서비스를 이용하고 있다면 Mrs Eaves OT *fonts.adobe.com/fonts/mrs-eaves* 폰트(9개 폰트 패밀리)와 Mrs Eaves XL Serif OT *fonts.adobe.com/fonts/mrs-eaves-xl* 폰트(12개 폰트 패밀리)를 무료로 사용할 수 있습니다. 미시즈 이브 폰트가 Baskerville 폰트의 변형이므로 구글 폰트에 있는 Libre Baskerville 폰트(3개 폰트 패밀리)를 무료 폰트로 추천할 수 있습니다.

Gotham

Gotham Boook 73p, 0

Gotham

Metropolis Regular 76p, 0

2000년: 뉴욕의 감성을 복구한 전문가용 패밀리 폰트, 고담

고담은 미국의 디자이너 토비아스 프레레 존스*Tobias Frere-Jones 1970-*가 디자인한 기하학적 산세리프 폰트입니다. 고담은 전문가용으로 개발된 폰트이며 4종류의 폭, 8단계의 두께, 3가지 디자인(인쇄용, 화면용, 둥근 모서리)이 결합된 거대한 패밀리 폰트로 구성되어 있습니다. 고담 폰트는 소문자 높이가 높고 개구부 입구가 넓은 특징을 가집니다.

고담은 새롭고 신선한 산세리프 폰트가 필요했던 GQ 매거진의 요청에 의해 시작된 프로젝트에서 탄생했습니다. 프레레 존스는 어린 시절부터 뉴욕의 맨하튼을 걸으며 오래된 건물의 간판에서 볼 수 있는 타이포그래피에 관심을 기울였으며, 뉴욕의 오래된 레터링 디자인을 잊혀지지 않게 보존하고 싶었다고 합니다. 그래서인지 고담은 뉴욕을 상징하는 매우 미국적인 폰트가 되었습니다.

고담 폰트는 2000년에 토비아스 프레레 존스의 이전 사업 파트너였던 조나단 호플러의 회사 Hoefler&Co.에 의해 발표되었습니다. 고담 폰트는 등장하자 마자 버락 오바마의 2008년 대선 캠페인 등 여러 유명한 이벤트에 사용되면서 주목을 받았습니다.

Hoefler&Co의 Gotham 폰트는 자사의 홈페이지*www.typography.com/fonts/gotham*에서 구입할 수 있습니다. 패밀리 폰트의 수가 매우 많으며 가격도 비쌉니다.(풀 패키지 966달러) 어도비 폰트 서비스를 이용하고 있다면 매우 비슷한 Proxima Nova *fonts.adobe.com/fonts/proxima-nova* 폰트(48개 폰트 패밀리)를 무료로 사용할 수 있습니다. 고담 폰트를 대체할 수 있는 무료 폰트로는 Metropolis 폰트(18개 폰트 패밀리)를 추천합니다.

Google Font
Sans Serif Best 20

구글 폰트 분석기Google Fonts analytics 덕분에 전 세계 웹사이트에서 많이 사용되고 있는 구글 폰트들이 무엇인지 손쉽게 알 수 있습니다. 1,000개에 가까운 구글 폰트들을 모두 살펴보고 사용하는 것은 너무 힘든 일이므로 가장 많이 사용되는 폰트들을 살펴보는 것은 당연합니다.

상위 순위 폰트들 중에서도 먼저 산세리프San Serif 폰트 베스트 20개를 정리하여 보았습니다. 이들은 최근 1년 동안 가장 많이 선택된 무료 영문 폰트인데(여러분이 이 책을 볼 때는 조금 달라질 수 있습니다) 이 폰트들 중에는 역사적으로 유명한 폰트들을 대신할 수 있는 것도 있습니다.

구글 폰트 분석기는 웹사이트에 사용되고 있는 폰트들의 순위를 측정합니다. 웹사이트에는 간결한 산세리프 폰트가 더 어울리므로 상위권에 있는 폰트들은 세리프 폰트보다 산세리프 폰트들이 더 많습니다. 따라서 사실상 구글 폰트 전체 베스트 20이라고 해도 지나친 말은 아닙니다.

오른쪽 페이지에서 패밀리 폰트가 많을수록(폰트 이름 오른쪽에 표시한 작은 숫자가 패밀리 폰트의 수) 복잡한 프로젝트의 메인 폰트로 사용하기에 적당합니다. 다양한 굵기와 스타일이 존재하기 때문입니다. 한글 본문 폰트에 어울리는 영숫자를 가진 영문 폰트를 찾을 때도 유리합니다.

일반적으로 본문용 영문 폰트 패밀리는 바른 글자(Roman)와 기울인 글자(Italic)를 모두 포함합니다. 이런 경우에는 패밀리를 구성하는 폰트의 수는 짝수가 됩니다. 만약 이것이 홀수라면 그 폰트 패밀리에는 이탤릭 폰트가 없을 가능성이 높습니다.

1 Roboto [12]

Aa Ee Rr
Aa Ee Rr
Aa Ee Rr
abcdefghijklm
nopqrstuvwxyz
1234567890 ○180p

2 Open Sans [10]

Aa Ee Rr
Aa Ee Rr
Aa Ee Rr
abcdefghijklm
nopqrstuvwxyz
1234567890 ○152p

3 Lato [10]

Aa Ee Rr
Aa Ee Rr
Aa Ee Rr
abcdefghijklm
nopqrstuvwxyz
1234567890 ○128p

4 Montserrat [18]

Aa Ee Rr
Aa Ee Rr
Aa Ee Rr
abcdefghijklm
nopqrstuvwxyz
1234567890 ○132p

5 Source Sans [12]

Aa Ee Rr
Aa Ee Rr
Aa Ee Rr
abcdefghijklm
nopqrstuvwxyz
1234567890 ○188p

6 Oswald [6]

Aa Ee Rr
Aa Ee Rr
Aa Ee Rr
abcdefghijklm
nopqrstuvwxyz
1234567890 ○156p

7 Raleway [18]

Aa Ee Rr
Aa Ee Rr
Aa Ee Rr
abcdefghijklm
nopqrstuvwxyz
1234567890 ○176p

8 Poppins [18]

Aa Ee Rr
Aa Ee Rr
Aa Ee Rr
abcdefghijklm
nopqrstuvwxyz
1234567890 ○164p

9 Noto Sans [4]

Aa Ee Rr
Aa Ee Rr
abcdefghijklm
nopqrstuvwxyz
1234567890 ○140p

10 PT Sans [4]

Aa Ee Rr
Aa Ee Rr
abcdefghijklm
nopqrstuvwxyz
1234567890 ○168p

11 Muli [14]

Aa Ee Rr
Aa Ee Rr
Aa Ee Rr
abcdefghijklm
nopqrstuvwxyz
1234567890 ○136p

12 Nunito [14]

Aa Ee Rr
Aa Ee Rr
Aa Ee Rr
abcdefghijklm
nopqrstuvwxyz
1234567890 ○144p

13 Fira Sans [18]

Aa Ee Rr
Aa Ee Rr
Aa Ee Rr
abcdefghijklm
nopqrstuvwxyz
1234567890 ○124p

14 Rubik [10]

Aa Ee Rr
Aa Ee Rr
Aa Ee Rr
abcdefghijklm
nopqrstuvwxyz
1234567890 ○184p

15 Work Sans [9]

Aa Ee Rr
Aa Ee Rr
Aa Ee Rr
abcdefghijklm
nopqrstuvwxyz
1234567890 ○192p

16 Quicksand [6]

Aa Ee Rr
Aa Ee Rr
Aa Ee Rr
abcdefghijklm
nopqrstuvwxyz
1234567890 ○172p

17 Arimo [4]

Aa Ee Rr
Aa Ee Rr
abcdefghijklm
nopqrstuvwxyz
1234567890 ○116p

18 Nunito Sans [14]

Aa Ee Rr
Aa Ee Rr
Aa Ee Rr
abcdefghijklm
nopqrstuvwxyz
1234567890 ○148p

19 Dosis [7]

Aa Ee Rr
Aa Ee Rr
Aa Ee Rr
abcdefghijklm
nopqrstuvwxyz
1234567890 ○120p

20 Oxygen [3]

Aa Ee Rr
Aa Ee Rr
Aa Ee Rr
abcdefghijklm
nopqrstuvwxyz
1234567890 ○160p

Google Font
Serif Best 20

구글 폰트 분석기*Google Fonts analytics* 덕분에 전 세계 웹사이트에서 많이 사용되고 있는 구글 폰트들이 무엇인지 손쉽게 알 수 있습니다. 1,000개에 가까운 구글 폰트들을 모두 살펴보고 사용하는 것은 너무 힘든 일이므로 가장 많이 사용되는 폰트들을 살펴보는 것은 당연합니다.

이번에는 세리프*Serif* 폰트 베스트 20개를 정리하여 보았습니다. 이들은 최근 1년 동안 가장 많이 선택된 무료 영문 폰트인데(여러분이 이 책을 볼 때는 조금 달라져 있을 겁니다) 이 폰트들 중에는 역사적으로 유명한 폰트들을 대신할 수 있는 것도 있습니다.

구글 폰트 분석기는 웹사이트에 사용되고 있는 폰트들의 순위를 측정합니다. 웹사이트에는 간결한 산세리프 폰트가 더 어울리므로 상위권에 있는 폰트들은 세리프 폰트보다 산세리프 폰트들이 더 많습니다. 따라서 세리프 폰트들의 순위는 산세리프 폰트들보다 아래에 있습니다.

오른쪽 페이지에서 패밀리 폰트가 많을수록(폰트 이름 오른쪽에 표시한 작은 숫자가 패밀리 폰트의 수) 복잡한 프로젝트의 메인 폰트로 사용하기에 적당합니다. 다양한 굵기와 스타일이 존재하기 때문입니다. 한글 본문 폰트에 어울리는 영숫자를 가진 영문 폰트를 찾을 때도 유리합니다. 제작 난이도 높아서 세리프 폰트의 패밀리 폰트 수는 적은 편입니다.

일반적으로 본문용 영문 폰트 패밀리는 바른 글자(Roman)와 기울인 글자(Italic)를 모두 포함합니다. 이런 경우에는 패밀리를 구성하는 폰트의 수는 짝수가 됩니다. 만약 이것이 홀수라면 그 폰트 패밀리에는 이탤릭 폰트가 없을 가능성이 높습니다.

1 Merriweather [8]

Aa Ee Rr
Aa Ee Rr
Aa Ee Rr

abcdefghijklm
nopqrstuvwxyz
1234567890 ○236p

2 Roboto Slab [4]

Aa Ee Rr
Aa Ee Rr
Aa Ee Rr

abcdefghijklm
nopqrstuvwxyz
1234567890 ○252p

3 Playfair Display [6]

Aa Ee Rr
Aa Ee Rr
Aa Ee Rr

abcdefghijklm
nopqrstuvwxyz
1234567890 ○244p

4 PT Serif [4]

Aa Ee Rr
Aa Ee Rr

abcdefghijklm
nopqrstuvwxyz
1234567890 ○248p

5 Lora [4]

Aa Ee Rr
Aa Ee Rr

abcdefghijklm
nopqrstuvwxyz
1234567890 ○232p

6 Alegreya [10]

Aa Ee Rr
Aa Ee Rr

abcdefghijklm
nopqrstuvwxyz
1234567890 ○196p

7 Noto Serif [4]

Aa Ee Rr
Aa Ee Rr

abcdefghijklm
nopqrstuvwxyz
1234567890 ○240p

8 Libre Baskerville [3]

Aa Ee Rr
Aa Ee Rr

abcdefghijklm
nopqrstuvwxyz
1234567890○228p

9 Crimson Text [6]

Aa Ee Rr
Aa Ee Rr
Aa Ee Rr

abcdefghijklm
nopqrstuvwxyz
1234567890 ○218p

10 Bitter [3]

Aa Ee Rr
Aa Ee Rr

abcdefghijklm
nopqrstuvwxyz
1234567890 ○208p

11 Arvo [4]

Aa Ee Rr
Aa Ee Rr

abcdefghijklm
nopqrstuvwxyz
1234567890 ○204p

12 Source Serif Pro [12]

Aa Ee Rr
Aa Ee Rr

abcdefghijklm
nopqrstuvwxyz
1234567890 ○260p

13 Bree Serif [1]

Aa Ee Rr

abcdefghijklm
nopqrstuvwxyz
1234567890 ○212p

14 EB Garamond [10]

Aa Ee Rr
Aa Ee Rr
Aa Ee Rr

abcdefghijklm
nopqrstuvwxyz
1234567890 ○224p

15 Rokkitt [9]

Aa Ee Rr
Aa Ee Rr
Aa Ee Rr

abcdefghijklm
nopqrstuvwxyz
1234567890 ○256p

16 Domine [2]

Aa Ee Rr
Aa Ee Rr

abcdefghijklm
nopqrstuvwxyz
1234567890 ○222p

17 Crete Round [2]

Aa Ee Rr

abcdefghijklm
nopqrstuvwxyz
1234567890 ○216p

18 Vollkorn [8]

Aa Ee Rr
Aa Ee Rr
Aa Ee Rr

abcdefghijklm
nopqrstuvwxyz
1234567890 ○262p

19 CINZEL [3]

AA EE RR
AA EE RR
AA EE RR

ABCDEFGHIJKLM
NOPQRSTUVWXY
1234567890 ○214p

20 Amiri [4]

Aa Ee Rr
Aa Ee Rr

abcdefghijklm
nopqrstuvwxyz
1234567890 ○200p

Arimo

Arimo Bold 116p, 0

Arimo Regular
Arimo Italic
Arimo Bold
Arimo Bold Italic

20/24p, 0

ABCDEFGHIJKLMNOPQRSTUVWXYZ
ABCDEFGHIJKLMNOPQRSTUVWXYZ
abcefghijklmnopqrstuvwxyz abc@gmail.com
abcefghijklmnopqrstuvwxyz abc@gmail.com
1234567890 +−×÷=#%&*, . : ; ! ? ( )[ ]{ } ' ' " " ®©
1234567890 +−×÷=#%&, . : ; ! ? ( )[ ]{ } ' ' " " ®©*

ABCDEFGHIJKLMNOPQRSTUVWXYZ
ABCDEFGHIJKLMNOPQRSTUVWXYZ
abcefghijklmnopqrstuvwxyz abc@gmail.com
abcefghijklmnopqrstuvwxyz abc@gmail.com
1234567890 +−×÷=#%&*, . : ; ! ? ( )[ ]{ } ' ' " " ®©
1234567890 +−×÷=#%&*, . : ; ! ? ( )[ ]{ } ' ' " " ®©

14/

"I loved her against *reason*, against *promise*, against *peace*, against *hope*, against *happiness*, against *all discouragement* that could be."
— **Charles Dickens, *Great Expectations***

Regular 10/14p, 0 | Bold 9/14p, 10

| License | Apache License, Version 2.0 | | Link | fonts.google.com/specimen/Arimo |
| Font tag | Sans serif, Text, Arial, Helvetica, Google | | Pair | Open Sans, Roboto, Oswald, Montserrat, Lora |

Deep into that darkness peering,
long I stood there, wondering, fearing, doubting,
dreaming dreams no mortal ever dared to dream before.
— **Edgar Allan Poe, *Complete Tales and Poems***

Regular 13/17p, 10 | Bold 10/14p, 0

SPARKLING ARTS

www.sparklingarts.com

Founder

CAROLINE LEE

carolinelee@sparklingarts.com

010.2345.6789

Bold 18p, 50

Regular 9p, 100

Regular 10p, 100

Bold 16/20p, 50

Italic 9p, 0

Italic 11p, 100

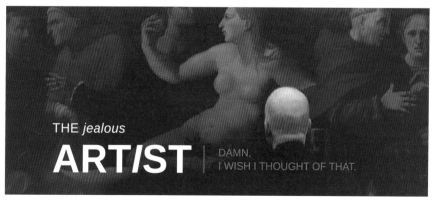

THE *jealous*
ART/ST
DAMN,
I WISH I THOUGHT OF THAT.

Regular 10p, 30 | Italic 10p, 30 | Bold 30/30p, 10 | Regular 8/10p, 0

ADVENTURE FOR THE YOUNG AT HEART

Go outside and explore

At any rate, That is Happiness; To be dissolved into something
COMPLETE AND GREAT.

Arimo Regular 23.3-23.3-Bold 27.2p, 20 | Regular 10p, 10

— Willa Cather, *My Ántonia*

"Stay close to anything that makes you feel you are glad to be alive. Plant the seeds for a sustainable future. *Connect, respect and listen to nature,* **for nature is our greatest teacher."**

Bold 10/15p, 30

LOOK UP, KEEP GOING

Bold 14p, 100

Lorem ipsum dolor sit amet, consectetur adipiscing elit, sed do eiusmod tempor incididunt ut labore et dolore magna aliqua. Ut enim ad minim veniam, nostrud exercitation ullamco laboris nisi aliquip ex ea commodo consequat. Duis aute irure dolor in reprehenderit in voluptate velit esse cillum dolore eu fugiat nulla pariatur. Excepteur sint occaecat cupidatat non proident, sunt in culpa qui officia deserunt mollit anim id est laborum.

"Aliquam fermentum est. Praesent posuere lorem quis quam viverra tempus. Suspendisse varius nunc nec sapien convallis rutrum. Donec vitae tincidunt tortor, nec tempor tortor."

Ultrices sagittis orci a scelerisque purus. Diam maecenas ultricies mi eget mauris. Nam aliquam sem et tortor consequat id porta nibh. Tempor orci dapibus ultrices in iaculis nunc sed augue lacus. Sit amet massa vitae tortor condimentum.

Mi sit amet mauris commodo quis. Adipiscing at in tellus integer feugiat scelerisque varius morbi in enim. Elementum nibh tellus molestie nunc non. Nisi porta lorem mollis aliquam ut porttitor leo a. Sed sed risus pretium quam vulputate dignissim. Nunc mi ipsum faucibus vitae aliquet nec ullam corper. Scelerisque viverra mauris in aliquam sem fringilla.

In nisl nisi scelerisque eu. Odio facilisis mauris sit amet massa. Porttitor lacus luctus accumsan tortor posuere ac ut consequat. Nibh venenatis cras sed felis. Vestibulum sed arcu non odio euismod. Vitae aliquet nec ullamcorper sit amet. Amet mauris commodo quis imperdiet massa tincidunt nunc. Condimentum mattis pellentesque id nibh. Egestas purus viverra accumsan in nisl nisi scelerisque eu. Euismod in pellentesque massa placerat duis ultricies. Eget egestas purus viverra accumsan in. Id venenatis a condimentum vitae pellentesque habitant morbi. Dignissim convallis aenean et tortor Est ullamcorper eget nulla facilisi dignissim diam quis. Dui nunc mattis enim elementum sagittis.

Regular 7/9p, 0 | Bold 8/11p, 50

⤹ Bold 14/17p, 100 | Regular 8/25p, 25

Dosis

Dosis Bold 100p, 0

Dosis Extra Light
Dosis Light
Dosis Regular
Dosis Medium

Dosis SemiBold
Dosis Bold
Dosis Extra bold 20/24p, 0

ABCDEFGHIJKLMNOPQRSTUVWXYZ
1234567890 abcefghijklmnopqrstuvwxyz
+−×÷=#%&*,.:;!?
( )[ ]{ }' ' " " ®©

ABCDEFGHIJKLMNOPQRSTUVWXYZ
1234567890 abcefghijklmnopqrstuvwxyz
+−×÷=#%&*,.:;!?
( )[ ]{ }' ' " " ®©

ABCDEFGHIJKLMNOPQRSTUVWXYZ
1234567890 abcefghijklmnopqrstuvwxyz
+−×÷=#%&*,.:;!?
( )[ ]{ }' ' " " ®©

ABCDEFGHIJKLMNOPQRSTUVWXYZ
1234567890 abcefghijklmnopqrstuvwxyz
+−×÷=#%&*,.:;!?
( )[ ]{ }' ' " " ®©

ABCDEFGHIJKLMNOPQRSTUVWXYZ
1234567890 abcefghijklmnopqrstuvwxyz
+−×÷=#%&*,.:;!?
( )[ ]{ }' ' " " ®©

ABCDEFGHIJKLMNOPQRSTUVWXYZ
1234567890 abcefghijklmnopqrstuvwxyz
+−×÷=#%&*,.:;!?
( )[ ]{ }' ' " " ®©

ABCDEFGHIJKLMNOPQRSTUVWXYZ
1234567890 abcefghijklmnopqrstuvwxyz
+−×÷=#%&*,.:;!?
( )[ ]{ }' ' " " ®©

14/20p, 0

License	Open Font License	Link	fonts.google.com/specimen/Dosis
Font tag	Sans serif, round, ITC Conduit, Google	Pair	Open Sans, Roboto, Montserrat, Lato, Raleway

Deep into that darkness peering,
long I stood there, wondering, fearing, doubting,
dreaming dreams no mortal ever dared to dream before.
— **Edgar Allan Poe, Complete Tales and Poems**

Regular 13/17p, 10 | Bold 10/14p, 0

SPARKLING ARTS

www.sparklingarts.com

Founder
CAROLINE LEE

carolinelee@sparklingarts.com

010.2345.6789

Bold 18p, 50

Light 9p, 100

Regular 10p, 100

Extra Bold 16/20p, 50

Medium 9p, 0

Extra Light 11p, 100

THE jealous
ARTIST

DAMN,
I WISH I THOUGHT OF THAT.

Medium 10p, 30 | Extra Bold 30/30p, 20 | Light 8/10p, 0

ADVENTURE FOR THE YOUNG AT HEART

Go outside and explore

At any rate, That is Happiness;
To be dissolved into something
COMPLETE AND GREAT.

Dosis Medium 27.5-Bold 25.5-ExtraBold 33.1p, 20 | Regular 10p, 10

— Willa Cather, My Ántonia

"Stay close to anything that makes you feel you are glad to be alive. Plant the seeds for a sustainable future. Connect, respect and listen to nature, for nature is our greatest teacher."

SemiBold 10/15p, 30

LOOK UP, KEEP GOING

Extra Bold 14p, 100

Lorem ipsum dolor sit amet, consectetur adipiscing elit, sed do eiusmod tempor incididunt ut labore et dolore magna aliqua. Ut enim ad minim veniam, nostrud exercitation ullamco laboris nisi aliquip ex ea commodo consequat. Duis aute irure dolor in reprehenderit in voluptate velit esse cillum dolore eu fugiat nulla pariatur. Excepteur sint occaecat cupidatat non proident, sunt in culpa qui officia deserunt mollit anim id est laborum.

"Aliquam fermentum est. Praesent posuere lorem quis quam viverra tempus. Suspendisse varius nunc nec sapien convallis rutrum. Donec vitae tincidunt tortor, tortor."

Ultrices sagittis orci a scelerisque purus. Diam maecenas ultricies mi eget mauris. Nam aliquam sem et tortor consequat id porta nibh. Tempor orci dapibus ultrices in iaculis nunc sed augue lacus. Sit amet massa vitae tortor condimentum.

Regular 7/9p, 0 | SemiBold 8/11p, 50

Mi sit amet mauris commodo quis. Adipiscing at in tellus integer feugiat scelerisque varius morbi in enim. Elementum nibh tellus molestie nunc non. Nisi porta lorem mollis aliquam ut porttitor leo a. Sed sed risus pretium quam vulputate dignissim. Nunc mi ipsum faucibus vitae aliquet nec ullam corper. Scelerisque viverra mauris in aliquam sem fringilla.

In nisl nisi scelerisque eu. Odio facilisis mauris sit amet massa. Porttitor lacus luctus accumsan tortor posuere ac ut consequat. Nibh venenatis cras sed felis. Vestibulum sed arcu non odio euismod. Vitae aliquet nec ullamcorper sit amet. Amet mauris commodo quis imperdiet massa tincidunt nunc. Condimentum mattis pellentesque id nibh. Egestas purus viverra accumsan in nisl nisi scelerisque eu. Euismod in pellentesque massa placerat duis ultricies. Eget egestas purus viverra accumsan in. Id venenatis a condimentum vitae pellentesque habitant morbi. Dignissim convallis aenean et tortor Est ullamcorper eget nulla facilisi dignissim diam quis. Dui nunc mattis enim elementum sagittis.

Extra Bold 14/17p, 100 | Regular 8/25p, 25

Fira Sans

Fira Sans SemiBold 83p, 0

Fira Sans Thin	*Fira Sans Thin Italic*
Fira Sans ExtraLight	*Fira Sans ExtraLight Italic*
Fira Sans Light	*Fira Sans Light Italic*
Fira Sans Regular	*Fira Sans Italic*
Fira Sans Medium	***Fira Sans Medium Italic***
Fira Sans SemiBold	***Fira Sans SemiBold Italic***
Fira Sans Bold	***Fira Sans Bold Italic***
Fira Sans ExtraBold	***Fira Sans ExtraBold Italic***
Fira Sans Black	***Fira Sans Black Italic***

ABCDEFGHIJKLMNOPQRSTUVW abcdefghijklmnopqrstuvwxyz 1234567
ABCDEFGHIJKLMNOPQRSTUVW abcdefghijklmnopqrstuvwxyz 1234567

ABCDEFGHIJKLMNOPQRSTUVW abcdefghijklmnopqrstuvwxyz 123456
ABCDEFGHIJKLMNOPQRSTUVW abcdefghijklmnopqrstuvwxyz 123456

ABCDEFGHIJKLMNOPQRSTUVW abcdefghijklmnopqrstuvwxyz 123456
ABCDEFGHIJKLMNOPQRSTUVW abcdefghijklmnopqrstuvwxyz 123456

ABCDEFGHIJKLMNOPQRSTUVW abcdefghijklmnopqrstuvwxyz 1234
ABCDEFGHIJKLMNOPQRSTUVW abcdefghijklmnopqrstuvwxyz 12345

ABCDEFGHIJKLMNOPQRSTUVW abcdefghijklmnopqrstuvwxyz 1234
ABCDEFGHIJKLMNOPQRSTUVW abcdefghijklmnopqrstuvwxyz 1234

ABCDEFGHIJKLMNOPQRSTUVW abcdefghijklmnopqrstuvwxyz 1234
ABCDEFGHIJKLMNOPQRSTUVW abcdefghijklmnopqrstuvwxyz 1234

ABCDEFGHIJKLMNOPQRSTUVW abcdefghijklmnopqrstuvwxyz 123
ABCDEFGHIJKLMNOPQRSTUVW abcdefghijklmnopqrstuvwxyz 1234

ABCDEFGHIJKLMNOPQRSTUVW abcdefghijklmnopqrstuvwxyz 123
ABCDEFGHIJKLMNOPQRSTUVW abcdefghijklmnopqrstuvwxyz 1234

ABCDEFGHIJKLMNOPQRSTUVW abcdefghijklmnopqrstuvwxyz 123
ABCDEFGHIJKLMNOPQRSTUVW abcdefghijklmnopqrstuvwxyz 1234

| License | Open Font License | Link | fonts.google.com/specimen/Fira+Sans |
| Font tag | Sans serif, Text, Vista Sans, Google | Pair | Roboto, Open Sans, Montserrat, Playfair Display, Merriwether |

Deep into that darkness peering,
long I stood there, wondering, fearing, doubting,
dreaming dreams no mortal ever dared to dream before.
— **Edgar Allan Poe,** *Complete Tales and Poems*

Light 12/17p, 10 | Medium 10/14p, 0

SPARKLING ARTS

www.sparklingarts.com

Founder

CAROLINE LEE

carolinelee@sparklingarts.com

010.2345.6789

Black 18p, 50

Thin 9p, 100

Medium 10p, 100

Bold 16/20p, 50

Italic 9p, 0

Light Italic 11p, 100

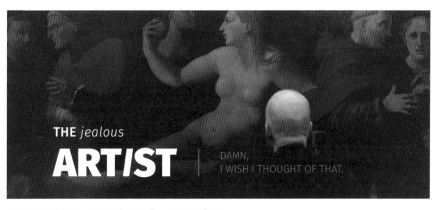

THE *jealous*

ART/ST

DAMN,
I WISH I THOUGHT OF THAT.

Medium 10p, 30 | Light Italic 10p, 30 | Black 30/30p, 10 | Light 8/10p, 0

ADVENTURE FOR THE YOUNG AT HEART

Go outside and explore

At any rate, That is Happiness;
To be dissolved into something
COMPLETE AND GREAT.

Fira Sans Medium 23.2p-Bold 22.5p-Black 31.4p, 20 | Regular 10p, 10

– Willa Cather, *My Ántonia*

"Stay close to anything that makes you feel you are glad to be alive. Plant the seeds for a sustainable future. *Connect, respect and listen to nature,* for nature is our greatest teacher."

Medium 10/15p, 30

LOOK UP, KEEP GOING

Black 14p, 100

Lorem ipsum dolor sit amet, consectetur adipiscing elit, sed do eiusmod tempor incididunt ut labore et dolore magna aliqua. Ut enim ad minim veniam, nostrud exercitation ullamco laboris nisi aliquip ex ea commodo consequat. Duis aute irure dolor in reprehenderit in voluptate velit esse cillum dolore eu fugiat nulla pariatur. Excepteur sint occaecat cupidatat non proident, sunt in culpa qui officia deserunt mollit anim id est laborum.

"Aliquam fermentum est. Praesent posuere lorem quis quam viverra tempus. Suspendisse varius nunc nec sapien convallis rutrum. Donec vitae tincidunt tortor, nec tempor tortor."

Ultrices sagittis orci a scelerisque purus. Diam maecenas ultricies mi eget mauris. Nam aliquam sem et tortor consequat id porta nibh. Tempor orci dapibus ultrices in iaculis nunc sed augue lacus. Sit amet massa vitae tortor condimentum.

Regular 7/9p, 0 | Medium 8/11p, 50

Mi sit amet mauris commodo quis. Adipiscing at in tellus integer feugiat scelerisque varius morbi in enim. Elementum nibh tellus molestie nunc non. Nisi porta lorem mollis aliquam ut porttitor leo a. Sed sed risus pretium quam vulputate dignissim. Nunc mi ipsum faucibus vitae aliquet nec ullam corper. Scelerisque viverra mauris in aliquam sem fringilla.

In nisl nisi scelerisque eu. Odio facilisis mauris sit amet massa. Porttitor lacus luctus accumsan tortor posuere ac ut consequat. Nibh venenatis cras sed felis. Vestibulum sed arcu non odio euismod. Vitae aliquet nec ullamcorper sit amet. Amet mauris commodo quis imperdiet massa tincidunt nunc. Condimentum mattis pellentesque id nibh. Egestas purus viverra accumsan in nisl nisi scelerisque eu. Euismod in pellentesque massa placerat duis ultricies. Eget egestas purus viverra accumsan in. Id venenatis a condimentum vitae pellentesque habitant morbi. Dignissim convallis aenean et tortor Est ullamcorper eget nulla facilisi dignissim diam quis. Dui nunc mattis enim elementum sagittis.

Black 14/17p, 100 | Light 8/25p, 25

Lato

Lato Bold 120p, 0

Lato Hairline	*Lato Hairline Italic*
Lato Light	*Lato Light Italic*
Lato Regular	*Lato Italic*
Lato Bold	***Lato Bold Italic***
Lato Black	***Lato Black Italic***

18/24p

ABCDEFGHIJKLMNOPQRSTUVWXYZ abcdefghijklmnopqrstuvwxyz
ABCDEFGHIJKLMNOPQRSTUVWXYZ abcdefghijklmnopqrstuvwxyz
1234567890 1234567890 +−×÷=#%&*,.:;!? ()[]{}'' " "®©

ABCDEFGHIJKLMNOPQRSTUVWXYZ abcdefghijklmnopqrstuvwxy
ABCDEFGHIJKLMNOPQRSTUVWXYZ abcdefghijklmnopqrstuvwxyz
1234567890 1234567890 +−×÷=#%&*, . : ; ! ? ( )[ ]{ } ' ' " " ®©

ABCDEFGHIJKLMNOPQRSTUVWXYZ abcdefghijklmnopqrstuvw
ABCDEFGHIJKLMNOPQRSTUVWXYZ abcdefghijklmnopqrstuvwxyz
1234567890 1234567890 +−×÷=#%&*,.:;!? ()[]{}'' " "®©

ABCDEFGHIJKLMNOPQRSTUVWXYZ abcdefghijklmnopqrstuvw
ABCDEFGHIJKLMNOPQRSTUVWXYZ abcdefghijklmnopqrstuvwxyz
1234567890 1234567890 +−×÷=#%&*, . : ; ! ? ( )[ ]{ } ' ' " " ®©

ABCDEFGHIJKLMNOPQRSTUVWXYZ abcdefghijklmnopqrstuv
ABCDEFGHIJKLMNOPQRSTUVWXYZ abcdefghijklmnopqrstuvwxy
1234567890 1234567890 +−×÷=#%&*,.:;!? ()[]{}'' " "®©

11/16p

| License | Apache License, Version 2.0 | | Link | fonts.google.com/specimen/Lato |
| Font tag | Sans serif, Text, Avenir, Google | | Pair | Open Sans, Roboto, Raleway, Oswald, Source Sans Pro |

Deep into that darkness peering,
long I stood there, wondering, fearing, doubting,
dreaming dreams no mortal ever dared to dream before.
— Edgar Allan Poe, *Complete Tales and Poems*

Light 13/17p, 10 | Regular 10/14p, 0

SPARKLING ARTS

www.sparklingarts.com

Founder

CAROLINE LEE

carolinelee@sparklingarts.com

010.2345.6789

Black 18p, 50

Light 9p, 100

Hairline 10p, 100

Bold 16/20p, 50

Italic 9p, 0

Light Italic 11p, 100

THE *jealous*
ART*I*ST

DAMN,
I WISH I THOUGHT OF THAT.

Regular 10p, 30 | Light Italic 10p, 30 | Black 30/30p, 10 | Light 8/10p, 0

ADVENTURE FOR THE YOUNG AT HEART

Go outside and explore

At any rate, That is Happiness;
To be dissolved into something
COMPLETE AND GREAT.

— Willa Cather, *My Ántonia*

"Stay close to anything that makes you feel you are glad to be alive. Plant the seeds for a sustainable future. *Connect, respect and listen to nature,* for nature is our greatest teacher."

LOOK UP, KEEP GOING

Lorem ipsum dolor sit amet, consectetur adipiscing elit, sed do eiusmod tempor incididunt ut labore et dolore magna aliqua. Ut enim ad minim veniam, nostrud exercitation ullamco laboris nisi aliquip ex ea commodo consequat. Duis aute irure dolor in reprehenderit in voluptate velit esse cillum dolore eu fugiat nulla pariatur. Excepteur sint occaecat cupidatat non proident, sunt in culpa qui officia deserunt mollit anim id est laborum.

"Aliquam fermentum est. Praesent posuere lorem quis quam viverra tempus. Suspendisse varius nunc nec sapien convallis rutrum. Donec vitae tincidunt tortor, nec tempor tortor."

Ultrices sagittis orci a scelerisque purus. Diam maecenas ultricies mi eget mauris. Nam aliquam sem et tortor consequat id porta nibh. Tempor orci dapibus ultrices in iaculis nunc sed augue lacus. Sit amet massa vitae tortor condimentum.

Mi sit amet mauris commodo quis. Adipiscing at in tellus integer feugiat scelerisque varius morbi in enim. Elementum nibh tellus molestie nunc non. Nisi porta lorem mollis aliquam ut porttitor leo a. Sed sed risus pretium quam vulputate dignissim. Nunc mi ipsum faucibus vitae aliquet nec ullam corper. Scelerisque viverra mauris in aliquam sem fringilla.

In nisl nisi scelerisque eu. Odio facilisis mauris sit amet massa. Porttitor lacus luctus accumsan tortor posuere ac ut consequat. Nibh venenatis cras sed felis. Vestibulum sed arcu non odio euismod. Vitae aliquet nec ullamcorper sit amet. Amet mauris commodo quis imperdiet massa tincidunt nunc. Condimentum mattis pellentesque id nibh. Egestas purus viverra accumsan in nisl nisi scelerisque eu. Euismod in pellentesque massa placerat duis ultricies. Eget egestas purus viverra accumsan in. Id venenatis a condimentum vitae pellentesque habitant morbi. Dignissim convallis aenean et tortor Est ullamcorper eget nulla facilisi dignissim diam quis. Dui nunc mattis enim elementum sagittis.

Montserrat

Montserrat SemiBold 60p, 0

Montserrat Thin	*Thin Italic*
Montserrat ExtraLight	*ExtraLight Italic*
Montserrat Light	*Light Italic*
Montserrat Regular	*Italic*
Montserrat Medium	*Medium Italic*
Montserrat SemiBold	*SemiBold Italic*
Montserrat Bold	***Bold Italic***
Montserrat ExtraBold	***ExtraBold Italic***
Montserrat Black	***Black Italic***

16/18p

ABCDEFGHIJKLMNOPQRSTUVW abcdefghijklmnopqrstuvwxyz 123456789
ABCDEFGHIJKLMNOPQRSTUVW abcdefghijklmnopqrstuvwxyz 123456789

ABCDEFGHIJKLMNOPQRSTUVW abcdefghijklmnopqrstuvwxyz 123456789
ABCDEFGHIJKLMNOPQRSTUVW abcdefghijklmnopqrstuvwxyz 123456789

ABCDEFGHIJKLMNOPQRSTUVW abcdefghijklmnopqrstuvwxyz 123456789
ABCDEFGHIJKLMNOPQRSTUVW abcdefghijklmnopqrstuvwxyz 12345678

ABCDEFGHIJKLMNOPQRSTUVW abcdefghijklmnopqrstuvwxyz 12345678
ABCDEFGHIJKLMNOPQRSTUVW abcdefghijklmnopqrstuvwxyz 12345678

ABCDEFGHIJKLMNOPQRSTUVW abcdefghijklmnopqrstuvwxyz 1234567
ABCDEFGHIJKLMNOPQRSTUVW abcdefghijklmnopqrstuvwxyz 1234567

ABCDEFGHIJKLMNOPQRSTUVW abcdefghijklmnopqrstuvwxyz 123456
ABCDEFGHIJKLMNOPQRSTUVW abcdefghijklmnopqrstuvwxyz 123456

ABCDEFGHIJKLMNOPQRSTUVW abcdefghijklmnopqrstuvwxyz 12345
ABCDEFGHIJKLMNOPQRSTUVW abcdefghijklmnopqrstuvwxyz 12345

ABCDEFGHIJKLMNOPQRSTUVW abcdefghijklmnopqrstuvwxyz 1234
ABCDEFGHIJKLMNOPQRSTUVW abcdefghijklmnopqrstuvwxyz 1234

ABCDEFGHIJKLMNOPQRSTUVW abcdefghijklmnopqrstuvwxyz 1234
ABCDEFGHIJKLMNOPQRSTUVW abcdefghijklmnopqrstuvwxyz 1234

9/13p

License — Open Font License
Font tag — Sans serif, Text, Proxima Nova, Google

Link — fonts.google.com/specimen/Montserrat
Pair — Open Sans, Roboto, Raleway, Oswald, Lato

Deep into that darkness peering,
long I stood there, wondering, fearing, doubting,
dreaming dreams no mortal ever dared to dream before.
— **Edgar Allan Poe,** *Complete Tales and Poems*

Light 11/16p, 0 | SemiBold 10/16p, 0

Black 18p, 30

ExtraLight 9p, 100

Medium 10p, 100

ExtraBold 16/20p, 50

Italic 9p, 0

Light Italic 11p, 100

Medium 10p, 30 | Light Italic 10p, 30 | Black 30/30p, 10 | Light 8/10p, 0

ADVENTURE FOR THE YOUNG AT HEART

Go outside and explore

At any rate, That is Happiness;
To be dissolved into something
COMPLETE AND GREAT.

Montserrat Medium 21p-Bold 19.6p-Black 25.2p, 20 | Regular 10p, 10

— Willa Cather, *My Ántonia*

"Stay close to anything that makes you feel you are glad to be alive. Plant the seeds for a sustainable future. *Connect, respect and listen to nature,* for nature is our greatest teacher."

SemiBold 10/15p, 30

LOOK UP, KEEP GOING

Black 14p, 100

Lorem ipsum dolor sit amet, consectetur adipiscing elit, sed do eiusmod tempor incididunt ut labore et dolore magna aliqua. Ut enim ad minim veniam, nostrud exercitation ullamco laboris nisi aliquip ex ea commodo consequat. Duis aute irure dolor in reprehenderit in voluptate velit esse cillum dolore eu fugiat nulla pariatur. Excepteur sint occaecat cupidatat non proident, sunt in culpa qui officia deserunt mollit anim id est laborum.

"Aliquam fermentum est. Praesent posuere lorem quis quam viverra tempus. Suspendisse varius nunc nec sapien convallis rutrum. Donec vitae tincidunt tortor, nec tortor."

Ultrices sagittis orci a scelerisque purus. Diam maecenas ultricies mi eget mauris. Nam aliquam sem et tortor consequat id porta nibh. Tempor orci dapibus ultrices in iaculis nunc sed augue lacus. Sit amet massa vitae tortor condimentum.

Regular 7/9p, 0 | SemiBold 8/11p, 50

Mi sit amet mauris commodo quis. Adipiscing at in tellus integer feugiat scelerisque varius morbi in enim. Elementum nibh tellus molestie nunc non. Nisi porta lorem mollis aliquam ut porttitor leo a. Sed sed risus pretium quam vulputate dignissim. Nunc mi ipsum faucibus vitae aliquet nec ullam corper. Scelerisque viverra mauris in aliquam sem fringilla.

In nisl nisi scelerisque eu. Odio facilisis mauris sit amet massa. Porttitor lacus luctus accumsan tortor posuere ac ut consequat. Nibh venenatis cras sed felis. Vestibulum sed arcu non odio euismod. Vitae aliquet nec ullamcorper sit amet. Amet mauris commodo quis imperdiet massa tincidunt nunc. Condimentum mattis pellentesque id nibh. Egestas purus viverra accumsan in nisl nisi scelerisque eu. Euismod in pellentesque massa placerat duis ultricies. Eget egestas purus viverra accumsan in. Id venenatis a condimentum vitae pellentesque habitant morbi. Dignissim convallis aenean et tortor Est ullamcorper eget nulla facilisi dignissim diam quis. Dui nunc mattis enim elementum sagittis.

Black 14/17p, 100 | Light 8/25p, 25

Muli

Muli Bold 100p, 0

Muli ExtraLight
Muli Light
Muli Regular
Muli SemiBold
Muli Bold
Muli ExtraBold
Muli Black

Muli ExtraLight Italic
Muli Light Italic
Muli Italic
Muli SemiBold Italic
Muli Bold Italic
Muli ExtraBold Italic
Muli Black Italic

16/18p

ABCDEFGHIJKLMNOPQRSTUVW abcdefghijklmnopqrstuvwxyz 123456
ABCDEFGHIJKLMNOPQRSTUVW abcdefghijklmnopqrstuvwxyz 123456
+−×÷=#%&*,.:;!?()[]{}''""®©   +−×÷=#%&*,.:;!?()[]{}''""®©

ABCDEFGHIJKLMNOPQRSTUVW abcdefghijklmnopqrstuvwxyz 123456
ABCDEFGHIJKLMNOPQRSTUVW abcdefghijklmnopqrstuvwxyz 123456
+−×÷=#%&*,.:;!?()[]{}''""®©   +−×÷=#%&*,.:;!?()[]{}''""®©

ABCDEFGHIJKLMNOPQRSTUVW abcdefghijklmnopqrstuvwxyz 12345
ABCDEFGHIJKLMNOPQRSTUVW abcdefghijklmnopqrstuvwxyz 12345
+−×÷=#%&*,.:;!?()[]{}''""®©   +−×÷=#%&*,.:;!?()[]{}''""®©

ABCDEFGHIJKLMNOPQRSTUVW abcdefghijklmnopqrstuvwxyz 1234!
ABCDEFGHIJKLMNOPQRSTUVW abcdefghijklmnopqrstuvwxyz 1234!
+−×÷=#%&*,.:;!?()[]{}''""®©   +−×÷=#%&*,.:;!?()[]{}''""®©

ABCDEFGHIJKLMNOPQRSTUVW abcdefghijklmnopqrstuvwxyz 1234
ABCDEFGHIJKLMNOPQRSTUVW abcdefghijklmnopqrstuvwxyz 1234
+−×÷=#%&*,.:;!?()[]{}''""®©   +−×÷=#%&*,.:;!?()[]{}''""®©

ABCDEFGHIJKLMNOPQRSTUVW abcdefghijklmnopqrstuvwxyz 123
ABCDEFGHIJKLMNOPQRSTUVW abcdefghijklmnopqrstuvwxyz 123
+−×÷=#%&*,.:;!?()[]{}''""®©   +−×÷=#%&*,.:;!?()[]{}''""

ABCDEFGHIJKLMNOPQRSTUVW abcdefghijklmnopqrstuvwxyz 12
ABCDEFGHIJKLMNOPQRSTUVW abcdefghijklmnopqrstuvwxyz 12
+−×÷=#%&*,.:;!?()[]{}''""®©   +−×÷=#%&*,.:;!?()[]{}''

11/14p

| License | Open Font License |
| Font tag | Sans serif, Text, Forma DJR Text , Google |

| Link | fonts.google.com/specimen/Muli |
| Pair | Open Sans, Roboto, Montserrat, Lato, Playfair Display |

Deep into that darkness peering,
long I stood there, wondering, fearing, doubting,
dreaming dreams no mortal ever dared to dream before.
— **Edgar Allan Poe, Complete Tales and Poems**

Light 12/17p, 10 | Bold 10/14p, 0

Black 18p, 50

ExtraLight 9p, 100

Regular 10p, 100

Bold 16/20p, 50

Italic 9p, 0

Light Italic 11p, 100

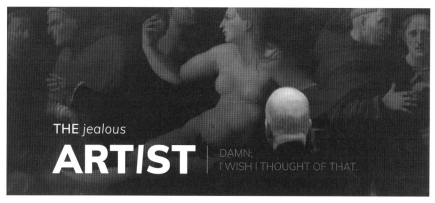

SemiBold 10p, 30 | Light Italic 10p, 30 | Black 30/30p, 10 | Light 8/10p, 0

ADVENTURE FOR THE YOUNG AT HEART

Go outside and explore

At any rate, That is Happiness;
To be dissolved into something
COMPLETE AND GREAT.

Muli SemiBold 21.7p-Bold 21.8p-Black 27p, 20 | Regular 10p, 10

— Willa Cather, *My Ántonia*

"Stay close to anything that makes you feel you are glad to be alive. Plant the seeds for a sustainable future. Connect, *respect and listen to nature*, for nature is our greatest teacher."

Bold 10/15p, 30

LOOK UP, KEEP GOING

Black 14p, 100

Lorem ipsum dolor sit amet, consectetur adipiscing elit, sed do eiusmod tempor incididunt ut labore et dolore magna aliqua. Ut enim ad minim veniam, nostrud exercitation ullamco laboris nisi aliquip ex ea commodo consequat. Duis aute irure dolor in reprehenderit in voluptate velit esse cillum dolore eu fugiat nulla pariatur. Excepteur sint occaecat cupidatat non proident, sunt in culpa qui officia deserunt mollit anim id est laborum.

"Aliquam fermentum est. Praesent posuere lorem quis quam viverra tempus. Suspendisse varius nunc nec sapien convallis rutrum. Donec vitae tincidunt tortor, nec tempor tortor."

Ultrices sagittis orci a scelerisque purus. Diam maecenas ultricies mi eget mauris. Nam aliquam sem et tortor consequat id porta nibh. Tempor orci dapibus ultrices in iaculis nunc sed augue lacus. Sit amet massa vitae tortor condimentum.

Regular 7/9p, 0 | Bold 8/11p, 50

Mi sit amet mauris commodo quis. Adipiscing at in tellus integer feugiat scelerisque varius morbi in enim. Elementum nibh tellus molestie nunc non. Nisi porta lorem mollis aliquam ut porttitor leo a. Sed sed risus pretium quam vulputate dignissim. Nunc mi ipsum faucibus vitae aliquet nec ullam corper. Scelerisque viverra mauris in aliquam sem fringilla.

In nisl nisi scelerisque eu. Odio facilisis mauris sit amet massa. Porttitor lacus luctus accumsan tortor posuere ac ut consequat. Nibh venenatis cras sed felis. Vestibulum sed arcu non odio euismod. Vitae aliquet nec ullamcorper sit amet. Amet mauris commodo quis imperdiet massa tincidunt nunc. Condimentum mattis pellentesque id nibh. Egestas purus viverra accumsan in nisl nisi scelerisque eu. Euismod in pellentesque massa placerat duis ultricies. Eget egestas purus viverra accumsan in. Id venenatis a condimentum vitae pellentesque habitant morbi. Dignissim convallis aenean et tortor Est ullamcorper eget nulla facilisi dignissim diam quis. Dui nunc mattis enim elementum sagittis.

Black 14/17p, 100 | Light 8/25p, 25

Noto Sans

Noto Sans Bold 67p, 0

Noto Sans Regular
Noto Sans Italic
Noto Sans Bold
Noto Sans Bold Italic

20/24p, 0

ABCDEFGHIJKLMNOPQRSTUVWXYZ
ABCDEFGHIJKLMNOPQRSTUVWXYZ
abcefghijklmnopqrstuvwxyz abc@gmail.com
abcefghijklmnopqrstuvwxyz abc@gmail.com
1234567890 +−×÷=#%&*, . : ; ! ? ( )[ ]{ } ' ' " " ®©
1234567890 +−×÷=#%&, . : ; ! ? ( )[ ]{ } ' ' " " ®©*

ABCDEFGHIJKLMNOPQRSTUVWXYZ
ABCDEFGHIJKLMNOPQRSTUVWXYZ
abcefghijklmnopqrstuvwxyz abc@gmail.com
abcefghijklmnopqrstuvwxyz abc@gmail.com
1234567890 +−×÷=#%&*, . : ; ! ? ( )[ ]{ } ' ' " " ®©
1234567890 +−×÷=#%&*, . : ; ! ? ( )[ ]{ } ' ' " " ®©

14/20p, 0

"I loved her against *reason*, against *promise*, against *peace*, against *hope*, against *happiness*, against *all discouragement* that could be."
— Charles Dickens, *Great Expectations*

Regular 10/14p, 0 | Bold 9/14p, 10

License Apache License, Version 2.0
Font tag Sans serif, Text, Myriad, Google

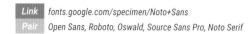

Link fonts.google.com/specimen/Noto+Sans
Pair Open Sans, Roboto, Oswald, Source Sans Pro, Noto Serif

Deep into that darkness peering,
long I stood there, wondering, fearing, doubting,
dreaming dreams no mortal ever dared to dream before.
— **Edgar Allan Poe, *Complete Tales and Poems***

Regular 12/17p, 10 | Bold 10/14p, 0

SPARKLING ARTS

www.sparklingarts.com

Founder
CAROLINE LEE

carolinelee@sparklingarts.com

010.2345.6789

Bold 18p, 50

Regular 9p, 100

Regular 10p, 100

Bold 16/20p, 50

Italic 9p, 0

Italic 11p, 100

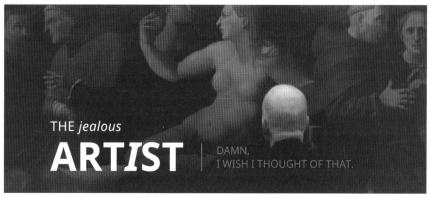

THE *jealous*
ARTIST | DAMN, I WISH I THOUGHT OF THAT.

Regular 10p, 30 | Italic 10p, 30 | Bold 30/30p, 10 | Regular 8/10p, 0

ADVENTURE FOR THE YOUNG AT HEART

Go outside and explore

At any rate, That is Happiness; To be dissolved into something
COMPLETE AND GREAT.

Noto Sans Regular 22.4-21.8-Bold 28p, 20 | Regular 10p, 10

— Willa Cather, *My Ántonia*

"Stay close to anything that makes you feel you are glad to be alive. Plant the seeds for a sustainable future. *Connect, respect and listen to nature,* for nature is our greatest teacher."

Bold 10/15p, 30

LOOK UP, KEEP GOING

Bold 14p, 100

Lorem ipsum dolor sit amet, consectetur adipiscing elit, sed do eiusmod tempor incididunt ut labore et dolore magna aliqua. Ut enim ad minim veniam, nostrud exercitation ullamco laboris nisi aliquip ex ea commodo consequat. Duis aute irure dolor in reprehenderit in voluptate velit esse cillum dolore eu fugiat nulla pariatur. Excepteur sint occaecat cupidatat non proident, sunt in culpa qui officia deserunt mollit anim id est laborum.

"Aliquam fermentum est. Praesent posuere lorem quis quam viverra tempus. Suspendisse varius nunc nec sapien convallis rutrum. Donec vitae tincidunt tortor, nec tortor."

Ultrices sagittis orci a scelerisque purus. Diam maecenas ultricies mi eget mauris. Nam aliquam sem et tortor consequat id porta nibh. Tempor orci dapibus ultrices in iaculis nunc sed augue lacus. Sit amet massa vitae tortor condimentum.

Regular 7/9p, 0 | Bold 8/11p, 50

Mi sit amet mauris commodo quis. Adipiscing at in tellus integer feugiat scelerisque varius morbi in enim. Elementum nibh tellus molestie nunc non. Nisi porta lorem mollis aliquam ut porttitor leo a. Sed sed risus pretium quam vulputate dignissim. Nunc mi ipsum faucibus vitae aliquet nec ullam corper. Scelerisque viverra mauris in aliquam sem fringilla.

In nisl nisi scelerisque eu. Odio facilisis mauris sit amet massa. Porttitor lacus luctus accumsan tortor posuere ac ut consequat. Nibh venenatis cras sed felis. Vestibulum sed arcu non odio euismod. Vitae aliquet nec ullamcorper sit amet. Amet mauris commodo quis imperdiet massa tincidunt nunc. Condimentum mattis pellentesque id nibh. Egestas purus viverra accumsan in nisl nisi scelerisque eu. Euismod in pellentesque massa placerat duis ultricies. Eget egestas purus viverra accumsan in. Id venenatis a condimentum vitae pellentesque habitant morbi. Dignissim convallis aenean et tortor Est ullamcorper eget nulla facilisi dignissim diam quis. Dui nunc mattis enim elementum sagittis.

Bold 14/17p, 100 | Regular 8/25p, 25

Nunito

Nunito ExtraLight	Nunito ExtraLight Italic
Nunito Light	Nunito Light Italic
Nunito Regular	Nunito Italic
Nunito SemiBold	Nunito SemiBold Italic
Nunito Bold	Nunito Bold Italic
Nunito ExtraBold	Nunito ExtraBold Italic
Nunito Black	Nunito Black Italic

ABCDEFGHIJKLMNOPQRSTUVW abcdefghijklmnopqrstuvwxyz 123456789
ABCDEFGHIJKLMNOPQRSTUVW abcdefghijklmnopqrstuvwxyz 123456789
+−×÷=#%&*,.:;!? ()[]{}''"" ®©   +−×÷=#%&*,.:;!? ()[]{}''"" ®©

ABCDEFGHIJKLMNOPQRSTUVW abcdefghijklmnopqrstuvwxyz 12345678
ABCDEFGHIJKLMNOPQRSTUVW abcdefghijklmnopqrstuvwxyz 12345678
+−×÷=#%&*,.:;!? ()[]{}''"" ®©   +−×÷=#%&*,.:;!? ()[]{}''"" ®©

ABCDEFGHIJKLMNOPQRSTUVW abcdefghijklmnopqrstuvwxyz 1234567
ABCDEFGHIJKLMNOPQRSTUVW abcdefghijklmnopqrstuvwxyz 1234567
+−×÷=#%&*,.:;!? ()[]{}''"" ®©   +−×+=#%&*,.:;!? ()[]{}''"" ®©

ABCDEFGHIJKLMNOPQRSTUVW abcdefghijklmnopqrstuvwxyz 1234567
ABCDEFGHIJKLMNOPQRSTUVW abcdefghijklmnopqrstuvwxyz 1234567
+−×÷=#%&*,.:;!? ()[]{}''"" ®©   +−×-=‡%&*,.:;!? ()[]{}''"" ®©

ABCDEFGHIJKLMNOPQRSTUVW abcdefghijklmnopqrstuvwxyz 123456
ABCDEFGHIJKLMNOPQRSTUVW abcdefghijklmnopqrstuvwxyz 123456
+−×÷=#%&*,.:;!? ()[]{}''"" ®©   +−×+=‡%&*,.:;!? ()[]{}''"" ®©

ABCDEFGHIJKLMNOPQRSTUVW abcdefghijklmnopqrstuvwxyz 12345
ABCDEFGHIJKLMNOPQRSTUVW abcdefghijklmnopqrstuvwxyz 12345
+−×÷=#%&*,.:;!? ()[]{}''"" ®©   +−×÷=#%&*,.:;!? ()[]{}''"" ®

ABCDEFGHIJKLMNOPQRSTUVW abcdefghijklmnopqrstuvwxyz 1234!
ABCDEFGHIJKLMNOPQRSTUVW abcdefghijklmnopqrstuvwxyz 1234!
+−×÷=#%&*,.:;!? ()[]{}''"" ®©   +−×÷=#%&*,.:;!? ()[]{}''""

License	Open Font License
Font tag	Sans serif, Text, Proxima Soft, Google

Link	fonts.google.com/specimen/Nunito
Pair	Open Sans, Roboto, Montserrat, Oswald, Lato

Deep into that darkness peering,
long I stood there, wondering, fearing, doubting,
dreaming dreams no mortal ever dared to dream before.
— **Edgar Allan Poe, Complete Tales and Poems**

Light 12/17p, 10 | Bold 10/14p, 0

SPARKLING ARTS

010.2345.6789

www.sparklingarts.com

Founder
CAROLINE LEE

carolinelee@sparklingarts.com

Black 18p, 50

ExtraLight 9p, 100

Regular 10p, 100

Bold 16/20p, 50

Italic 9p, 0

Light Italic 11p, 100

THE jealous
ARTIST DAMN,
I WISH I THOUGHT OF THAT.

SemiBold 10p, 30 | Light Italic 10p, 30 | Black 30/30p, 10 | Light 8/10p, 0

ADVENTURE FOR THE YOUNG AT HEART

Go outside and explore

At any rate, That is Happiness; To be dissolved into something
COMPLETE AND GREAT.

Nunito SemiBold 22.9p-Bold 22.3p-Black 27.3p, 20 | Regular 10p, 10

— Willa Cather, My Ántonia

"Stay close to anything that makes you feel you are glad to be alive. Plant the seeds for a sustainable future. Connect, respect and listen to nature, for nature is our greatest teacher."

Bold 10/15p, 30

LOOK UP, KEEP GOING

Black 14p, 100

Lorem ipsum dolor sit amet, consectetur adipiscing elit, sed do eiusmod tempor incididunt ut labore et dolore magna aliqua. Ut enim ad minim veniam, nostrud exercitation ullamco laboris nisi aliquip ex ea commodo consequat. Duis aute irure dolor in reprehenderit in voluptate velit esse cillum dolore eu fugiat nulla pariatur. Excepteur sint occaecat cupidatat non proident, sunt in culpa qui officia deserunt mollit anim id est laborum.

"Aliquam fermentum est. Praesent posuere lorem quis quam viverra tempus. Suspendisse varius nunc nec sapien convallis rutrum. Donec vitae tincidunt tortor, nec tempor tortor."

Ultrices sagittis orci a scelerisque purus. Diam maecenas ultricies mi eget mauris. Nam aliquam sem et tortor consequat id porta nibh. Tempor orci dapibus ultrices in iaculis nunc sed augue lacus. Sit amet massa vitae tortor condimentum.

Mi sit amet mauris commodo quis. Adipiscing at in tellus integer feugiat scelerisque varius morbi in enim. Elementum nibh tellus molestie nunc non. Nisi porta lorem mollis aliquam ut porttitor leo a. Sed sed risus pretium quam vulputate dignissim. Nunc mi ipsum faucibus vitae aliquet nec ullam corper. Scelerisque viverra mauris in aliquam sem fringilla.

In nisl nisi scelerisque eu. Odio facilisis mauris sit amet massa. Porttitor lacus luctus accumsan tortor posuere ac ut consequat. Nibh venenatis cras sed felis. Vestibulum sed arcu non odio euismod. Vitae aliquet nec ullamcorper sit amet. Amet mauris commodo quis imperdiet massa tincidunt nunc. Condimentum mattis pellentesque id nibh. Egestas purus viverra accumsan in nisl nisi scelerisque eu. Euismod in pellentesque massa placerat duis ultricies. Eget egestas purus viverra accumsan in. Id venenatis a condimentum vitae pellentesque habitant morbi. Dignissim convallis aenean et tortor Est ullamcorper eget nulla facilisi dignissim diam quis. Dui nunc mattis enim elementum sagittis.

Regular 7/9p, 0 | Bold 8/11p, 50

Black 14/17p, 100 | Light 8/25p, 25

Nunito Sans

Nunito Sans Bold 60p, 0

Nunito Sans ExtraLight   *ExtraLight Italic*
Nunito Sans Light   *Light Italic*
Nunito Sans Regular   *Italic*
Nunito Sans SemiBold   *SemiBold Italic*
Nunito Sans Bold   ***Bold Italic***
Nunito Sans ExtraBold ***ExtraBold Italic***
Nunito Sans Black   ***Black Italic***   16/18p

ABCDEFGHIJKLMNOPQRSTUVW abcdefghijklmnopqrstuvwxyz 123456789(
ABCDEFGHIJKLMNOPQRSTUVW abcdefghijklmnopqrstuvwxyz 123456789(
+−×÷=#%&*,.:;!?()[]{}''""®©   +−×÷=#%&*,.:;!?()[]{}''""®©

ABCDEFGHIJKLMNOPQRSTUVW abcdefghijklmnopqrstuvwxyz 123456789
ABCDEFGHIJKLMNOPQRSTUVW abcdefghijklmnopqrstuvwxyz 123456789
+−×÷=#%&*,.:;!?()[]{}''""®©   +−×÷=#%&*,.:;!?()[]{}''""®©

ABCDEFGHIJKLMNOPQRSTUVW abcdefghijklmnopqrstuvwxyz 12345678
ABCDEFGHIJKLMNOPQRSTUVW abcdefghijklmnopqrstuvwxyz 12345678
+−×÷=#%&*,.:;!?()[]{}''""®©   +−×÷=#%&*,.:;!?()[]{}''""®©

ABCDEFGHIJKLMNOPQRSTUVW abcdefghijklmnopqrstuvwxyz 1234567
ABCDEFGHIJKLMNOPQRSTUVW abcdefghijklmnopqrstuvwxyz 1234567
+−×÷=#%&*,.:;!?()[]{}''""®©   +−×÷=#%&*,.:;!?()[]{}''""®©

ABCDEFGHIJKLMNOPQRSTUVW abcdefghijklmnopqrstuvwxyz 1234567
ABCDEFGHIJKLMNOPQRSTUVW abcdefghijklmnopqrstuvwxyz 1234567
+−×÷=#%&*,.:;!?()[]{}''""®©   +−×÷=#%&*,.:;!?()[]{}''""®©

ABCDEFGHIJKLMNOPQRSTUVW abcdefghijklmnopqrstuvwxyz 123456
ABCDEFGHIJKLMNOPQRSTUVW abcdefghijklmnopqrstuvwxyz 123456
+−×÷=#%&*,.:;!?()[]{}''""®©   +−×÷=#%&*,.:;!?()[]{}''""®

ABCDEFGHIJKLMNOPQRSTUVW abcdefghijklmnopqrstuvwxyz 12345
ABCDEFGHIJKLMNOPQRSTUVW abcdefghijklmnopqrstuvwxyz 12345
+−×÷=#%&*,.:;!?()[]{}''""®©   +−×÷=#%&*,.:;!?()[]{}''""®

10/14p

| License | Open Font License | Link | fonts.google.com/specimen/Nunito+Sans |
| Font tag | Sans serif, Text, Avenir, Google | Pair | Roboto, Montserrat, Open Sans, Lato, Raleway |

Deep into that darkness peering,
long I stood there, wondering, fearing, doubting,
dreaming dreams no mortal ever dared to dream before.
— **Edgar Allan Poe, *Complete Tales and Poems***

Light 12/17p, 10 | Bold 10/14p, 0

SPARKLING ARTS

www.sparklingarts.com

Founder
CAROLINE LEE

carolinelee@sparklingarts.com

010.2345.6789

Black 18p, 50

ExtraLight 9p, 100

Regular 10p, 100

Bold 16/20p, 50

Italic 9p, 0

Light Italic 11p, 100

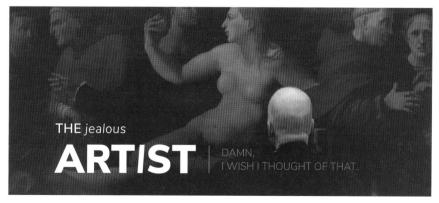

THE jealous
ART/ST | DAMN,
I WISH I THOUGHT OF THAT.

SemiBold 10p, 30 | Light Italic 10p, 30 | Black 30/30p, 10 | Light 8/10p, 0

ADVENTURE FOR THE YOUNG AT HEART

Go outside and explore

At any rate, That is Happiness;
To be dissolved into something
COMPLETE AND GREAT.

Nunito Sans SemiBold 22.9p·Bold 22.3p·Black 27.3p, 20 ¦ Regular 10p, 10 — Willa Cather, My Ántonia

"Stay close to anything that makes you feel you are glad to be alive. Plant the seeds for a sustainable future. Connect, respect and listen to nature, for nature is our greatest teacher."

Bold 10/15p, 30

LOOK UP, KEEP GOING

Black 14p, 100

Lorem ipsum dolor sit amet, consectetur adipiscing elit, sed do eiusmod tempor incididunt ut labore et dolore magna aliqua. Ut enim ad minim veniam, nostrud exercitation ullamco laboris nisi aliquip ex ea commodo consequat. Duis aute irure dolor in reprehenderit in voluptate velit esse cillum dolore eu fugiat nulla pariatur. Excepteur sint occaecat cupidatat non proident, sunt in culpa qui officia deserunt mollit anim id est laborum.

"Aliquam fermentum est. Praesent posuere lorem quis quam viverra tempus. Suspendisse varius nunc nec sapien convallis rutrum. Donec vitae tincidunt tortor, nec tempor tortor."

Ultrices sagittis orci a scelerisque purus. Diam maecenas ultricies mi eget mauris. Nam aliquam sem et tortor consequat id porta nibh. Tempor orci dapibus ultrices in iaculis nunc sed augue lacus. Sit amet massa vitae tortor condimentum.

Mi sit amet mauris commodo quis. Adipiscing at in tellus integer feugiat scelerisque varius morbi in enim. Elementum nibh tellus molestie nunc non. Nisi porta lorem mollis aliquam ut porttitor leo a. Sed sed risus pretium quam vulputate dignissim. Nunc mi ipsum faucibus vitae aliquet nec ullam corper. Scelerisque viverra mauris in aliquam sem fringilla.

In nisl nisi scelerisque eu. Odio facilisis mauris sit amet massa. Porttitor lacus luctus accumsan tortor posuere ac ut consequat. Nibh venenatis cras sed felis. Vestibulum sed arcu non odio euismod. Vitae aliquet nec ullamcorper sit amet. Amet mauris commodo quis imperdiet massa tincidunt nunc. Condimentum mattis pellentesque id nibh. Egestas purus viverra accumsan in nisl nisi scelerisque eu. Euismod in pellentesque massa placerat duis ultricies. Eget egestas purus viverra accumsan in. Id venenatis a condimentum vitae pellentesque habitant morbi. Dignissim convallis aenean et tortor Est ullamcorper eget nulla facilisi dignissim diam quis. Dui nunc mattis enim elementum sagittis.

Regular 7/9p, 0 ¦ Bold 8/11p, 50

Open Sans

Open Sans Bold 65p, 0

Open Sans Light | *Light Italic*
Open Sans Regular | *Italic*
Open Sans SemiBold | *SemiBold Italic*
Open Sans Bold | ***Bold Italic***
Open Sans ExtraBold | ***ExtraBold***

18/24p

ABCDEFGHIJKLMNOPQRSTUVWXYZ abcdefghijklmnopqrstuvwxyz
ABCDEFGHIJKLMNOPQRSTUVWXYZ abcdefghijklmnopqrstuvwxyz
1234567890 *1234567890* +−×÷=#%&*, . : ; ! ? ( )[ ]{ } ' ' " " ®©

ABCDEFGHIJKLMNOPQRSTUVWXYZ abcdefghijklmnopqrstuvwxyz
ABCDEFGHIJKLMNOPQRSTUVWXYZ abcdefghijklmnopqrstuvwxyz
1234567890 *1234567890* +−×÷=#%&*, . : ; ! ? ( )[ ]{ } ' ' " " ®©

ABCDEFGHIJKLMNOPQRSTUVWXYZ abcdefghijklmnopqrstuvwxyz
ABCDEFGHIJKLMNOPQRSTUVWXYZ abcdefghijklmnopqrstuvwxyz
1234567890 *1234567890* +−×÷=#%&*, . : ; ! ? ( )[ ]{ } ' ' " " ®©

ABCDEFGHIJKLMNOPQRSTUVWXYZ abcdefghijklmnopqrstuvwx
ABCDEFGHIJKLMNOPQRSTUVWXYZ abcdefghijklmnopqrstuvwxyz
1234567890 *1234567890* +−×÷=#%&*, . : ; ! ? ( )[ ]{ } ' ' " " ®©

ABCDEFGHIJKLMNOPQRSTUVWXYZ abcdefghijklmnopqrstuvw
ABCDEFGHIJKLMNOPQRSTUVWXYZ abcdefghijklmnopqrstuvwxy
1234567890 *1234567890* +−×÷=#%&*, . : ; ! ? ( )[ ]{ } ' ' " " ®©

11/16p

| License | Apache License, Version 2.0 | | Link | fonts.google.com/specimen/Open+Sans |
| Font tag | Sans serif, Text, Myriad, Google | | Pair | Roboto, Open Sans, Oswald, Montserrat, Raleway |

Deep into that darkness peering,
long I stood there, wondering, fearing, doubting,
dreaming dreams no mortal ever dared to dream before.
— Edgar Allan Poe, *Complete Tales and Poems*

Light 12/17p, 10 | SemiBold 10/14p, 0

SPARKLING ARTS

www.sparklingarts.com

Founder
CAROLINE LEE

carolinelee@sparklingarts.com

010.2345.6789

ExtraBold 18p, 50

Light 9p, 100

Light 10p, 100

Bold 16/20p, 50

Italic 9p, 0

Light Italic 11p, 100

THE *jealous*
ART/ST | DAMN,
I WISH I THOUGHT OF THAT.

Regular 10p, 30 | Light Italic 10p, 30 | ExtraBold 30/30p, 10 | Light 8/10p, 0

ADVENTURE FOR THE YOUNG AT HEART

Go outside and explore

At any rate, That is Happiness; To be dissolved into something COMPLETE AND GREAT.

Open Sans SemiBold 21.8p·Bold 20.7p·ExtraBold 27.5p, 20 | Regular 10p, 10 — Willa Cather, *My Ántonia*

"Stay close to anything that makes you feel you are glad to be alive. Plant the seeds for a sustainable future. *Connect, respect and listen to nature,* for nature is our greatest teacher."

SemiBold 10/15p, 30

LOOK UP, KEEP GOING

ExtraBold 14p, 100

Lorem ipsum dolor sit amet, consectetur adipiscing elit, sed do eiusmod tempor incididunt ut labore et dolore magna aliqua. Ut enim ad minim veniam, nostrud exercitation ullamco laboris nisi aliquip ex ea commodo consequat. Duis aute irure dolor in reprehenderit in voluptate velit esse cillum dolore eu fugiat nulla pariatur. Excepteur sint occaecat cupidatat non proident, sunt in culpa qui officia deserunt mollit anim id est laborum.

"Aliquam fermentum est. Praesent posuere lorem quis quam viverra tempus. Suspendisse varius nunc nec sapien convallis rutrum. Donec vitae tincidunt tortor, nec tempor tortor."

Ultrices sagittis orci a scelerisque purus. Diam maecenas ultricies mi eget mauris. Nam aliquam sem et tortor consequat id porta nibh. Tempor orci dapibus ultrices in iaculis nunc sed augue lacus. Sit amet massa vitae tortor condimentum.

Regular 7/9p, 0 | SemiBold 8/11p, 50

Mi sit amet mauris commodo quis. Adipiscing at in tellus integer feugiat scelerisque varius morbi in enim. Elementum nibh tellus molestie nunc non. Nisi porta lorem mollis aliquam ut porttitor leo a. Sed sed risus pretium quam vulputate dignissim. Nunc mi ipsum faucibus vitae aliquet nec ullam corper. Scelerisque viverra mauris in aliquam sem fringilla.

In nisl nisi scelerisque eu. Odio facilisis mauris sit amet massa. Porttitor lacus luctus accumsan tortor posuere ac ut consequat. Nibh venenatis cras sed felis. Vestibulum sed arcu non odio euismod. Vitae aliquet nec ullamcorper sit amet. Amet mauris commodo quis imperdiet massa tincidunt nunc. Condimentum mattis pellentesque id nibh. Egestas purus viverra accumsan in nisl nisi scelerisque eu. Euismod in pellentesque massa placerat duis ultricies. Eget egestas purus viverra accumsan in. Id venenatis a condimentum vitae pellentesque habitant morbi. Dignissim convallis aenean et tortor Est ullamcorper eget nulla facilisi dignissim diam quis. Dui nunc mattis enim elementum sagittis.

ExtraBold 14/17p, 100 | Light 8/25p, 25

Oswald

Oswald Regualr 90p, 0

Oswald Extra Light
Oswald Light
Oswald Regular
Oswald Medium
Oswald DemiBold
Oswald Bold

20/24p, 0

ABCDEFGHIJKLMNOPQRSTUVWXYZ
1234567890 abcefghijklmnopqrstuvwxyz

+-×÷=#%&*,.:;!?
()[]{}''"" ®©

ABCDEFGHIJKLMNOPQRSTUVWXYZ
1234567890 abcefghijklmnopqrstuvwxyz

+-×÷=#%&*,.:;!?
()[]{}''"" ®©

ABCDEFGHIJKLMNOPQRSTUVWXYZ
1234567890 abcefghijklmnopqrstuvwxyz

+-×÷=#%&*,.:;!?
()[]{}''"" ®©

ABCDEFGHIJKLMNOPQRSTUVWXYZ
1234567890 abcefghijklmnopqrstuvwxyz

+-×÷=#%&*,.:;!?
()[]{}''"" ®©

ABCDEFGHIJKLMNOPQRSTUVWXYZ
1234567890 abcefghijklmnopqrstuvwxyz

+-×÷=#%&*,.:;!?
()[]{}''"" ®©

ABCDEFGHIJKLMNOPQRSTUVWXYZ
1234567890 abcefghijklmnopqrstuvwxyz

+-×÷=#%&*,.:;!?
()[]{}''"" ®©

14/20p, 0

| License | Open Font License | Link | fonts.google.com/specimen/Oswald |
| Font tag | Sans serif, text, League Gothic, Google | Pair | Open Sans, Roboto, Lato, Montserrat, Raleway |

Deep into that darkness peering,
long I stood there, wondering, fearing, doubting,
dreaming dreams no mortal ever dared to dream before.
— Edgar Allan Poe, Complete Tales and Poems

Light 15/18p, 10 | Medium 11/15p, 0

SPARKLING ARTS

www.sparklingarts.com

Founder
CAROLINE LEE

carolinelee@sparklingarts.com

010.2345.6789

Bold 18p, 50

Light 9p, 100

Regular 10p, 100

Bold 16/20p, 50

Light 9p, 0

Extra Light 11p, 100

THE jealous
ARTIST | DAMN,
I WISH I THOUGHT OF THAT.

Medium 10p, 30 | Regular 10p, 30 | Bold 30/30p, 20 | Light 8/10p, 0

ADVENTURE FOR THE YOUNG AT HEART

Go outside and explore

At any rate, That is Happiness; To be dissolved into something
COMPLETE AND GREAT.

Oswald Regular 28.7 ·Medium 26.7 ·Bold 34.5p, 20 | Regular 10p, 10

— Willa Cather, My Ántonia

"Stay close to anything that makes you feel you are glad to be alive. Plant the seeds for a sustainable future. Connect, respect and listen to nature, for nature is our greatest teacher."

Medium 10/15p, 30

LOOK UP, KEEP GOING

Bold 14p, 100

Lorem ipsum dolor sit amet, consectetur adipiscing elit, sed do eiusmod tempor incididunt ut labore et dolore magna aliqua. Ut enim ad minim veniam, nostrud exercitation ullamco laboris nisi aliquip ex ea commodo consequat. Duis aute irure dolor in reprehenderit in voluptate velit esse cillum dolore eu fugiat nulla pariatur. Excepteur sint occaecat cupidatat non proident, sunt in culpa qui officia deserunt mollit anim id est laborum.

"Aliquam fermentum est. Praesent posuere lorem quis quam viverra tempus. Suspendisse varius nunc nec sapien convallis rutrum. Donec vitae tincidunt tortor, nec tortor."

Ultrices sagittis orci a scelerisque purus. Diam maecenas ultricies mi eget mauris. Nam aliquam sem et tortor consequat id porta nibh. Tempor orci dapibus ultrices in iaculis nunc sed augue lacus. Sit amet massa vitae tortor condimentum.

Light 8/10p, 0 | Medium 8/11p, 50

Mi sit amet mauris commodo quis. Adipiscing at in tellus integer feugiat scelerisque varius morbi in enim. Elementum nibh tellus molestie nunc non. Nisi porta lorem mollis aliquam ut porttitor leo a. Sed sed risus pretium quam vulputate dignissim. Nunc mi ipsum faucibus vitae aliquet nec ullam corper. Scelerisque viverra mauris in aliquam sem fringilla.

In nisl nisi scelerisque eu. Odio facilisis mauris sit amet massa. Porttitor lacus luctus accumsan tortor posuere ac ut consequat. Nibh venenatis cras sed felis. Vestibulum sed arcu non odio euismod. Vitae aliquet nec ullamcorper sit amet. Amet mauris commodo quis imperdiet massa tincidunt nunc. Condimentum mattis pellentesque id nibh. Egestas purus viverra accumsan in nisl nisi scelerisque eu. Euismod in pellentesque massa placerat duis ultricies. Eget egestas purus viverra accumsan in. Id venenatis a condimentum vitae pellentesque habitant morbi. Dignissim convallis aenean et tortor Est ullamcorper eget nulla facilisi dignissim diam quis. Dui nunc mattis enim elementum sagittis.

Oxygen

Oxygen Bold 90p, 0

Oxygen Light
Oxygen Regular
Oxygen Bold

24/28p, 0

ABCDEFGHIJKLMNOPQRSTUVWXYZ
abcefghijklmnopqrstuvwxyz abc@gmail.com
The quick brown fox jumps over the lazy dog
1234567890 +−×÷=#%&*, . : ; ! ? ( )[ ]{ } ' ' " " ®©

ABCDEFGHIJKLMNOPQRSTUVWXYZ
abcefghijklmnopqrstuvwxyz abc@gmail.com
The quick brown fox jumps over the lazy dog
1234567890 +−×÷=#%&*, . : ; ! ? ( )[ ]{ } ' ' " " ®©

ABCDEFGHIJKLMNOPQRSTUVWXYZ
abcefghijklmnopqrstuvwxyz abc@gmail.com
The quick brown fox jumps over the lazy dog
1234567890 +−×÷=#%&*, . : ; ! ? ( )[ ]{ } ' ' " " ®©

14/20p, 0

"I loved her against reason, against promise, against peace, against
hope, against happiness, against all discouragement that could be."
— **Charles Dickens, Great Expectations**

Light 10/14p, 0 | Bold 9/14p, 10

License	Open Font License	Link	fonts.google.com/specimen/Oxygen
Font tag	Sans serif, Web, Linux, Google	Pair	Open Sans, Lato, Source Sans Pro, Montserrat, Raleway

Deep into that darkness peering,
long I stood there, wondering, fearing, doubting,
dreaming dreams no mortal ever dared to dream before.
— **Edgar Allan Poe, Complete Tales and Poems**

Right 12/17p, 10 | Bold 10/14p, 0

SPARKLING ARTS

www.sparklingarts.com

Founder
CAROLINE LEE

carolinelee@sparklingarts.com

010.2345.6789

Bold 18p, 50

Light 9p, 100

Regular 10p, 100

Bold 16/20p, 50

Light 9p, 0

Light 11p, 100

THE jealous
ARTIST DAMN,
I WISH I THOUGHT OF THAT.

Regular 10p, 30 | Bold 30/30p, 10 | Light 8/10p, 0

ADVENTURE FOR THE YOUNG AT HEART

Go outside and explore

At any rate, That is Happiness;
To be dissolved into something
COMPLETE AND GREAT.

Oxygen Light 23.5-222.7-Bold 28.8p, 20 | Regular 10p, 10

— Willa Cather, My Ántonia

"Stay close to anything that makes you feel you are glad to be alive. Plant the seeds for a sustainable future. Connect, respect and listen to nature, for nature is our greatest teacher."

Bold 10/15p, 30

LOOK UP, KEEP GOING

Bold 14p, 100

Lorem ipsum dolor sit amet, consectetur adipiscing elit, sed do eiusmod tempor incididunt ut labore et dolore magna aliqua. Ut enim ad minim veniam, nostrud exercitation ullamco laboris nisi aliquip ex ea commodo consequat. Duis aute irure dolor in reprehenderit in voluptate velit esse cillum dolore eu fugiat nulla pariatur. Excepteur sint occaecat cupidatat non proident, sunt in culpa qui officia deserunt mollit anim id est laborum.

"Aliquam fermentum est. Praesent posuere lorem quis quam viverra tempus. Suspendisse varius nunc nec sapien convallis rutrum. Donec vitae tincidunt tortor, nec tempor tortor."

Ultrices sagittis orci a scelerisque purus. Diam maecenas ultricies mi eget mauris. Nam aliquam sem et tortor consequat id porta nibh. Tempor orci dapibus ultrices in iaculis nunc sed augue lacus. Sit amet massa vitae tortor condimentum.

Light 7/9p, 0 | Bold 8/11p, 50

Mi sit amet mauris commodo quis. Adipiscing at in tellus integer feugiat scelerisque varius morbi in enim. Elementum nibh tellus molestie nunc non. Nisi porta lorem mollis aliquam ut porttitor leo a. Sed sed risus pretium quam vulputate dignissim. Nunc mi ipsum faucibus vitae aliquet nec ullam corper. Scelerisque viverra mauris in aliquam sem fringilla.

In nisl nisi scelerisque eu. Odio facilisis mauris sit amet massa. Porttitor lacus luctus accumsan tortor posuere ac ut consequat. Nibh venenatis cras sed felis. Vestibulum sed arcu non odio euismod. Vitae aliquet nec ullamcorper sit amet. Amet mauris commodo quis imperdiet massa tincidunt nunc. Condimentum mattis pellentesque id nibh. Egestas purus viverra accumsan in nisl nisi scelerisque eu. Euismod in pellentesque massa placerat duis ultricies. Eget egestas purus viverra accumsan in. Id venenatis a condimentum vitae pellentesque habitant morbi. Dignissim convallis aenean et tortor Est ullamcorper eget nulla facilisi dignissim diam quis. Dui nunc mattis enim elementum sagittis.

Bold 14/17p, 100 | Regular 8/25p, 25

Poppins

Poppins SemiBold 83p, 0

Poppins Thin	*Thin Italic*
Poppins ExtraLight	*ExtraLight Italic*
Poppins Light	*Light Italic*
Poppins Regular	*Italic*
Poppins Medium	*Medium Italic*
Poppins SemiBold	***SemiBold Italic***
Poppins Bold	***Bold Italic***
Poppins ExtraBold	***ExtraBold Italic***
Poppins Black	***Black Italic***

16/18p

ABCDEFGHIJKLMNOPQRSTUVW abcdefghijklmnopqrstuvwxyz 123456

ABCDEFGHIJKLMNOPQRSTUVW abcdefghijklmnopqrstuvwxyz 123456

ABCDEFGHIJKLMNOPQRSTUVW abcdefghijklmnopqrstuvwxyz 12345

ABCDEFGHIJKLMNOPQRSTUVW abcdefghijklmnopqrstuvwxyz 12345

ABCDEFGHIJKLMNOPQRSTUVW abcdefghijklmnopqrstuvwxyz 1234

ABCDEFGHIJKLMNOPQRSTUVW abcdefghijklmnopqrstuvwxyz 1234

ABCDEFGHIJKLMNOPQRSTUVW abcdefghijklmnopqrstuvwxyz 123

ABCDEFGHIJKLMNOPQRSTUVW abcdefghijklmnopqrstuvwxyz 123

ABCDEFGHIJKLMNOPQRSTUVW abcdefghijklmnopqrstuvwxyz 12

ABCDEFGHIJKLMNOPQRSTUVW abcdefghijklmnopqrstuvwxyz 12

ABCDEFGHIJKLMNOPQRSTUVW abcdefghijklmnopqrstuvwxyz

ABCDEFGHIJKLMNOPQRSTUVW abcdefghijklmnopqrstuvwxyz

ABCDEFGHIJKLMNOPQRSTUVW abcdefghijklmnopqrstuvwxy

ABCDEFGHIJKLMNOPQRSTUVW abcdefghijklmnopqrstuvwxy

ABCDEFGHIJKLMNOPQRSTUVW abcdefghijklmnopqrstuvwx

ABCDEFGHIJKLMNOPQRSTUVW abcdefghijklmnopqrstuvwx

ABCDEFGHIJKLMNOPQRSTUVW abcdefghijklmnopqrstuvwx

ABCDEFGHIJKLMNOPQRSTUVW abcdefghijklmnopqrstuvwx

11/14p

License Open Font License
Font tag Sans serif, Text, Sofia Pro, Google

Link fonts.google.com/specimen/Poppins
Pair Roboto, Open Sans, Raleway, Playfair Display, Oswald

Deep into that darkness peering,
long I stood there, wondering, fearing, doubting,
dreaming dreams no mortal ever dared to dream before.
— **Edgar Allan Poe,** *Complete Tales and Poems*

Light 11/15p, 10 | SemiBold 10/14p, 0

SPARKLING ARTS

www.sparklingarts.com

Founder
CAROLINE LEE

carolinelee@sparklingarts.com

010.2345.6789

Black 18p, 50

Thin 9p, 100

Medium 10p, 100

Bold 16/20p, 50

Italic 9p, 0

Light Italic 11p, 100

THE *jealous*
ART/ST

DAMN,
I WISH I THOUGHT OF THAT.

Medium 10p, 30 | Light Italic 10p, 30 | Black 30/30p, 10 | Light 8/10p, 0

ADVENTURE FOR THE YOUNG AT HEART

Go outside and explore

At any rate, That is Happiness;
To be dissolved into something
COMPLETE AND GREAT.

— Willa Cather, *My Ántonia*

"Stay close to anything that makes you feel you are glad to be alive. Plant the seeds for a sustainable future. *Connect, respect and listen to nature*, for nature is our greatest teacher."

LOOK UP, KEEP GOING

Lorem ipsum dolor sit amet, consectetur adipiscing elit, sed do eiusmod tempor incididunt ut labore et dolore magna aliqua. Ut enim ad minim veniam, nostrud exercitation ullamco laboris nisi aliquip ex ea commodo consequat. Duis aute irure dolor in reprehenderit in voluptate velit esse cillum dolore eu fugiat nulla pariatur. Excepteur sint occaecat cupidatat non proident, sunt in culpa qui officia deserunt mollit anim id est laborum.

"Aliquam fermentum est. Praesent posuere lorem quis quam viverra tempus. Suspendisse varius nunc nec sapien convallis rutrum. Donec vitae tincidunt tortor, nec tortor."

Ultrices sagittis orci a scelerisque purus. Diam maecenas ultricies mi eget mauris. Nam aliquam sem et tortor consequat id porta nibh. Tempor orci dapibus ultrices in iaculis nunc sed augue lacus. Sit amet massa vitae tortor condimentum.

Mi sit amet mauris commodo quis. Adipiscing at in tellus integer feugiat scelerisque varius morbi in enim. Elementum nibh tellus molestie nunc non. Nisi porta lorem mollis aliquam ut porttitor leo a. Sed sed risus pretium quam vulputate dignissim. Nunc mi ipsum faucibus vitae aliquet nec ullam corper. Scelerisque viverra mauris in aliquam sem fringilla.

In nisl nisi scelerisque eu. Odio facilisis mauris sit amet massa. Porttitor lacus luctus accumsan tortor posuere ac ut consequat. Nibh venenatis cras sed felis. Vestibulum sed arcu non odio euismod. Vitae aliquet nec ullamcorper sit amet. Amet mauris commodo quis imperdiet massa tincidunt nunc. Condimentum mattis pellentesque id nibh. Egestas purus viverra accumsan in nisl nisi scelerisque eu. Euismod in pellentesque massa placerat duis ultricies. Eget egestas purus viverra accumsan in. Id venenatis a condimentum vitae pellentesque habitant morbi. Dignissim convallis aenean et tortor Est ullamcorper eget nulla facilisi dignissim diam quis. Dui nunc mattis enim elementum sagittis.

PT Sans

PT Sans Bold 102p, 0

PT Sans Regular
PT Sans Italic
PT Sans Bold
PT Sans Bold Italic

20/24p, 0

ABCDEFGHIJKLMNOPQRSTUVWXYZ
ABCDEFGHIJKLMNOPQRSTUVWXYZ
abcefghijklmnopqrstuvwxyz abc@gmail.com
abcefghijklmnopqrstuvwxyz abc@gmail.com
1234567890 +−×÷=#%&*,.:;!?()[]{}''""®©
1234567890 +−×÷=#%&,.:;!?()[]{}''""®©*

ABCDEFGHIJKLMNOPQRSTUVWXYZ
ABCDEFGHIJKLMNOPQRSTUVWXYZ
abcefghijklmnopqrstuvwxyz abc@gmail.com
abcefghijklmnopqrstuvwxyz abc@gmail.com
1234567890 +−×÷=#%&*,.:;!?()[]{}''""®©
1234567890 +−×÷=#%&*,.:;!?()[]{}''""®©

14/20p, 0

"I loved her against *reason*, against *promise*, against *peace*, against *hope*, against *happiness*, against *all discouragement* that could be."

— Charles Dickens, *Great Expectations*

Regular 10/14p, 0 | Bold 9/14p, 10

License	Apache License, Version 2.0	Link	fonts.google.com/specimen/PT+Sans
Font tag	Sans serif, Text, Gesta, Google	Pair	Open Sans, Roboto, Lato, Montserrat, Raleway

Deep into that darkness peering,
long I stood there, wondering, fearing, doubting,
dreaming dreams no mortal ever dared to dream before.

— Edgar Allan Poe, *Complete Tales and Poems*

Regular 12/17p, 10 | Bold 10/14p, 0

SPARKLING ARTS — Bold 18p, 50

www.sparklingarts.com — Regular 9p, 100

Founder — Regular 10p, 100

CAROLINE LEE — Bold 16/20p, 50

carolinelee@sparklingarts.com — Italic 9p, 0

010.2345.6789 — Italic 11p, 100

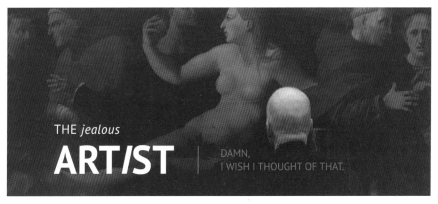

THE *jealous* ART/ST — DAMN, I WISH I THOUGHT OF THAT.

Regular 10p, 30 | Italic 10p, 30 | Bold 30/30p, 10 | Regular 8/10p, 0

ADVENTURE FOR THE YOUNG AT HEART

Go outside and explore

At any rate, That is Happiness; To be dissolved into something
COMPLETE AND GREAT.

PT Sans Regular 24.7·23.9·Bold 32p, 20 | Regular 10p, 10

— Willa Cather, *My Ántonia*

"Stay close to anything that makes you feel you are glad to be alive. Plant the seeds for a sustainable future. *Connect, respect and listen to nature,* for nature is our greatest teacher."

Bold 10/15p, 30

LOOK UP, KEEP GOING

Bold 14p, 100

Lorem ipsum dolor sit amet, consectetur adipiscing elit, sed do eiusmod tempor incididunt ut labore et dolore magna aliqua. Ut enim ad minim veniam, nostrud exercitation ullamco laboris nisi aliquip ex ea commodo consequat. Duis aute irure dolor in reprehenderit in voluptate velit esse cillum dolore eu fugiat nulla pariatur. Excepteur sint occaecat cupidatat non proident, sunt in culpa qui officia deserunt mollit anim id est laborum.

"Aliquam fermentum est. Praesent posuere lorem quis quam viverra tempus. Suspendisse varius nunc nec sapien convallis rutrum. Donec vitae tincidunt tortor, nec tempor tortor."

Ultrices sagittis orci a scelerisque purus. Diam maecenas ultricies mi eget mauris. Nam aliquam sem et tortor consequat id porta nibh. Tempor orci dapibus ultrices in iaculis nunc sed augue lacus. Sit amet massa vitae tortor condimentum.

Mi sit amet mauris commodo quis. Adipiscing at in tellus integer feugiat scelerisque varius morbi in enim. Elementum nibh tellus molestie nunc non. Nisi porta lorem mollis aliquam ut porttitor leo a. Sed sed risus pretium quam vulputate dignissim. Nunc mi ipsum faucibus vitae aliquet nec ullam corper. Scelerisque viverra mauris in aliquam sem fringilla.

In nisl nisi scelerisque eu. Odio facilisis mauris sit amet massa. Porttitor lacus luctus accumsan tortor posuere ac ut consequat. Nibh venenatis cras sed felis. Vestibulum sed arcu non odio euismod. Vitae aliquet nec ullamcorper sit amet. Amet mauris commodo quis imperdiet massa tincidunt nunc. Condimentum mattis pellentesque id nibh. Egestas purus viverra accumsan in nisl nisi scelerisque eu. Euismod in pellentesque massa placerat duis ultricies. Eget egestas purus viverra accumsan in. Id venenatis a condimentum vitae pellentesque habitant morbi. Dignissim convallis aenean et tortor Est ullamcorper eget nulla facilisi dignissim diam quis. Dui nunc mattis enim elementum sagittis.

Regular 7/9p, 0 | Bold 8/11p, 50

Bold 14/17p, 100 | Regular 8/25p, 25

Quicksand

Quicksand SemiBold 68p, 0

Quicksand Light
Quicksand Regular
Quicksand Medium
Quicksand SemiBold
Quicksand Bold

20/24p, 0

ABCDEFGHIJKLMNOPQRSTUVWXYZ
abcefghijklmnopqrstuvwxyz abc@gmail.com
1234567890 +−×÷=#%&*, . : ; ! ? ( )[ ]{ } ' ' " " ®©

ABCDEFGHIJKLMNOPQRSTUVWXYZ
abcefghijklmnopqrstuvwxyz abc@gmail.com
1234567890 +−×÷=#%&*, . : ; ! ? ( )[ ]{ } ' ' " " ®©

ABCDEFGHIJKLMNOPQRSTUVWXYZ
abcefghijklmnopqrstuvwxyz abc@gmail.com
1234567890 +−×÷=#%&*, . : ; ! ? ( )[ ]{ } ' ' " " ®©

ABCDEFGHIJKLMNOPQRSTUVWXYZ
abcefghijklmnopqrstuvwxyz abc@gmail.com
1234567890 +−×÷=#%&*, . : ; ! ? ( )[ ]{ } ' ' " " ®©

ABCDEFGHIJKLMNOPQRSTUVWXYZ
abcefghijklmnopqrstuvwxyz abc@gmail.com
1234567890 +−×÷=#%&*, . : ; ! ? ( )[ ]{ } ' ' " " ®©

12/15p, 0

"I loved her against reason, against promise, against peace, against
hope, against happiness, against all discouragement that could be."
— Charles Dickens, Great Expectations

Light 10/14p, 0 | Medium 9/14p, 10

License	Open Font License	Link	fonts.google.com/specimen/Quicksand
Font tag	Sans serif, Heading, Google	Pair	Open Sans, Roboto, Montserrat, Raleway, Lato

Deep into that darkness peering,
long I stood there, wondering, fearing, doubting,
dreaming dreams no mortal ever dared to dream before.
— Edgar Allan Poe, Complete Tales and Poems

Light 12/17p, 10 | Medium 11/15p, 0

SPARKLING ARTS

www.sparklingarts.com

Founder
CAROLINE LEE

carolinelee@sparklingarts.com

010.2345.6789

Bold 18p, 50

Light 9p, 100

Medium 10p, 100

Bold 16/20p, 50

Light 9p, 0

Light 11p, 100

THE jealous
ARTIST
DAMN,
I WISH I THOUGHT OF THAT.

Medium 10p, 30 | Regular 10p, 30 | Bold 30/30p, 20 | Light 8/10p, 0

ADVENTURE FOR THE YOUNG AT HEART

Go outside and explore

At any rate, That is Happiness;
To be dissolved into something
COMPLETE AND GREAT.

Quicksand Regular 22.8·SemiBold 21.9·Bold 28.9p, 20 | Regular 10p, 10 — Willa Cather, My Ántonia

"Stay close to anything that makes you feel
you are glad to be alive. Plant the seeds for a
sustainable future. Connect, respect and listen
to nature, for nature is our greatest teacher."

SemiBold 10/15p, 30

LOOK UP, KEEP GOING

Bold 14p, 100

Lorem ipsum dolor sit amet, consectetur adipiscing elit, sed do eiusmod tempor incididunt ut labore et dolore magna aliqua. Ut enim ad minim veniam, nostrud exercitation ullamco laboris nisi aliquip ex ea commodo consequat. Duis aute irure dolor in reprehenderit in voluptate velit esse cillum dolore eu fugiat nulla pariatur. Excepteur sint occaecat cupidatat non proident, sunt in culpa qui officia deserunt mollit anim id est laborum.

"Aliquam fermentum est. Praesent posuere lorem quis quam viverra tempus. Suspendisse varius nunc nec sapien convallis rutrum. Donec vitae tincidunt tortor, nec tortor."

Ultrices sagittis orci a scelerisque purus. Diam maecenas ultricies mi eget mauris. Nam aliquam sem et tortor consequat id porta nibh. Tempor orci dapibus ultrices in iaculis nunc sed augue lacus. Sit amet massa vitae tortor condimentum.

Light 7/9p, 0 | Semibold 8/11p, 50

Mi sit amet mauris commodo quis. Adipiscing at in tellus integer feugiat scelerisque varius morbi in enim. Elementum nibh tellus molestie nunc non. Nisi porta lorem mollis aliquam ut porttitor leo a. Sed sed risus pretium quam vulputate dignissim. Nunc mi ipsum faucibus vitae aliquet nec ullam corper. Scelerisque viverra mauris in aliquam sem fringilla.

In nisl nisi scelerisque eu. Odio facilisis mauris sit amet massa. Porttitor lacus luctus accumsan tortor posuere ac ut consequat. Nibh venenatis cras sed felis. Vestibulum sed arcu non odio euismod. Vitae aliquet nec ullamcorper sit amet. Amet mauris commodo quis imperdiet massa tincidunt nunc. Condimentum mattis pellentesque id nibh. Egestas purus viverra accumsan in nisl nisi scelerisque eu. Euismod in pellentesque massa placerat duis ultricies. Eget egestas purus viverra accumsan in. Id venenatis a condimentum vitae pellentesque habitant morbi. Dignissim convallis aenean et tortor Est ullamcorper eget nulla facilisi dignissim diam quis. Dui nunc mattis enim elementum sagittis.

Bold 14/17p, 100 | Regular 8/25p, 25

Raleway

Raleway Bold 83p, 0

Raleway Thin	Thin Italic
Raleway ExtraLight	ExtraLight Italic
Raleway Light	Light Italic
Raleway Regular	Italic
Raleway Medium	Medium Italic
Raleway SemiBold	SemiBold Italic
Raleway Bold	Bold Italic
Raleway ExtraBold	ExtraBold Italic
Raleway Black	Black Italic

ABCDEFGHIJKLMNOPQRSTUVW abcdefghijklmnopqrstuvwxyz 123

ABCDEFGHIJKLMNOPQRSTUVW abcdefghijklmnopqrstuvwxyz 123456

ABCDEFGHIJKLMNOPQRSTUVW abcdefghijklmnopqrstuvwxyz 123

ABCDEFGHIJKLMNOPQRSTUVW abcdefghijklmnopqrstuvwxyz 12345

ABCDEFGHIJKLMNOPQRSTUVW abcdefghijklmnopqrstuvwxyz 12.

ABCDEFGHIJKLMNOPQRSTUVW abcdefghijklmnopqrstuvwxyz 12345

ABCDEFGHIJKLMNOPQRSTUVW abcdefghijklmnopqrstuvwxyz 12

ABCDEFGHIJKLMNOPQRSTUVW abcdefghijklmnopqrstuvwxyz 1234

ABCDEFGHIJKLMNOPQRSTUVW abcdefghijklmnopqrstuvwxyz 1

ABCDEFGHIJKLMNOPQRSTUVW abcdefghijklmnopqrstuvwxyz 1234

ABCDEFGHIJKLMNOPQRSTUVW abcdefghijklmnopqrstuvwxyz 1

ABCDEFGHIJKLMNOPQRSTUVW abcdefghijklmnopqrstuvwxyz 123

ABCDEFGHIJKLMNOPQRSTUVW abcdefghijklmnopqrstuvwxyz :

ABCDEFGHIJKLMNOPQRSTUVW abcdefghijklmnopqrstuvwxyz 12.

ABCDEFGHIJKLMNOPQRSTUVW abcdefghijklmnopqrstuvwxyz

ABCDEFGHIJKLMNOPQRSTUVW abcdefghijklmnopqrstuvwxyz 12

ABCDEFGHIJKLMNOPQRSTUVW abcdefghijklmnopqrstuvwxy

ABCDEFGHIJKLMNOPQRSTUVW abcdefghijklmnopqrstuvwxyz 1

| License | Open Font License |
| Font tag | Sans serif, Text, Heading, Google |

| Link | fonts.google.com/specimen/Raleway |
| Pair | Open Sans, Roboto, Lato, Montserrat, Oswald |

Deep into that darkness peering,
long I stood there, wondering, fearing, doubting,
dreaming dreams no mortal ever dared to dream before.

— Edgar Allan Poe, *Complete Tales and Poems*

Light 11/15p, 10 | SemiBold 10/14p, 0

SPARKLING ARTS

www.sparklingarts.com

Founder
CAROLINE LEE

carolinelee@sparklingarts.com

010.2345.6789

Black 18p, 50

Thin 9p, 100

Medium 10p, 100

Bold 16/20p, 50

Italic 9p, 0

Light Italic 11p, 100

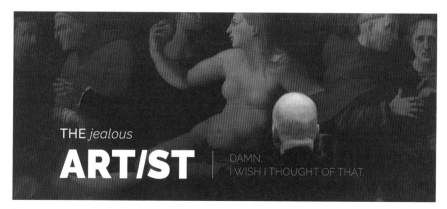

THE *jealous*
ART/ST
DAMN,
I WISH I THOUGHT OF THAT.

Medium 10p, 30 | Light Italic 10p, 30 | Black 30/30p, 10 | Light 8/10p, 0

ADVENTURE FOR THE YOUNG AT HEART

Go outside and explore

At any rate, That is Happiness;
To be dissolved into something
COMPLETE AND GREAT.

Raleway Medium 22.8p·Bold 21.5p·Black 28.4p, 20 | Regular 10p, 10　　　　　— Willa Cather, *My Ántonia*

"Stay close to anything that makes you feel you are glad to be alive. Plant the seeds for a sustainable future. *Connect, respect and listen to nature,* for nature is our greatest teacher."

SemiBold 10/15p, 30

LOOK UP, KEEP GOING

Black 14p, 100

Lorem ipsum dolor sit amet, consectetur adipiscing elit, sed do eiusmod tempor incididunt ut labore et dolore magna aliqua. Ut enim ad minim veniam, nostrud exercitation ullamco laboris nisi aliquip ex ea commodo consequat. Duis aute irure dolor in reprehenderit in voluptate velit esse cillum dolore eu fugiat nulla pariatur. Excepteur sint occaecat cupidatat non proident, sunt in culpa qui officia deserunt mollit anim id est laborum.

"Aliquam fermentum est. Praesent posuere lorem quis quam viverra tempus. Suspendisse varius nunc nec sapien convallis rutrum. Donec vitae tincidunt tortor, nec tortor."

Ultrices sagittis orci a scelerisque purus. Diam maecenas ultricies mi eget mauris. Nam aliquam sem et tortor consequat id porta nibh. Tempor orci dapibus ultrices in iaculis nunc sed augue lacus. Sit amet massa vitae tortor condimentum.

Regular 6.5/9p, 0 | SemiBold 8/11p, 50

Mi sit amet mauris commodo quis. Adipiscing at in tellus integer feugiat scelerisque varius morbi in enim. Elementum nibh tellus molestie nunc non. Nisi porta lorem mollis aliquam ut porttitor leo a. Sed sed risus pretium quam vulputate dignissim. Nunc mi ipsum faucibus vitae aliquet nec ullam corper. Scelerisque viverra mauris in aliquam sem fringilla.

In nisl nisi scelerisque eu. Odio facilisis mauris sit amet massa. Porttitor lacus luctus accumsan tortor posuere ac ut consequat. Nibh venenatis cras sed felis. Vestibulum sed arcu non odio euismod. Vitae aliquet nec ullamcorper sit amet. Amet mauris commodo quis imperdiet massa tincidunt nunc. Condimentum mattis pellentesque id nibh. Egestas purus viverra accumsan in nisl nisi scelerisque eu. Euismod in pellentesque massa placerat duis ultricies. Eget egestas purus viverra accumsan in. Id venenatis a condimentum vitae pellentesque habitant morbi. Dignissim convallis aenean et tortor Est ullamcorper eget nulla facilisi dignissim diam quis. Dui nunc mattis enim elementum sagittis.

Black 14/17p, 100 | Light 8/25p, 25

Roboto

Roboto Bold 100p, 0

Roboto Thin	*Roboto Thin Italic*
Roboto Light	*Roboto Light Italic*
Roboto Regular	*Roboto Italic*
Roboto Medium	*Roboto Medium Italic*
Roboto Bold	***Roboto Bold Italic***
Roboto Black	***Roboto Black Italic***

18/24p

AaBbCcDdEeFfGgHhIiJjKkLlMmNnOoPpQqRrSsTtUuVvWwXxYyZz
AaBbCcDdEeFfGgHhIiJjKkLlMmNnOoPpQqRrSsTtUuVvWwXxYyZz
1234567890 *1234567890* +−×÷=#%&*,.:;!?()[]{}''""®©

AaBbCcDdEeFfGgHhIiJjKkLlMmNnOoPpQqRrSsTtUuVvWwXxYyZz
AaBbCcDdEeFfGgHhIiJjKkLlMmNnOoPpQqRrSsTtUuVvWwXxYyZz
1234567890 *1234567890* +−×÷=#%&*,.:;!?()[]{}''""®©

AaBbCcDdEeFfGgHhIiJjKkLlMmNnOoPpQqRrSsTtUuVvWwXxYyZz
AaBbCcDdEeFfGgHhIiJjKkLlMmNnOoPpQqRrSsTtUuVvWwXxYyZz
1234567890 *1234567890* +−×÷=#%&*,.:;!?()[]{}''""®©

AaBbCcDdEeFfGgHhIiJjKkLlMmNnOoPpQqRrSsTtUuVvWwXxYyZz
AaBbCcDdEeFfGgHhIiJjKkLlMmNnOoPpQqRrSsTtUuVvWwXxYyZz
1234567890 *1234567890* +−×÷=#%&*,.:;!?()[]{}''""®©

AaBbCcDdEeFfGgHhIiJjKkLlMmNnOoPpQqRrSsTtUuVvWwXxYyZz
AaBbCcDdEeFfGgHhIiJjKkLlMmNnOoPpQqRrSsTtUuVvWwXxYyZz
1234567890 *1234567890* +−×÷=#%&*,.:;!?()[]{}''""®©

11/16p

| License | Apache License, Version 2.0 | Link | fonts.google.com/specimen/Roboto |
| Font tag | Sans serif, Text, DIN, Google | Pair | Open Sans, Lato, Montserrat, Raleway |

Deep into that darkness peering,
long I stood there, wondering, fearing, doubting,
dreaming dreams no mortal ever dared to dream before.
— **Edgar Allan Poe, *Complete Tales and Poems***

Light 13/17p, 10 | Bold 10/14p, 0

SPARKLING ARTS

www.sparklingarts.com

Founder
CAROLINE LEE

carolinelee@sparklingarts.com

010.2345.6789

Black 18p, 50

Thin 9p, 100

Medium 10p, 100

Bold 16/20p, 50

Italic 9p, 0

Light Italic 11p, 100

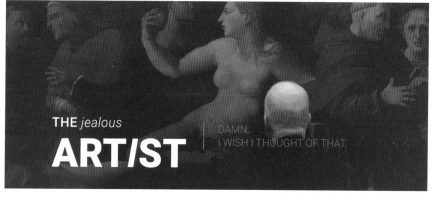

THE *jealous*
ART/ST

DAMN,
I WISH I THOUGHT OF THAT.

Medium 10p, 30 | Light Italic 10p, 30 | Black 30/30p, 10 | Light 8/10p, 0

ADVENTURE FOR THE YOUNG AT HEART

Go outside and explore

At any rate, That is Happiness; To be dissolved into something
COMPLETE AND GREAT.

Roboto Medium 23.4p-Bold 22.8p-Black 29.1p, 20 | Regular 10p, 10

— Willa Cather, *My Ántonia*

"Stay close to anything that makes you feel you are glad to be alive. Plant the seeds for a sustainable future. *Connect, respect and listen to nature,* for nature is our greatest teacher."

Bold 10/15p, 30

LOOK UP, KEEP GOING

Black 14p, 100

Lorem ipsum dolor sit amet, consectetur adipiscing elit, sed do eiusmod tempor incididunt ut labore et dolore magna aliqua. Ut enim ad minim veniam, nostrud exercitation ullamco laboris nisi aliquip ex ea commodo consequat. Duis aute irure dolor in reprehenderit in voluptate velit esse cillum dolore eu fugiat nulla pariatur. Excepteur sint occaecat cupidatat non proident, sunt in culpa qui officia deserunt mollit anim id est laborum.

"Aliquam fermentum est. Praesent posuere lorem quis quam viverra tempus. Suspendisse varius nunc nec sapien convallis rutrum. Donec vitae tincidunt tortor, nec tempor tortor."

Ultrices sagittis orci a scelerisque purus. Diam maecenas ultricies mi eget mauris. Nam aliquam sem et tortor consequat id porta nibh. Tempor orci dapibus ultrices in iaculis nunc sed augue lacus. Sit amet massa vitae tortor condimentum.

Mi sit amet mauris commodo quis. Adipiscing at in tellus integer feugiat scelerisque varius morbi in enim. Elementum nibh tellus molestie nunc non. Nisi porta lorem mollis aliquam ut porttitor leo a. Sed sed risus pretium quam vulputate dignissim. Nunc mi ipsum faucibus vitae aliquet nec ullam corper. Scelerisque viverra mauris in aliquam sem fringilla.

In nisl nisi scelerisque eu. Odio facilisis mauris sit amet massa. Porttitor lacus luctus accumsan tortor posuere ac ut consequat. Nibh venenatis cras sed felis. Vestibulum sed arcu non odio euismod. Vitae aliquet nec ullamcorper sit amet. Amet mauris commodo quis imperdiet massa tincidunt nunc. Condimentum mattis pellentesque id nibh. Egestas purus viverra accumsan in nisl nisi scelerisque eu. Euismod in pellentesque massa placerat duis ultricies. Eget egestas purus viverra accumsan in. Id venenatis a condimentum vitae pellentesque habitant morbi. Dignissim convallis aenean et tortor Est ullamcorper eget nulla facilisi dignissim diam quis. Dui nunc mattis enim elementum sagittis.

Regular 7/9p, 0 | Medium 8/11p, 50

Black 14/17p, 100 | Light 8/25p, 25

Rubik

Rubik Bold 100p, 0

Rubik Light
Rubik Regular
Rubik Medium
Rubik Bold
Rubik Black

Light Italic
Italic
Medium Italic
Bold Italic
Black Italic

18/24p

ABCDEFGHIJKLMNOPQRSTUVWXYZ abcdefghijklmnopqrstuvwxyz
ABCDEFGHIJKLMNOPQRSTUVWXYZ abcdefghijklmnopqrstuvwxyz
1234567890 *1234567890* +−×÷=#%&*,.:;!?()[]{}''"" ®©

ABCDEFGHIJKLMNOPQRSTUVWXYZ abcdefghijklmnopqrstuvwxyz
ABCDEFGHIJKLMNOPQRSTUVWXYZ abcdefghijklmnopqrstuvwxyz
1234567890 *1234567890* +−×÷=#%&*,.:;!?()[]{}''"" ®©

ABCDEFGHIJKLMNOPQRSTUVWXYZ abcdefghijklmnopqrstuvwx
ABCDEFGHIJKLMNOPQRSTUVWXYZ abcdefghijklmnopqrstuvwx
1234567890 *1234567890* +−×÷=#%&*,.:;!?()[]{}''"" ®©

ABCDEFGHIJKLMNOPQRSTUVWXYZ abcdefghijklmnopqrstuvw
ABCDEFGHIJKLMNOPQRSTUVWXYZ abcdefghijklmnopqrstuvw
1234567890 *1234567890* +−×÷=#%&*,.:;!?()[]{}''"" ®©

ABCDEFGHIJKLMNOPQRSTUVWXYZ abcdefghijklmnopqrstu
ABCDEFGHIJKLMNOPQRSTUVWXYZ abcdefghijklmnopqrstu
1234567890 *1234567890* +−×÷=#%&*,.:;!?()[]{}''"" ®©

11/16p

184

| License | Open Font License | Link | fonts.google.com/specimen/Rubik |
| Font tag | Sans serif, Heading, Neue Haas Unica | Pair | Roboto, Open Sans, Montserrat, Lato, Playfair Display |

Deep into that darkness peering,
long I stood there, wondering, fearing, doubting,
dreaming dreams no mortal ever dared to dream before.
— **Edgar Allan Poe,** *Complete Tales and Poems*

Light 12/17p, 10 ¦ Medium 10/14p, 0

SPARKLING ARTS

www.sparklingarts.com

Founder
CAROLINE LEE

carolinelee@sparklingarts.com

010.2345.6789

Black 18p, 50

Light 9p, 100

Regular 10p, 100

Bold 16/20p, 50

Italic 9p, 0

Light Italic 11p, 100

THE *jealous*
ART/ST

DAMN,
I WISH I THOUGHT OF THAT.

Regular 10p, 30 ¦ Light Italic 10p, 30 ¦ Black 30/30p, 10 ¦ Light 8/10p, 0

ADVENTURE FOR THE YOUNG AT HEART

Go outside and explore

At any rate, That is Happiness;
To be dissolved into something
COMPLETE AND GREAT.

Rubik Medium 21.9p-Bold 20.8p-ExtraBold 26.8p, 20 | Regular 10p, 10

— Willa Cather, *My Ántonia*

"Stay close to anything that makes you feel you are glad to be alive. Plant the seeds for a sustainable future. *Connect, respect and listen to nature,* for nature is our greatest teacher."

Medium 10/15p, 30

LOOK UP, KEEP GOING

Black 14p, 100

Lorem ipsum dolor sit amet, consectetur adipiscing elit, sed do eiusmod tempor incididunt ut labore et dolore magna aliqua. Ut enim ad minim veniam, nostrud exercitation ullamco laboris nisi aliquip ex ea commodo consequat. Duis aute irure dolor in reprehenderit in voluptate velit esse cillum dolore eu fugiat nulla pariatur. Excepteur sint occaecat cupidatat non proident, sunt in culpa qui officia deserunt mollit anim id est laborum.

"Aliquam fermentum est. Praesent posuere lorem quis quam viverra tempus. Suspendisse varius nunc nec sapien convallis rutrum. Donec vitae tincidunt tortor, nec tempor tortor."

Ultrices sagittis orci a scelerisque purus. Diam maecenas ultricies mi eget mauris. Nam aliquam sem et tortor consequat id porta nibh. Tempor orci dapibus ultrices in iaculis nunc sed augue lacus. Sit amet massa vitae tortor condimentum.

Regular 7/9p, 0 | Medium 8/11p, 50

Mi sit amet mauris commodo quis. Adipiscing at in tellus integer feugiat scelerisque varius morbi in enim. Elementum nibh tellus molestie nunc non. Nisi porta lorem mollis aliquam ut porttitor leo a. Sed sed risus pretium quam vulputate dignissim. Nunc mi ipsum faucibus vitae aliquet nec ullam corper. Scelerisque viverra mauris in aliquam sem fringilla.

In nisl nisi scelerisque eu. Odio facilisis mauris sit amet massa. Porttitor lacus luctus accumsan tortor posuere ac ut consequat. Nibh venenatis cras sed felis. Vestibulum sed arcu non odio euismod. Vitae aliquet nec ullamcorper sit amet. Amet mauris commodo quis imperdiet massa tincidunt nunc. Condimentum mattis pellentesque id nibh. Egestas purus viverra accumsan in nisl nisi scelerisque eu. Euismod in pellentesque massa placerat duis ultricies. Eget egestas purus viverra accumsan in. Id venenatis a condimentum vitae pellentesque habitant morbi. Dignissim convallis aenean et tortor Est ullamcorper eget nulla facilisi dignissim diam quis. Dui nunc mattis enim elementum sagittis.

Source Sans Pro

Source Sans Bold 47p, 0

Source Sans ExtraLight	*ExtraLight Italic*
Source Sans Light	*Light Italic*
Source Sans Regular	*Italic*
Source Sans SemiBold	*SemiBold Italic*
Source Sans Bold	***Bold Italic***
Source Sans Black	***Black Italic***

18/24p

AaBbCcDdEeFfGgHhIiJjKkLlMmNnOoPpQqRrSsTtUuVvWwXxYyZz
AaBbCcDdEeFfGgHhIiJjKkLlMmNnOoPpQqRrSsTtUuVvWwXxYyZz
1234567890 *1234567890* +−×÷=#%&*,.:;!? ()[]{}''" "®©

AaBbCcDdEeFfGgHhIiJjKkLlMmNnOoPpQqRrSsTtUuVvWwXxYyZz
AaBbCcDdEeFfGgHhIiJjKkLlMmNnOoPpQqRrSsTtUuVvWwXxYyZz
1234567890 *1234567890* +−×÷=#%&*,.:;!? ()[]{}''" "®©

AaBbCcDdEeFfGgHhIiJjKkLlMmNnOoPpQqRrSsTtUuVvWwXxYyZz
AaBbCcDdEeFfGgHhIiJjKkLlMmNnOoPpQqRrSsTtUuVvWwXxYyZz
1234567890 *1234567890* +−×÷=#%&*,.:;!? ()[]{}''" "®©

AaBbCcDdEeFfGgHhIiJjKkLlMmNnOoPpQqRrSsTtUuVvWwXxYyZz
AaBbCcDdEeFfGgHhIiJjKkLlMmNnOoPpQqRrSsTtUuVvWwXxYyZz
1234567890 ***1234567890*** **+−×÷=#%&*,.:;!? ()[]{}''" "®©**

AaBbCcDdEeFfGgHhIiJjKkLlMmNnOoPpQqRrSsTtUuVvWwXxYyZz
AaBbCcDdEeFfGgHhIiJjKkLlMmNnOoPpQqRrSsTtUuVvWwXxYyZz
1234567890 ***1234567890*** **+−×÷=#%&*,.:;!? ()[]{}''" "®©**

AaBbCcDdEeFfGgHhIiJjKkLlMmNnOoPpQqRrSsTtUuVvWwXxYyZz
AaBbCcDdEeFfGgHhIiJjKkLlMmNnOoPpQqRrSsTtUuVvWwXxYyZz
1234567890 ***1234567890*** **+−×÷=#%&*,.:;!? ()[]{}''" "®©**

11/16p

| License | Open Font License |
| Font tag | Sans serif, Text, FF Dagny Pro, Google |

| Link | fonts.google.com/specimen/Source+Sans+Pro |
| Pair | Open Sans, Lato, Roboto, Merriweather,Montserrat |

Deep into that darkness peering,
long I stood there, wondering, fearing, doubting,
dreaming dreams no mortal ever dared to dream before.
— **Edgar Allan Poe,** *Complete Tales and Poems*

Light 13/17p, 10 | SemiBold 10/14p, 0

SPARKLING ARTS

www.sparklingarts.com

Founder
CAROLINE LEE

carolinelee@sparklingarts.com

010.2345.6789

Light Italic 11p, 100

Black 18p, 50

ExtraLight 9p, 100

Regular 10p, 100

Bold 16/20p, 50

Italic 9p, 0

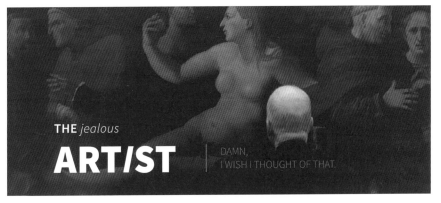

THE *jealous*
ART/ST

DAMN,
I WISH I THOUGHT OF THAT.

SemiBold 10p, 30 | Light Italic 10p, 30 | Black 30/30p, 10 | Light 8/10p, 0

ADVENTURE FOR THE YOUNG AT HEART

Go outside and explore

At any rate, That is Happiness; To be dissolved into something COMPLETE AND GREAT.

Source Sans SemiBold 24.6p·Bold 23.4p·Black 31.3p, 20 | Regular 10p, 10

— Willa Cather, *My Ántonia*

"Stay close to anything that makes you feel you are glad to be alive. Plant the seeds for a sustainable future. *Connect, respect and listen to nature,* for nature is our greatest teacher."

SemiBold 10/15p, 30

LOOK UP, KEEP GOING

Black 14p, 100

Lorem ipsum dolor sit amet, consectetur adipiscing elit, sed do eiusmod tempor incididunt ut labore et dolore magna aliqua. Ut enim ad minim veniam, nostrud exercitation ullamco laboris nisi aliquip ex ea commodo consequat. Duis aute irure dolor in reprehenderit in voluptate velit esse cillum dolore eu fugiat nulla pariatur. Excepteur sint occaecat cupidatat non proident, sunt in culpa qui officia deserunt mollit anim id est laborum.

"Aliquam fermentum est. Praesent posuere lorem quis quam viverra tempus. Suspendisse varius nunc nec sapien convallis rutrum. Donec vitae tincidunt tortor, nec tempor tortor."

Ultrices sagittis orci a scelerisque purus. Diam maecenas ultricies mi eget mauris. Nam aliquam sem consequat id porta nibh. Tempor orci in iaculis nunc sed augue lacus. Sit amet massa vitae tortor condimentum.

Regular 7/9p, 0 | Semibold 8/11p, 50

Mi sit amet mauris commodo quis. Adipiscing at in tellus integer feugiat scelerisque varius morbi in enim. Elementum nibh tellus molestie nunc non. Nisi porta lorem mollis aliquam ut porttitor leo a. Sed sed risus pretium quam vulputate dignissim. Nunc mi ipsum faucibus vitae aliquet nec ullam corper. Scelerisque viverra mauris in aliquam sem fringilla.

In nisl nisi scelerisque eu. Odio facilisis mauris sit amet massa. Porttitor lacus luctus accumsan tortor posuere ac ut consequat. Nibh venenatis cras sed felis. Vestibulum sed arcu non odio euismod. Vitae aliquet nec ullamcorper sit amet. Amet mauris commodo quis imperdiet massa tincidunt nunc. Condimentum mattis pellentesque id nibh. Egestas purus viverra accumsan in nisl nisi scelerisque eu. Euismod in pellentesque massa placerat duis ultricies. Eget egestas purus viverra accumsan in. Id venenatis a condimentum vitae pellentesque habitant morbi. Dignissim convallis aenean et tortor Est ullamcorper eget nulla facilisi dignissim diam quis. Dui nunc mattis enim elementum sagittis.

Black 14/17p, 100 | Light 8/25p, 25

Work Sans

Work Sans Bold 63p, 0

Work Sans Thin
Work Sans ExtraLight
Work Sans Light
Work Sans Regular
Work Sans Medium

Work Sans SemiBold
Work Sans Bold
Work Sans Extrabold
Work Sans Black

16/22p, 0

ABCDEFGHIJKLMNOPQRSTUVWXYZ
1234567890 abcefghijklmnopqrstuvwxyz
+−×÷=#%&*,.:;!?
( )[ ]{ } ' ' " " ®©

ABCDEFGHIJKLMNOPQRSTUVWXYZ
1234567890 abcefghijklmnopqrstuvwxyz
+−×÷=#%&*,.:;!?
( )[ ]{ } ' ' " " ®©

ABCDEFGHIJKLMNOPQRSTUVWXYZ
1234567890 abcefghijklmnopqrstuvwxyz
+−×÷=#%&*,.:;!?
( )[ ]{ } ' ' " " ®©

ABCDEFGHIJKLMNOPQRSTUVWXYZ
1234567890 abcefghijklmnopqrstuvwxyz
+−×÷=#%&*,.:;!?
( )[ ]{ } ' ' " " ®©

ABCDEFGHIJKLMNOPQRSTUVWXYZ
1234567890 abcefghijklmnopqrstuvwxyz
+−×÷=#%&*,.:;!?
( )[ ]{ } ' ' " " ®©

ABCDEFGHIJKLMNOPQRSTUVWXYZ
1234567890 abcefghijklmnopqrstuvwxyz
+−×÷=#%&*,.:;!?
( )[ ]{ } ' ' " " ®©

ABCDEFGHIJKLMNOPQRSTUVWXYZ
1234567890 abcefghijklmnopqrstuvwxyz
+−×÷=#%&*,.:;!?
( )[ ]{ } ' ' " " ®©

ABCDEFGHIJKLMNOPQRSTUVWXYZ
1234567890 abcefghijklmnopqrstuvwxyz
+−×÷=#%&*,.:;!?
( )[ ]{ } ' ' " " ®©

ABCDEFGHIJKLMNOPQRSTUVWXYZ
1234567890 abcefghijklmnopqrstuvwxyz
+−×÷=#%&*,.:;!?
( )[ ]{ } ' ' " " ®©

11/16p, 0

| License | Open Font License | Link | fonts.google.com/specimen/Work+Sans |
| Font tag | Sans serif, Akzidenz Grotesk, Google | Pair | Roboto, Montserrat, Lato, Poppins, Playfair Display |

Deep into that darkness peering,
long I stood there, wondering, fearing, doubting,
dreaming dreams no mortal ever dared to dream before.

— Edgar Allan Poe, Complete Tales and Poems

Light 12/16p, 10 | SemiBold 10/14p, 0

Black 18p, 50

Light 9p, 100

Regular 10p, 100

Bold 16/20p, 50

Medium 9p, 0

Extralight 11p, 100

Medium 10p, 30 | Light 10p, 30 | Extra Bold 30/30p, 20 | Light 8/10p, 0

ADVENTURE FOR THE YOUNG AT HEART

Go outside and explore

At any rate, That is Happiness;
To be dissolved into something
COMPLETE AND GREAT.

Work Sans Medium 21.3-Bold 20.9-Black 27.4p, 20 | Regular 10p, 10 — Willa Cather, My Ántonia

"Stay close to anything that makes you feel you are glad to be alive. Plant the seeds for a sustainable future. Connect, respect and listen to nature, for nature is our greatest teacher." SemiBold 10/15p, 30

LOOK UP, KEEP GOING ExtraBold 14p, 100

Lorem ipsum dolor sit amet, consectetur adipiscing elit, sed do eiusmod tempor incididunt ut labore et dolore magna aliqua. Ut enim ad minim veniam, nostrud exercitation ullamco laboris nisi aliquip ex ea commodo consequat. Duis aute irure dolor in reprehenderit in voluptate velit esse cillum dolore eu fugiat nulla pariatur. Excepteur sint occaecat cupidatat non proident, sunt in culpa qui officia deserunt mollit anim id est laborum.

"Aliquam fermentum est. Praesent posuere lorem quis quam viverra tempus. Suspendisse varius nunc nec sapien convallis rutrum. Donec vitae tincidunt tortor, tortor."

Ultrices sagittis orci a scelerisque purus. Diam maecenas ultricies mi eget mauris. Nam aliquam sem et tortor consequat id porta nibh. Tempor orci dapibus ultrices in iaculis nunc sed augue lacus. Sit amet massa vitae tortor condimentum.

Regular 7/9p, 0 | SemiBold 8/11p, 50

Mi sit amet mauris commodo quis. Adipiscing at in tellus integer feugiat scelerisque varius morbi in enim. Elementum nibh tellus molestie nunc non. Nisi porta lorem mollis aliquam ut porttitor leo a. Sed sed risus pretium quam vulputate dignissim. Nunc mi ipsum faucibus vitae aliquet nec ullam corper. Scelerisque viverra mauris in aliquam sem fringilla.

In nisl nisi scelerisque eu. Odio facilisis mauris sit amet massa. Porttitor lacus luctus accumsan tortor posuere ac ut consequat. Nibh venenatis cras sed felis. Vestibulum sed arcu non odio euismod. Vitae aliquet nec ullamcorper sit amet. Amet mauris commodo quis imperdiet massa tincidunt nunc. Condimentum mattis pellentesque id nibh. Egestas purus viverra accumsan in nisl nisi scelerisque eu. Euismod in pellentesque massa placerat duis ultricies. Eget egestas purus viverra accumsan in. Id venenatis a condimentum vitae pellentesque habitant morbi. Dignissim convallis aenean et tortor Est ullamcorper eget nulla facilisi dignissim diam quis. Dui nunc mattis enim elementum sagittis.

ExtraBold 14/17p, 100 | Regular 8/25p, 25 195

Alegreya

Alegreya Regular	*Italic*
Alegreya Medium	*Medium Italic*
Alegreya Bold	***Bold Italic***
Alegreya ExtraBold	***ExtraBold***
Alegreya Black	***Black Italic***

18/24p

ABCDEFGHIJKLMNOPQRSTUVWXYZ abcdefghijklmnopqrstuvwxyz
ABCDEFGHIJKLMNOPQRSTUVWXYZ abcdefghijklmnopqrstuvwxyz
1234567890 *1234567890* +−×÷=#%&*,.:;!?()[]{}''""®©

ABCDEFGHIJKLMNOPQRSTUVWXYZ abcdefghijklmnopqrstuvwxyz
ABCDEFGHIJKLMNOPQRSTUVWXYZ abcdefghijklmnopqrstuvwxyz
1234567890 *1234567890* +−×÷=#%&*,.:;!?()[]{}''""®©

ABCDEFGHIJKLMNOPQRSTUVWXYZ abcdefghijklmnopqrstuvwxyz
ABCDEFGHIJKLMNOPQRSTUVWXYZ abcdefghijklmnopqrstuvwxyz
1234567890 ***1234567890*** **+−×÷=#%&*,.:;!?()[]{}''""®©**

ABCDEFGHIJKLMNOPQRSTUVWXYZ abcdefghijklmnopqrstuvwxyz
ABCDEFGHIJKLMNOPQRSTUVWXYZ abcdefghijklmnopqrstuvwxyz
1234567890 ***1234567890*** **+−×÷=#%&*,.:;!?()[]{}''""®©**

ABCDEFGHIJKLMNOPQRSTUVWXYZ abcdefghijklmnopqrstuvwxyz
ABCDEFGHIJKLMNOPQRSTUVWXYZ abcdefghijklmnopqrstuvwxyz
1234567890 ***1234567890*** **+−×÷=#%&*,.:;!?()[]{}''""®©**

11/16p

| License | Open Font License | | Link | fonts.google.com/specimen/Alegreya |
| Font tag | Serif, Text, Literature, Elmhurst, Google | | Pair | Roboto, Lato, Lora, Raleway, Ubuntu |

Deep into that darkness peering,
long I stood there, wondering, fearing, doubting,
dreaming dreams no mortal ever dared to dream before.
— **Edgar Allan Poe,** *Complete Tales and Poems*

Regular 12/17p, 10 | Bold 10/14p, 0

SPARKLING ARTS

www.sparklingarts.com

Founder
CAROLINE LEE

carolinelee@sparklingarts.com

010.2345.6789

Black 18p, 50

Regular 9p, 100

Medium 10p, 100

Bold 16/20p, 50

Italic 9p, 0

Italic 11p, 100

THE *jealous*
ARTIST | DAMN,
I WISH I THOUGHT OF THAT.

Regular 10p, 30 | Italic 10p, 30 | Black 30/30p, 10 | Regular 8/10p, 0

ADVENTURE FOR THE YOUNG AT HEART

Go outside and explore

At any rate, That is Happiness; To be dissolved into something COMPLETE AND GREAT.

Alegreya Medium 25.5p-Bold 24.9p-Black 29.8p, 20 | Regular 10p, 10

— Willa Cather, *My Ántonia*

"Stay close to anything that makes you feel you are glad to be alive. Plant the seeds for a sustainable future. *Connect, respect and listen to nature*, for nature is our greatest teacher."

Bold 10/15p, 30

LOOK UP, KEEP GOING

ExtraBold 14p, 100

Lorem ipsum dolor sit amet, consectetur adipiscing elit, sed do eiusmod tempor incididunt ut labore et dolore magna aliqua. Ut enim ad minim veniam, nostrud exercitation ullamco laboris nisi aliquip ex ea commodo consequat. Duis aute irure dolor in reprehenderit in voluptate velit esse cillum dolore eu fugiat nulla pariatur. Excepteur sint occaecat cupidatat non proident, sunt in culpa qui officia deserunt mollit anim id est laborum.

"Aliquam fermentum est. Praesent posuere lorem quis quam viverra tempus. Suspendisse varius nunc nec sapien convallis rutrum. Donec vitae tincidunt tortor, nec tempor tortor."

Ultrices sagittis orci a scelerisque purus. Diam maecenas ultricies mi eget mauris. Nam aliquam sem et tortor consequat id porta nibh. Tempor orci dapibus ultrices in iaculis nunc sed augue lacus. Sit amet massa vitae tortor condimentum.

Mi sit amet mauris commodo quis. Adipiscing at in tellus integer feugiat scelerisque varius morbi in enim. Elementum nibh tellus molestie nunc non. Nisi porta lorem mollis aliquam ut porttitor leo a. Sed sed risus pretium quam vulputate dignissim. Nunc mi ipsum faucibus vitae aliquet nec ullam corper. Scelerisque viverra mauris in aliquam sem fringilla.

In nisl nisi scelerisque eu. Odio facilisis mauris sit amet massa. Porttitor lacus luctus accumsan tortor posuere ac ut consequat. Nibh venenatis cras sed felis. Vestibulum sed arcu non odio euismod. Vitae aliquet nec ullamcorper sit amet. Amet mauris commodo quis imperdiet massa tincidunt nunc. Condimentum mattis pellentesque id nibh. Egestas purus viverra accumsan in nisl nisi scelerisque eu. Euismod in pellentesque massa placerat duis ultricies. Eget egestas purus viverra accumsan in. Id venenatis a condimentum vitae pellentesque habitant morbi. Dignissim convallis aenean et tortor Est ullamcorper eget nulla facilisi dignissim diam quis. Dui nunc mattis enim elementum sagittis.

Regular 7/9p, 0 | Bold 8/11p, 50

Black 14/17p, 100 | Regular 8/25p, 25

Amiri

Amiri Bold 63p, 0

Amiri Regular
Amiri Italic
Amiri Bold
Amiri Bold Italic

20/24p, 0

ABCDEFGHIJKLMNOPQRSTUVWXYZ
ABCDEFGHIJKLMNOPQRSTUVWXYZ
abcefghijklmnopqrstuvwxyz abc@gmail.com
abcefghijklmnopqrstuvwxyz abc@gmail.com
1234567890 +−×÷=#%&*, . : ; ! ? ( ) [ ] { } ' ' " " ®©
1234567890 +−×÷=#%&, . : ; ! ? ( ) [ ] { } ' ' " " ®©*

ABCDEFGHIJKLMNOPQRSTUVWXYZ
ABCDEFGHIJKLMNOPQRSTUVWXYZ
abcefghijklmnopqrstuvwxyz abc@gmail.com
abcefghijklmnopqrstuvwxyz abc@gmail.com
1234567890 +−×÷=#%&*, . : ; ! ? ( ) [ ] { } ' ' " " ®©
1234567890 +−×÷=#%&*, . : ; ! ? ( ) [ ] { } ' ' " " ®©

14/20p, 0

"I loved her against *reason*, against *promise*, against *peace*, against
hope, against *happiness*, against *all discouragement* that could be."
— **Charles Dickens**, ***Great Expectations***

Regular 10/14p, 0 | Bold 9/14p, 10

License	Open Font License	Link	fonts.google.com/specimen/Amiri
Font tag	Serif, Text, , Arabic, Sabon, Google	Pair	Roboto, Open Sans, Montserrat, Lora, Raleway

Deep into that darkness peering,
long I stood there, wondering, fearing, doubting,
dreaming dreams no mortal ever dared to dream before.

— **Edgar Allan Poe,** *Complete Tales and Poems*

Regular 13/17p, 10 | Bold 10/14p, 0

Bold 18p, 50

Regular 9p, 100

Regular 10p, 100

Bold 16/20p, 50

Italic 9p, 0

Italic 11p, 100

Regular 10p, 30 | Italic 10p, 30 | Bold 30/30p, 10 | Regular 8/10p, 0

ADVENTURE FOR THE YOUNG AT HEART

Go outside and explore

At any rate, That is Happiness; To be dissolved into something COMPLETE AND GREAT.

Amiri Regular 25.9-25.6-Bold 28.4p, 20 | Regular 10p, 10

— Willa Cather, *My Ántonia*

"Stay close to anything that makes you feel you are glad to be alive. **Plant the seeds for a sustainable future.** *Connect, respect and listen to nature,* **for nature is our greatest teacher.**"

Bold 10/15p, 30

LOOK UP, KEEP GOING

Bold 14p, 100

Lorem ipsum dolor sit amet, consectetur adipiscing elit, sed do eiusmod tempor incididunt ut labore et dolore magna aliqua. Ut enim ad minim veniam, nostrud exercitation ullamco laboris nisi aliquip ex ea commodo consequat. Duis aute irure dolor in reprehenderit in voluptate velit esse cillum dolore eu fugiat nulla pariatur. Excepteur sint occaecat cupidatat non proident, sunt in culpa qui officia deserunt mollit anim id est laborum.

"Aliquam fermentum est. Praesent posuere lorem quis quam viverra tempus. Suspendisse varius nunc nec sapien convallis rutrum. Donec vitae tincidunt tortor, nec tempor tortor."

Ultrices sagittis orci a scelerisque purus. Diam maecenas ultricies mi eget mauris. Nam aliquam sem et tortor consequat id porta nibh. Tempor orci dapibus ultrices in iaculis nunc sed augue lacus. Sit amet massa vitae tortor condimentum.

Mi sit amet mauris commodo quis. Adipiscing at in tellus integer feugiat scelerisque varius morbi in enim. Elementum nibh tellus molestie nunc non. Nisi porta lorem mollis aliquam ut porttitor leo a. Sed sed risus pretium quam vulputate dignissim. Nunc mi ipsum faucibus vitae aliquet nec ullam corper. Scelerisque viverra mauris in aliquam sem fringilla.

In nisl nisi scelerisque eu. Odio facilisis mauris sit amet massa. Porttitor lacus luctus accumsan tortor posuere ac ut consequat. Nibh venenatis cras sed felis. Vestibulum sed arcu non odio euismod. Vitae aliquet nec ullamcorper sit amet. Amet mauris commodo quis imperdiet massa tincidunt nunc. Condimentum mattis pellentesque id nibh. Egestas purus viverra accumsan in nisl nisi scelerisque eu. Euismod in pellentesque massa placerat duis ultricies. Eget egestas purus viverra accumsan in. Id venenatis a condimentum vitae pellentesque habitant morbi. Dignissim convallis aenean et tortor Est ullamcorper eget nulla facilisi dignissim diam quis. Dui nunc mattis enim elementum sagittis.

Regular 7/9p, 0 | Bold 8/11p, 50

Bold 14/17p, 100 | Regular 8/25p, 25

Arvo

Arvo Bold 100p, 0

Arvo Regular
Arvo Italic
Arvo Bold
Arvo Bold Italic

20/24p, 0

ABCDEFGHIJKLMNOPQRSTUVWXYZ
ABCDEFGHIJKLMNOPQRSTUVWXYZ
abcefghijklmnopqrstuvwxyz abc@gmail.com
abcefghijklmnopqrstuvwxyz abc@gmail.com
1234567890 +−×÷=#%&*,.:;!?()[]{}''""®©
1234567890 +−×÷=#%&,.:;!?()[]{}''""®©*

ABCDEFGHIJKLMNOPQRSTUVWXYZ
ABCDEFGHIJKLMNOPQRSTUVWXYZ
abcefghijklmnopqrstuvwxyz abc@gmail.com
abcefghijklmnopqrstuvwxyz abc@gmail.com
1234567890 +−×÷=#%&*,.:;!?()[]{}''""®©
1234567890 +−×÷=#%&*,.:;!?()[]{}''""®©

14/20p, 0

"I loved her against *reason*, against *promise*, against *peace*, against hope, against *happiness*, against *all discouragement* that could be."
— **Charles Dickens, *Great Expectations***

Regular 10/14p, 0 | Bold 9/14p, 10

License — Open Font License
Font tag — Slab-Serif, Text, Questa Slab, Google

Link — fonts.google.com/specimen/Arvo
Pair — Open Sans, Roboto, Lato, Source Sans Pro, Montserrat

Deep into that darkness peering,
long I stood there, wondering, fearing, doubting,
dreaming dreams no mortal ever dared to dream before.
— **Edgar Allan Poe,** *Complete Tales and Poems*

Regular 11/16p, 10 | Bold 9/14p, 0

Bold 18p, 50

Regular 9p, 100

Regular 10p, 100

Bold 16/20p, 50

Italic 9p, 0

Italic 11p, 100

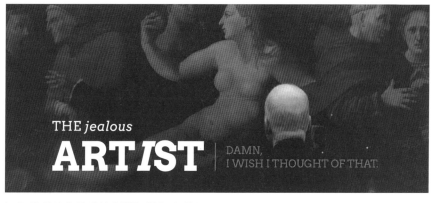

Regular 10p, 30 | Italic 10p, 30 | Bold 30/30p, 10 | Regular 8/10p, 0

ADVENTURE FOR THE YOUNG AT HEART

Go outside and explore

At any rate, That is Happiness; To be dissolved into something **COMPLETE AND GREAT.**

Arvo Regular 21.7-21.3·Bold 25.8p, 20 | Regular 10p, 10

— Willa Cather, *My Ántonia*

"Stay close to anything that makes you feel you are glad to be alive. Plant the seeds for a sustainable future. *Connect, respect and listen to nature*, for nature is our greatest teacher."

Bold 10/15p, 30

LOOK UP, KEEP GOING

Bold 14p, 100

Lorem ipsum dolor sit amet, consectetur adipiscing elit, sed do eiusmod tempor incididunt ut labore et dolore magna aliqua. Ut enim ad minim veniam, nostrud exercitation ullamco laboris nisi aliquip ex ea commodo consequat. Duis aute irure dolor in reprehenderit in voluptate velit esse cillum dolore eu fugiat nulla pariatur. Excepteur sint occaecat cupidatat non proident, sunt in culpa qui officia deserunt mollit anim id est laborum.

"Aliquam fermentum est. Praesent posuere lorem quis quam viverra tempus. Suspendisse varius nunc nec sapien convallis rutrum. Donec vitae tincidunt tortor, nec tempor tortor."

Ultrices sagittis orci a scelerisque purus. Diam maecenas ultricies mi eget mauris. Nam aliquam sem et tortor consequat id porta nibh. Tempor orci dapibus ultrices in iaculis nunc sed augue lacus. Sit amet massa vitae tortor condimentum.

Regular 7/9p, 0 | Bold 8/11p, 50

Mi sit amet mauris commodo quis. Adipiscing at in tellus integer feugiat scelerisque varius morbi in enim. Elementum nibh tellus molestie nunc non. Nisi porta lorem mollis aliquam ut porttitor leo a. Sed sed risus pretium quam vulputate dignissim. Nunc mi ipsum faucibus vitae aliquet nec ullam corper. Scelerisque viverra mauris in aliquam sem fringilla.

In nisl nisi scelerisque eu. Odio facilisis mauris sit amet massa. Porttitor lacus luctus accumsan tortor posuere ac ut consequat. Nibh venenatis cras sed felis. Vestibulum sed arcu non odio euismod. Vitae aliquet nec ullamcorper sit amet. Amet mauris commodo quis imperdiet massa tincidunt nunc. Condimentum mattis pellentesque id nibh. Egestas purus viverra accumsan in nisl nisi scelerisque eu. Euismod in pellentesque massa placerat duis ultricies. Eget egestas purus viverra accumsan in. Id venenatis a condimentum vitae pellentesque habitant morbi. Dignissim convallis aenean et tortor Est ullamcorper eget nulla facilisi dignissim diam quis. Dui nunc mattis enim elementum sagittis.

Bold 14/17p, 100 | Regular 8/25p, 25

Bitter

Bitter Bold 100p, 0

Bitter Regular
Bitter Italic
Bitter Bold

24/30p, 0

ABCDEFGHIJKLMNOPQRSTUVWXYZ
ABCDEFGHIJKLMNOPQRSTUVWXYZ
abcefghijklmnopqrstuvwxyz abc@gmail.com
abcefghijklmnopqrstuvwxyz abc@gmail.com
1234567890 +−×÷=#%&*, . : ; ! ? ( )[ ]{ } ' ' " " ®©
1234567890 +−×÷=#%&, . : ; ! ? ( )[ ]{ } ' ' " " ®©*

ABCDEFGHIJKLMNOPQRSTUVWXYZ
abcefghijklmnopqrstuvwxyz abc@gmail.com
1234567890 +−×÷=#%&*, . : ; ! ? ( )[ ]{ } ' ' " " ®©

14/20p, 0

"I loved her against *reason*, against *promise*, against *peace*, against *hope*, against *happiness*, against *all discouragement* that could be."
— **Charles Dickens, Great Expectations**

Regular 10/14p, 0 | Bold 9/14p, 10

| License | Open Font License |
| Font tag | Slab-Serif, Adelle, Screen, Google |

| Link | fonts.google.com/specimen/Bitter |
| Pair | Open Sans, Roboto, Source Sans Pro, Lato, Raleway |

Deep into that darkness peering,
long I stood there, wondering, fearing, doubting,
dreaming dreams no mortal ever dared to dream before.

— Edgar Allan Poe, Complete Tales and Poems

Regular 11/16p, 10   Bold 9/14p, 0

SPARKLING ARTS — Bold 18p, 50

www.sparklingarts.com — Regular 9p, 100

Founder — Regular 10p, 100

CAROLINE LEE — Bold 16/20p, 50

carolinelee@sparklingarts.com — Italic 9p, 0

010.2345.6789 — Italic 11p, 100

THE *jealous* ARTIST

DAMN,
I WISH I THOUGHT OF THAT.

Regular 10p, 30 | Italic 10p, 30 | Bold 30/30p, 10 | Regular 8/10p, 0

ADVENTURE FOR THE YOUNG AT HEART

Go outside and explore

At any rate, That is Happiness; To be dissolved into something
COMPLETE AND GREAT.

Bitter Regular 21.8-21.6-Bold 27.3p, 20 | Regular 10p, 10

— Willa Cather, *My Ántonia*

"Stay close to anything that makes you feel you are glad to be alive. Plant the seeds for a sustainable future. Connect, respect and listen to nature, for nature is our greatest teacher."

Bold 10/15p, 30

LOOK UP, KEEP GOING

Bold 14p, 100

Lorem ipsum dolor sit amet, consectetur adipiscing elit, sed do eiusmod tempor incididunt ut labore et dolore magna aliqua. Ut enim ad minim veniam, nostrud exercitation ullamco laboris nisi aliquip ex ea commodo consequat. Duis aute irure dolor in reprehenderit in voluptate velit esse cillum dolore eu fugiat nulla pariatur. Excepteur sint occaecat cupidatat non proident, sunt in culpa qui officia deserunt mollit anim id est laborum.

"Aliquam fermentum est. Praesent posuere lorem quis quam viverra tempus. Suspendisse varius nunc nec sapien convallis rutrum. Donec vitae tincidunt tortor, nec tempor tortor."

Ultrices sagittis orci a scelerisque purus. Diam maecenas ultricies mi eget mauris. Nam aliquam sem et tortor consequat id porta nibh. Tempor orci dapibus ultrices in iaculis nunc sed augue lacus. Sit amet massa vitae tortor condimentum.

Regular 7/9p, 0 | Bold 8/11p, 50

Mi sit amet mauris commodo quis. Adipiscing at in tellus integer feugiat scelerisque varius morbi in enim. Elementum nibh tellus molestie nunc non. Nisi porta lorem mollis aliquam ut porttitor leo a. Sed sed risus pretium quam vulputate dignissim. Nunc mi ipsum faucibus vitae aliquet nec ullam corper. Scelerisque viverra mauris in aliquam sem fringilla.

In nisl nisi scelerisque eu. Odio facilisis mauris sit amet massa. Porttitor lacus luctus accumsan tortor posuere ac ut consequat. Nibh venenatis cras sed felis. Vestibulum sed arcu non odio euismod. Vitae aliquet nec ullamcorper sit amet. Amet mauris commodo quis imperdiet massa tincidunt nunc. Condimentum mattis pellentesque id nibh. Egestas purus viverra accumsan in nisl nisi scelerisque eu. Euismod in pellentesque massa placerat duis ultricies. Eget egestas purus viverra accumsan in. Id venenatis a condimentum vitae pellentesque habitant morbi. Dignissim convallis aenean et tortor Est ullamcorper eget nulla facilisi dignissim diam quis. Dui nunc mattis enim elementum sagittis.

Bold 14/17p, 100 | Regular 8/25p, 25

Bree Serif

Bree Serif Bold 76p, 0

Bree Serif Regular

24/30p, 0

ABCDEFGHIJKLMNOPQRSTUVWXYZ

abcefghijklmnopqrstuvwxyz abc@gmail.com

1234567890 +−×÷=#%&*, . : ; ! ? ( )[ ]{ } ' ' " " ®©

14/20p, 0

Deep into that darkness peering,
long I stood there, wondering, fearing, doubting,
dreaming dreams no mortal ever dared to dream before.

— Edgar Allan Poe, Complete Tales and Poems

Regular 11/16p, 10 | 9/14p, 0

"I loved her against reason, against promise, against peace, against
hope, against happiness, against all discouragement that could be."

— Charles Dickens, Great Expectations

Regular 10/14p, 0 | 10/14p, 10

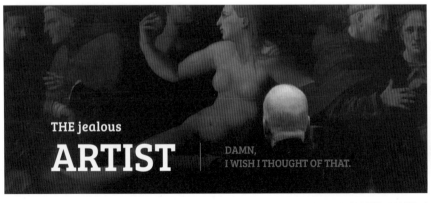

THE jealous

ARTIST

DAMN,
I WISH I THOUGHT OF THAT.

Regular 10p, 30 | 30/30p, 10 | 8/10p, 0

| License | Open Font License | | Link | fonts.google.com/specimen/Bree+Serif |
| Font tag | Slab-Serif, Handwriting, Editorial, Google | | Pair | Open Sans, Roboto, Lato, Source Sans Pro, Raleway |

At any rate, That is Happiness; To be dissolved into something COMPLETE AND GREAT.

Bree Serif Regular 23.4-23.5-30.7p, 20 | Regular 10p, 10

— Willa Cather, My Ántonia

"Stay close to anything that makes you feel you are glad to be alive. Plant the seeds for a sustainable future. Connect, respect and listen to nature, for nature is our greatest teacher."

Regular 10/15p, 30

LOOK UP, KEEP GOING

Regular 14p, 100

Lorem ipsum dolor sit amet, consectetur adipiscing elit, sed do eiusmod tempor incididunt ut labore et dolore magna aliqua. Ut enim ad minim veniam, nostrud exercitation ullamco laboris nisi aliquip ex ea commodo consequat. Duis aute irure dolor in reprehenderit in voluptate velit esse cillum dolore eu fugiat nulla pariatur. Excepteur sint occaecat cupidatat non proident, sunt in culpa qui officia deserunt mollit anim id est laborum.

"Aliquam fermentum est. Praesent posuere lorem quis quam viverra tempus. Suspendisse varius nunc nec sapien convallis rutrum. Donec vitae tincidunt tortor, nec tempor tortor."

Ultrices sagittis orci a scelerisque purus. Diam maecenas ultricies mi eget mauris. Nam aliquam sem et tortor consequat id porta nibh. Tempor orci dapibus ultrices in iaculis nunc sed augue lacus. Sit amet massa vitae tortor condimentum.

Regular 7/9p, 0 | 8/11p, 50

Mi sit amet mauris commodo quis. Adipiscing at in tellus integer feugiat scelerisque varius morbi in enim. Elementum nibh tellus molestie nunc non. Nisi porta lorem mollis aliquam ut porttitor leo a. Sed sed risus pretium quam vulputate dignissim. Nunc mi ipsum faucibus vitae aliquet nec ullam corper. Scelerisque viverra mauris in aliquam sem fringilla.

In nisl nisi scelerisque eu. Odio facilisis mauris sit amet massa. Porttitor lacus luctus accumsan tortor posuere ac ut consequat. Nibh venenatis cras sed felis. Vestibulum sed arcu non odio euismod. Vitae aliquet nec ullamcorper sit amet. Amet mauris commodo quis imperdiet massa tincidunt nunc. Condimentum mattis pellentesque id nibh. Egestas purus viverra accumsan in nisl nisi scelerisque eu. Euismod in pellentesque massa placerat duis ultricies. Eget egestas purus viverra accumsan in. Id venenatis a condimentum vitae pellentesque habitant morbi. Dignissim convallis aenean et tortor Est ullamcorper eget nulla facilisi dignissim diam quis. Dui nunc mattis enim elementum sagittis.

CINZEL

Cinzel Bold 92p, 0

CINZEL REGULAR
CINZEL BOLD
CINZEL BLACK

24/30p, 0

AABBCCDDEEFFGGHHIIJJKKLLMMNNOOPP
QQRRSSUUVVWWXXYYZZ ABC@GMAIL.COM
1234567890 + − × ÷ = # % & * , . : ; ! ? ( ) [ ] { } ' ' " " ® ©

AABBCCDDEEFFGGHHIIJJKKLLMMNNOOPP
QQRRSSUUVVWWXXYYZZ ABC@GMAIL.COM
1234567890 + − × ÷ = # % & * , . : ; ! ? ( ) [ ] { } ' ' " " ® ©

AABBCCDDEEFFGGHHIIJJKKLLMMNNOOPP
QQRRSSUUVVWWXXYYZZ ABC@GMAIL.COM
1234567890 + − × ÷ = # % & * , . : ; ! ? ( ) [ ] { } ' ' " " ®

14/20p, 0

"I LOVED HER AGAINST REASON, AGAINST PROMISE,
AGAINST PEACE, AGAINST HOPE, AGAINST HAPPINESS,
AGAINST ALL DISCOURAGEMENT THAT COULD BE."
— **CHARLES DICKENS, GREAT EXPECTATIONS**

Regular 10/14p, 0 | Bold 9/14p, 10

License	Open Font License
Font tag	Serif, Orpheus Pro, Contemporary, Google

Link	fonts.google.com/specimen/Cinzel
Pair	Roboto, Lato, Montserrat, Raleway, Oswald

AT ANY RATE, THAT IS HAPPINESS;
TO BE DISSOLVED INTO SOMETHING
COMPLETE AND GREAT.

Cinzel Regular 19.7-Bold 18.5-Black 25.3p, 20 | Regular 10p, 10

— WILLA CATHER, MY ÁNTONIA

SPARKLING ARTS

WWW.SPARKLINGARTS.COM

FOUNDER
CAROLINE LEE

CAROLINELEE@SPARKLINGARTS.COM

010.2345.6789

Black 17p, 50

Regular 9p, 100

Regular 10p, 100

Bold 15/20p, 50

Regular 9p, 0

Regular 11p, 100

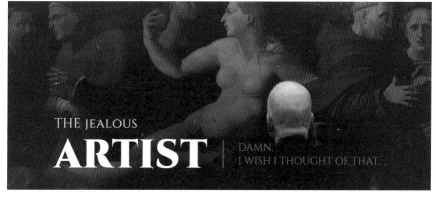

THE JEALOUS
ARTIST | DAMN,
I WISH I THOUGHT OF THAT.

Regular 10p, 30 | Black 30/30p, 10 | Regular 8/10p, 0

Crete Round

Crete Round Bold 60p, 0

Crete Round Regular
Crete Round Italic

24/30p, 0

ABCDEFGHIJKLMNOPQRSTUVWXYZ
abcefghijklmnopqrstuvwxyz abc@gmail.com
1234567890 +−×÷=#%&*,.:;!?()[]{} ' ' " " ®©

ABCDEFGHIJKLMNOPQRSTUVWXYZ
abcefghijklmnopqrstuvwxyz abc@gmail.com
1234567890 +−×÷=#%&,.:;!?()[]{} ' ' " " ®©*

14/20p, 0

"I loved her against reason, against *promise*, against *peace*, against *hope*, against *happiness*, against *all discouragement* that could be."
— Charles Dickens, *Great Expectations*

Regular 10/14p, 0 | 10/14p, 10

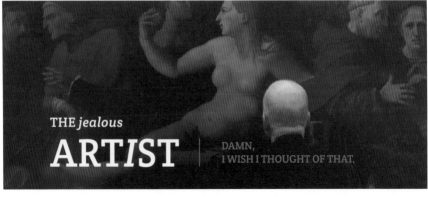

THE *jealous*
ARTIST | DAMN, I WISH I THOUGHT OF THAT.

Regular 10p, 30 | Italic 10p, 30 | Regular 30/30p, 10 | Regular 8/10p, 0

License Open Font License
Font tag Slab-Serif, Round, Contemporary, Lexia, Google

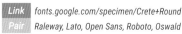

Link fonts.google.com/specimen/Crete+Round
Pair Raleway, Lato, Open Sans, Roboto, Oswald

At any rate, That is Happiness;
To be dissolved into something
COMPLETE AND GREAT.

Crete Round Regular 23.5-23.1-29.7p, 20 | Regular 10p, 10   — Willa Cather, My Ántonia

Deep into that darkness peering,
long I stood there, wondering, fearing, doubting,
dreaming dreams no mortal ever dared to dream before.

— Edgar Allan Poe, *Complete Tales and Poems*

Regular 11/15p, 10 | 9/14p, 0

LOOK UP, KEEP GOING

Regular 14p, 100

Lorem ipsum dolor sit amet, consectetur adipiscing elit, sed do eiusmod tempor incididunt ut labore et dolore magna aliqua. Ut enim ad minim veniam, nostrud exercitation ullamco laboris nisi aliquip ex ea commodo consequat. Duis aute irure dolor in reprehenderit in voluptate velit esse cillum dolore eu fugiat nulla pariatur. Excepteur sint occaecat cupidatat non proident, sunt in culpa qui officia deserunt mollit anim id est laborum.

"Aliquam fermentum est. Praesent posuere lorem quis quam viverra tempus. Suspendisse varius nunc nec sapien convallis rutrum. Donec vitae tincidunt tortor, nec tempor tortor."

Ultrices sagittis orci a scelerisque purus. Diam maecenas ultricies mi eget mauris. Nam aliquam sem et tortor consequat id porta nibh. Tempor orci dapibus ultrices in iaculis nunc sed augue lacus. Sit amet massa vitae tortor condimentum.

Mi sit amet mauris commodo quis. Adipiscing at in tellus integer feugiat scelerisque varius morbi in enim. Elementum nibh tellus molestie nunc non. Nisi porta lorem mollis aliquam ut porttitor leo a. Sed sed risus pretium quam vulputate dignissim. Nunc mi ipsum faucibus vitae aliquet nec ullam corper. Scelerisque viverra mauris in aliquam sem fringilla.

In nisl nisi scelerisque eu. Odio facilisis mauris sit amet massa. Porttitor lacus luctus accumsan tortor posuere ac ut consequat. Nibh venenatis cras sed felis. Vestibulum sed arcu non odio euismod. Vitae aliquet nec ullamcorper sit amet. Amet mauris commodo quis imperdiet massa tincidunt nunc. Condimentum mattis pellentesque id nibh. Egestas purus viverra accumsan in nisl nisi scelerisque eu. Euismod in pellentesque massa placerat duis ultricies. Eget egestas purus viverra accumsan in. Id venenatis a condimentum vitae pellentesque habitant morbi. Dignissim convallis aenean et tortor Est ullamcorper eget nulla facilisi dignissim diam quis. Dui nunc mattis enim elementum sagittis.

Regular 7/9p, 0 | 8/11p, 50

217

Crimson Text

Crimson Text Bold 58p, 0

Crimson Text Regular   *Italic*

Crimson Text SemiBold   ***SemiBold Italic***

Crimson Text Bold   ***Bold Italic***

18/24p, 10

ABCDEFGHIJKLMNOPQRSTUVWXYZ
abcdefghijklmnopqrstuvwxyz
1234567890 +−×÷=#%&*, . : ; ! ? ( )[ ]{ } ' ' " " ® ©

ABCDEFGHIJKLMNOPQRSTUVWXYZ
abcdefghijklmnopqrstuvwxyz
1234567890 +−×÷=#%&, . : ; ! ? ( )[ ]{ } ' ' " " ® ©*

ABCDEFGHIJKLMNOPQRSTUVWXYZ
abcdefghijklmnopqrstuvwxyz
1234567890 +−×÷=#%&*, . : ; ! ? ( )[ ]{ } ' ' "   ® ©

ABCDEFGHIJKLMNOPQRSTUVWXYZ
abcdefghijklmnopqrstuvwxyz
1234567890 +−×÷=#%&, . : . ! ? ( )[ ]{ } ' ' " " ® ©*

ABCDEFGHIJKLMNOPQRSTUVWXYZ
abcdefghijklmnopqrstuvwxyz
1234567890 +−×÷=#%&*, . : ; ! ? ( )[ ]{ } ' ' " " ® ©

ABCDEFGHIJKLMNOPQRSTUVWXYZ
abcdefghijklmnopqrstuvwxyz
1234567890 +−×÷=#%&*, . : ; ! ? ( )[ ]{ } ' ' " " ® ©

14/18p, 0

License Open Font license
Font tag Serif, Text, Old style, Garamond, Sabon, Google

Link fonts.google.com/specimen/Crimson+Text
Pair Open Sans, Montserrat, Lato, Roboto, Raleway

Deep into that darkness peering,
long I stood there, wondering, fearing, doubting,
dreaming dreams no mortal ever dared to dream before.

— **Edgar Allan Poe,** *Complete Tales and Poems*

Regular 13/18p, 10 ┊ Bold 10/14p, 0

SPARKLING ARTS — Bold 18p, 50

www.sparklingarts.com — Regular 9p, 100

Founder — Regular 10p, 100

CAROLINE LEE — SemiBold 16/20p, 50

carolinelee@sparklingarts.com — Italic 9p, 0

010.2345.6789 — Italic 11p, 100

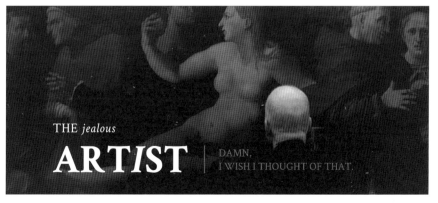

THE *jealous* ARTIST — DAMN, I WISH I THOUGHT OF THAT.

Regular 10p, 30 ┊ Italic 10p, 30 ┊ Bold 30/30p, 10 ┊ Regular 8/10p, 0

ADVENTURE FOR THE YOUNG AT HEART

Go outside and explore

At any rate, That is Happiness;
To be dissolved into something
COMPLETE AND GREAT.

Crimson Text Regular 26.4p·SemiBold 24.9p·Bold 28.6p, 20 | Regular 10p, 10

— Willa Cather, *My Ántonia*

"Stay close to anything that makes you feel you are glad to be alive. Plant the seeds for a sustainable future. *Connect, respect and listen to nature,* **for nature is our greatest teacher."**

SemiBold 10/15p, 30

LOOK UP, KEEP GOING

Bold 14p, 100

Lorem ipsum dolor sit amet, consectetur adipiscing elit, sed do eiusmod tempor incididunt ut labore et dolore magna aliqua. Ut enim ad minim veniam, nostrud exercitation ullamco laboris nisi aliquip ex ea commodo consequat. Duis aute irure dolor in reprehenderit in voluptate velit esse cillum dolore eu fugiat nulla pariatur. Excepteur sint occaecat cupidatat non proident, sunt in culpa qui officia deserunt mollit anim id est laborum.

"Aliquam fermentum est. Praesent posuere lorem quis quam viverra tempus. Suspendisse varius nunc nec sapien convallis rutrum. Donec vitae tincidunt tortor, nec tempor tortor.

Ultrices sagittis orci a scelerisque purus. Diam maecenas ultricies mi eget mauris. Nam aliquam sem et tortor consequat id porta nibh. Tempor orci dapibus ultrices in iaculis nunc sed augue lacus. Sit amet massa vitae tortor condimentum.

Mi sit amet mauris commodo quis. Adipiscing at in tellus integer feugiat scelerisque varius morbi in enim. Elementum nibh tellus molestie nunc non. Nisi porta lorem mollis aliquam ut porttitor leo a. Sed sed risus pretium quam vulputate dignissim. Nunc mi ipsum faucibus vitae aliquet nec ullam corper. Scelerisque viverra mauris in aliquam sem fringilla.

In nisl nisi scelerisque eu. Odio facilisis mauris sit amet massa. Porttitor lacus luctus accumsan tortor posuere ac ut consequat. Nibh venenatis cras sed felis. Vestibulum sed arcu non odio euismod. Vitae aliquet nec ullamcorper sit amet. Amet mauris commodo quis imperdiet massa tincidunt nunc. Condimentum mattis pellentesque id nibh. Egestas purus viverra accumsan in nisl nisi scelerisque eu. Euismod in pellentesque massa placerat duis ultricies. Eget egestas purus viverra accumsan in. Id consequat con dimentum vitae pellentesque habitant morbi. Dignissim convallis aenean et tortor Est ullamcorper eget nulla facilisi dignissim diam quis. Dui nunc mattis enim elementum sagittis.

Regular 7/9p, 0 | SemiBold 8/11p, 50

Bold 14/17p, 100 | Regular 8/25p, 25

Domine

Domine Bold 86p, 0

Domine Regular
Domine Bold

24/30p, 0

ABCDEFGHIJKLMNOPQRSTUVWXYZ
abcefghijklmnopqrstuvwxyz abc@gmail.com
1234567890 +−×÷=#%&*, . : ; ! ? ( )[ ]{ } ' ' " " ®©

**ABCDEFGHIJKLMNOPQRSTUVWXYZ
abcefghijklmnopqrstuvwxyz abc@gmail.com
1234567890 +−×÷=#%&*, . : ; ! ? ( )[ ]{ } ' ' " " ®©**

14/20p, 0

"I loved her against reason, against promise, against peace, against
hope, against happiness, against all discouragement that could be."
— **Charles Dickens, Great Expectations**

Regular 10/14p, 0 | 10/14p, 10

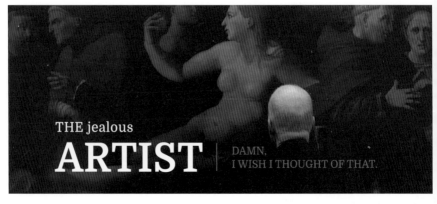

THE jealous
ARTIST DAMN,
I WISH I THOUGHT OF THAT.

Regular 10p, 30 | Bold 30/30p, 10 | Regular 8/10p, 0

License Open Font License
Font tag Slab-Serif, Round, Jubilat, Google

Link fonts.google.com/specimen/Domine
Pair Montserrat, Open Sans, Roboto, Playfair Display, Merriweather

At any rate, That is Happiness; To be dissolved into something COMPLETE AND GREAT.

Domine Regular 21.9-21.4 Bold 26.2p, 20 | Regular 10p, 10

— Willa Cather, My Ántonia

Deep into that darkness peering,
long I stood there, wondering, fearing, doubting,
dreaming dreams no mortal ever dared to dream before.

— Edgar Allan Poe, Complete Tales and Poems

Regular 11/15p, 10   9/14p, 0

LOOK UP, KEEP GOING

Bold 14p, 100

Lorem ipsum dolor sit amet, consectetur adipiscing elit, sed do eiusmod tempor incididunt ut labore et dolore magna aliqua. Ut enim ad minim veniam, nostrud exercitation ullamco laboris nisi aliquip ex ea commodo consequat. Duis velit esse cillum dolore eu fugiat nulla pariatur. Excepteur sint occaecat cupidatat non proident, sunt in culpa qui officia anim id est laborum.

"Aliquam fermentum est. Praesent posuere lorem quis quam viverra tempus. Suspendisse varius nunc nec sapien convallis rutrum. Donec vitae tincidunt tortor, nec tortor."

Ultrices sagittis orci a scelerisque purus. Diam maecenas ultricies mi eget mauris. Nam aliquam sem et tortor consequat id porta nibh. Tempor orci dapibus ultrices in iaculis nunc sed augue lacus. Sit amet massa vitae tortor condimentum.

Mi sit amet mauris commodo quis. Adipiscing at in tellus integer feugiat scelerisque varius morbi in enim. Elementum nibh tellus molestie nunc non. Nisi porta lorem mollis aliquam ut porttitor leo a. Sed sed risus pretium quam vulputate dignissim. Nunc mi ipsum faucibus vitae aliquet nec ullam corper. Scelerisque viverra mauris in aliquam sem fringilla.

In nisl nisi scelerisque eu. Odio facilisis mauris sit amet massa. Porttitor lacus luctus accumsan tortor posuere ac ut consequat. Nibh venenatis cras sed felis. Vestibulum sed arcu non odio euismod. Vitae aliquet nec ullamcorper sit amet. Condimentum mattis pellentesque id nibh. Egestas purus viverra accumsan in nisl nisi scelerisque eu. Euismod in pellentesque massa placerat duis ultricies. Eget egestas purus viverra accumsan in. Id venenatis a condimentum vitae pellentesque habitant morbi. Dignissim convallis aenean et tortor Est ullamcorper eget nulla facilisi dignissim diam quis. Dui nunc mattis enim elementum sagittis.

Regular 7/9p, 0 | Bold 8/11p, 50

EB Garamond

EB Garamond Bold 56p, 0

EB Garamond Regular	*Italic*
EB Garamond Medium	*Medium Italic*
EB Garamond SemiBold	*SemiBold Italic*
EB Garamond Bold	*Bold Italic*
EB Garamond ExtraBold	*ExtraBold*

18/24p

ABCDEFGHIJKLMNOPQRSTUVWXYZ abcdefghijklmnopqrstuvwxyz
ABCDEFGHIJKLMNOPQRSTUVWXYZ abcdefghijklmnopqrstuvwxyz
1234567890 *1234567890* +−×÷=#%&*,.:;!? ()[]{}''"" ®©

ABCDEFGHIJKLMNOPQRSTUVWXYZ abcdefghijklmnopqrstuvwxyz
ABCDEFGHIJKLMNOPQRSTUVWXYZ abcdefghijklmnopqrstuvwxyz
1234567890 *1234567890* +−×÷=#%&*,.:;!? ()[]{}''"" ®©

ABCDEFGHIJKLMNOPQRSTUVWXYZ abcdefghijklmnopqrstuvwxyz
ABCDEFGHIJKLMNOPQRSTUVWXYZ abcdefghijklmnopqrstuvwxyz
1234567890 *1234567890* +−×÷=#%&*,.:;!? ()[]{}''"" ®©

ABCDEFGHIJKLMNOPQRSTUVWXYZ abcdefghijklmnopqrstuvwxy
ABCDEFGHIJKLMNOPQRSTUVWXYZ abcdefghijklmnopqrstuvwxyz
1234567890 *1234567890* +−×÷=#%&*,.:;!? ()[]{}''"" ®©

ABCDEFGHIJKLMNOPQRSTUVWXYZ abcdef ghijklmnopqrstuvwx
ABCDEFGHIJKLMNOPQRSTUVWXYZ abcdefghijklmnopqrstuvwxy
1234567890 *1234567890* +−×÷=#%&*,.:;!? ()[]{}''"" ®©

11/16p

License	Apache License, Version 2.0	Link	fonts.google.com/specimen/EB+Garamond
Font tag	Sans serif, Text, Garamond, Google	Pair	Roboto, Montserrat, Lobster, Play, Oswald

Deep into that darkness peering,
long I stood there, wondering, fearing, doubting,
dreaming dreams no mortal ever dared to dream before.
— **Edgar Allan Poe,** *Complete Tales and Poems*

Regular 12/17p, 10 | Bold 10/14p, 0

SPARKLING ARTS — ExtraBold 18p, 50
www.sparklingarts.com — Regular 9p, 100
010.2345.6789 — Italic 11p, 100
Founder — Medium 10p, 100
CAROLINE LEE — Bold 16/20p, 50
carolinelee@sparklingarts.com — Italic 9p, 0

THE *jealous* ARTIST | DAMN, I WISH I THOUGHT OF THAT.

Regular 10p, 30 | Italic 10p, 30 | ExtraBold 30/30p, Optical 10 | Regular 8/10p, 0

ADVENTURE FOR THE YOUNG AT HEART

Go outside and explore

At any rate, That is Happiness; To be dissolved into something COMPLETE AND GREAT.

EB Garamond Medium 26p·SemiBold 25.3p·ExtraBold 27.1p, 20 | Regular 10p, 10

— Willa Cather, *My Ántonia*

"Stay close to anything that makes you feel you are glad to be alive. Plant the seeds for a sustainable future. *Connect, respect and listen to nature,* for nature is our greatest teacher."

SemiBold 10/15p, 30

LOOK UP, KEEP GOING

ExtraBold 14p, 100

Lorem ipsum dolor sit amet, consectetur adipiscing elit, sed do eiusmod tempor incididunt ut labore et dolore magna aliqua. Ut enim ad minim veniam, nostrud exercitation ullamco laboris nisi aliquip ex ea commodo consequat. Duis aute irure dolor in reprehenderit in voluptate velit esse cillum dolore eu fugiat nulla pariatur. Excepteur sint occaecat cupidatat non proident, sunt in culpa qui officia deserunt mollit anim id est laborum.

"Aliquam fermentum est. Praesent posuere lorem quis quam viverra tempus. Suspendisse varius nunc nec sapien convallis rutrum. Donec vitae tincidunt tortor, nec tempor tortor."

Ultrices sagittis orci a scelerisque purus. Diam maecenas ultricies mi eget mauris. Nam aliquam sem et tortor consequat id porta nibh. Tempor orci dapibus ultrices in iaculis nunc sed augue lacus. Sit amet massa vitae tortor condimentum.

Mi sit amet mauris commodo quis. Adipiscing at in tellus integer feugiat scelerisque varius morbi in enim. Elementum nibh tellus molestie nunc non. Nisi porta lorem mollis aliquam ut porttitor leo a. Sed sed risus pretium quam vulputate dignissim. Nunc mi ipsum faucibus vitae aliquet nec ullam corper. Scelerisque viverra mauris in aliquam sem fringilla.

In nisl nisi scelerisque eu. Odio facilisis mauris sit amet massa. Porttitor lacus luctus accumsan tortor posuere ac ut consequat. Nibh venenatis cras sed felis. Vestibulum sed arcu non odio euismod. Vitae aliquet nec ullamcorper sit amet. Amet mauris commodo quis imperdiet massa tincidunt nunc. Condimentum mattis pellentesque id nibh. Egestas purus viverra accumsan in nisl nisi scelerisque eu. Euismod in pellentesque massa placerat duis ultricies. Eget egestas purus viverra accumsan in. Id venenatis a condimentum vitae pellentesque habitant morbi. Dignissim convallis aenean et tortor Est ullamcorper eget nulla facilisi dignissim diam quis. Dui nunc mattis enim elementum sagittis.

Regular 7/9p, 0 | SemiBold 8/11p, 50

ExtraBold 14/17p, 100 | Regular 8/25p, 25

Libre Baskerville

Libre Baskerville Bold 37p, 0

Libre Baskerville Regular
Libre Baskerville Italic
Libre Baskerville Bold

24/30p, 0

ABCDEFGHIJKLMNOPQRSTUVWXYZ
abcefghijklmnopqrstuvwxyz abc@gmail.com
1234567890 +−×÷=#%&*, . : ; ! ? ( )[ ]{ } ' ' " " ®©
ABCDEFGHIJKLMNOPQRSTUVWXYZ
abcefghijklmnopqrstuvwxyz abc@gmail.com
1234567890 +−×÷=#%&, . : ; ! ? ( )[ ]{ } ' ' " " ®©*

ABCDEFGHIJKLMNOPQRSTUVWXYZ
abcefghijklmnopqrstuvwxyz abc@gmail.com
1234567890 +−×÷=#%&*, . : ; ! ? ( )[ ]{ } ' ' " " ®©

14/20p, 0

"I loved her against *reason*, against *promise*, against *peace*, against
hope, against *happiness*, against *all discouragement* that could be."
— Charles Dickens, Great Expectations

Regular 10/14p, 0 | Bold 9/14p, 10

License	Open Font License
Font tag	Serif, Text, Old style, Baskerville, Google

Link	fonts.google.com/specimen/Libre Baskerville
Pair	Roboto, Open Sans, Montserrat, Raleway, Lato

Deep into that darkness peering,
long I stood there, wondering, fearing, doubting,
dreaming dreams no mortal ever dared to dream before.

— Edgar Allan Poe, Complete Tales and Poems

Regular 11/16p, 10 | Bold 9/14p, 0

SPARKLING ARTS

www.sparklingarts.com

Founder
CAROLINE LEE

carolinelee@sparklingarts.com

010.2345.6789

Bold 16p, 50

Regular 9p, 100

Regular 10p, 100

Bold 16/20p, 50

Italic 9p, 0

Italic 11p, 100

THE *jealous*
ARTIST | DAMN,
I WISH I THOUGHT OF THAT.

Regular 10p, 30 | Italic 10p, 30 | Bold 30/30p, 10 | Regular 8/10p, 0

ADVENTURE FOR THE YOUNG AT HEART

Go outside and explore

At any rate, That is Happiness;
To be dissolved into something
COMPLETE AND GREAT.

— Willa Cather, *My Ántonia*

"Stay close to anything that makes you feel you are glad to be alive. Plant the seeds for a sustainable future. Connect, respect and listen to nature, for nature is our greatest teacher."

LOOK UP, KEEP GOING

Lorem ipsum dolor sit amet, consectetur adipiscing elit, sed do eiusmod tempor incididunt ut labore et dolore magna aliqua. Ut enim ad minim veniam, nostrud exercitation ullamco laboris nisi aliquip ex ea commodo consequat. Duis aute irure dolor in dolore eu fugiat nulla pariatur. Excepteur sint occaecat cupidatat non proident, sunt in culpa qui officia deserunt mollit anim id est laborum.

"Aliquam fermentum est. Praesent posuere lorem quis quam viverra tempus. Suspendisse nec convallis rutrum. Donec vitae tincidunt tortor, nec tempor tortor."

Ultrices sagittis orci a scelerisque purus. Diam maecenas ultricies mi eget mauris. Nam aliquam sem et tortor consequat id porta nibh. Tempor orci dapibus ultrices in iaculis nunc sed augue lacus. Sit amet massa vitae tortor condimentum.

Mi sit amet mauris commodo quis. Adipiscing at in tellus integer feugiat scelerisque varius morbi in enim. Elementum nibh tellus molestie nunc non. Nisi porta lorem mollis aliquam ut porttitor leo a. Sed sed risus pretium quam vulputate dignissim. Nunc mi ipsum faucibus vitae aliquet nec ullam corper. Scelerisque viverra mauris in aliquam sem fringilla.

In nisl nisi scelerisque eu. Odio facilisis mauris sit amet massa. Porttitor lacus luctus accumsan tortor posuere ac ut consequat. Nibh venenatis cras sed felis. Vestibulum sed arcu non odio euismod. Vitae aliquet nec ullamcorper sit amet. Amet mauris commodo quis imperdiet massa tincidunt nunc. Condimentum mattis pellentesque id nibh. Egestas purus viverra accumsan in nisl nisi scelerisque eu. Euismod in pellentesque massa placerat duis ultricies. Eget egestas purus viverra accumsan in. Id venenatis a condimentum vitae pellentesque habitant morbi. Dignissim convallis aenean et tortor Est ullamcorper eget nulla facilisi dignissim diam quis. Dui nunc mattis enim elementum sagittis.

Lora

Lora Bold 100p, 0

Lora Regular
Lora Italic
Lora Bold
Lora Bold Italic

20/24p, 0

ABCDEFGHIJKLMNOPQRSTUVWXYZ
ABCDEFGHIJKLMNOPQRSTUVWXYZ
abcefghijklmnopqrstuvwxyz abc@gmail.com
abcefghijklmnopqrstuvwxyz abc@gmail.com
1234567890 +−×:=#%&*, . : ; ! ? ( )[ ]{ } ' ' " " ®©
1234567890 +−×:=#%&, . : ; ! ? ( )[ ]{ } ' ' " " ®©*

ABCDEFGHIJKLMNOPQRSTUVWXYZ
ABCDEFGHIJKLMNOPQRSTUVWXYZ
abcefghijklmnopqrstuvwxyz abc@gmail.com
abcefghijklmnopqrstuvwxyz abc@gmail.com
1234567890 +−×:=#%&*, . : ; ! ? ( )[ ]{ } ' ' " " ®©
1234567890 +−×:=#%&*, . : ; ! ? ( )[ ]{ } ' ' " " ®©

14/20p, 0

"I loved her against *reason*, against *promise*, against *peace*, against *hope*, against *happiness*, against *all discouragement* that could be."
— **Charles Dickens, Great Expectations**

Regular 10/14p, 0 | Bold 9/14p, 10

License Open Font License
Font tag Serif, Text, , Latino URW, Google

Link fonts.google.com/specimen/Lora
Pair Roboto, Open Sans, Montserrat, Lora, Raleway

Deep into that darkness peering,
long I stood there, wondering, fearing, doubting,
dreaming dreams no mortal ever dared to dream before.
— **Edgar Allan Poe, *Complete Tales and Poems***

Regular 12/16p, 10 | Bold 10/14p, 0

SPARKLING ARTS

Bold 18p, 50

www.sparklingarts.com

Regular 9p, 100

Founder

Regular 10p, 100

CAROLINE LEE

Bold 16/20p, 50

carolinelee@sparklingarts.com

Italic 9p, 0

010.2345.6789

Italic 11p, 100

THE *jealous*
ARTIST
DAMN,
I WISH I THOUGHT OF THAT.

Regular 10p, 30 | Italic 10p, 30 | Bold 30/30p, 10 | Regular 8/10p, 0

ADVENTURE FOR THE YOUNG AT HEART

Go outside and explore

At any rate, That is Happiness; To be dissolved into something
COMPLETE AND GREAT.

Lora Regular 22.6-22.1-Bold 27.3p, 20 | Regular 10p, 10

— Willa Cather, *My Ántonia*

"Stay close to anything that makes you feel you are glad to be alive. Plant the seeds for a sustainable future. *Connect, respect and listen to nature,* **for nature is our greatest teacher."**

Bold 10/15p, 30

LOOK UP, KEEP GOING

Bold 14p, 100

Lorem ipsum dolor sit amet, consectetur adipiscing elit, sed do eiusmod tempor incididunt ut labore et dolore magna aliqua. Ut enim ad minim veniam, nostrud exercitation ullamco laboris nisi aliquip ex ea commodo consequat. Duis aute irure dolor in reprehenderit in voluptate velit esse cillum dolore eu fugiat nulla pariatur. Excepteur sint occaecat cupidatat non proident, sunt in culpa qui officia deserunt mollit anim id est laborum.

"Aliquam fermentum est. Praesent posuere lorem quis quam viverra tempus. Suspendisse varius nunc nec sapien convallis rutrum. Donec vitae tincidunt tortor, nec tempor tortor."

Ultrices sagittis orci a scelerisque purus. Diam maecenas ultricies mi eget mauris. Nam aliquam sem et tortor consequat id porta nibh. Tempor orci dapibus ultrices in iaculis nunc sed augue lacus. Sit amet massa vitae tortor condimentum.

Mi sit amet mauris commodo quis. Adipiscing at in tellus integer feugiat scelerisque varius morbi in enim. Elementum nibh tellus molestie nunc non. Nisi porta lorem mollis aliquam ut porttitor leo a. Sed sed risus pretium quam vulputate dignissim. Nunc mi ipsum faucibus vitae aliquet nec ullam corper. Scelerisque viverra mauris in aliquam sem fringilla.

In nisl nisi scelerisque eu. Odio facilisis mauris sit amet massa. Porttitor lacus luctus accumsan tortor posuere ac ut consequat. Nibh venenatis cras sed felis. Vestibulum sed arcu non odio euismod. Vitae aliquet nec ullamcorper sit amet. Amet mauris commodo quis imperdiet massa tincidunt nunc. Condimentum mattis pellentesque id nibh. Egestas purus viverra accumsan in nisl nisi scelerisque eu. Euismod in pellentesque massa placerat duis ultricies. Eget egestas purus viverra accumsan in. Id venenatis a condimentum vitae pellentesque habitant morbi. Dignissim convallis aenean et tortor Est ullamcorper eget nulla facilisi dignissim diam quis. Dui nunc mattis enim elementum sagittis.

Regular 7/9p, 0 | Bold 8/11p, 50

Bold 14/18p, 100 | Regular 8/25p, 25

Merriweather

Merriweather Bold 47p, 0

Merriweather Light
Merriweather Regular
Merriweather Bold
Merriweather Black

Light Italic
Italic
Bold Italic
Black Italic

18/24p

ABCDEFGHIJKLMNOPQRSTUVWXYZ abcdefghijklmnopqrstuvv
1234567890 +−×÷=#%&*,.:;!?()[]{}''""®©
ABCDEFGHIJKLMNOPQRSTUVWXYZ abcdefghijklmnopqrstuvwxyz
1234567890 +−×÷=#%&,.:;!?()[]{}''""®©*

ABCDEFGHIJKLMNOPQRSTUVWXYZ abcdefghijklmnopqrstuv
1234567890 +−×÷=#%&*,.:;!?()[]{}''""®©
ABCDEFGHIJKLMNOPQRSTUVWXYZ abcdefghijklmnopqrstuvwxy:
1234567890 +−×÷=#%&,.:;!?()[]{}''""®©*

ABCDEFGHIJKLMNOPQRSTUVWXYZ abcdefghijklmnopqrst
1234567890 +−×÷=#%&*,.:;!?()[]{}''""®©
ABCDEFGHIJKLMNOPQRSTUVWXYZ abcdefghijklmnopqrstuvwxy
1234567890 +−×÷=#%&*,.:;!?()[]{}''""®©

ABCDEFGHIJKLMNOPQRSTUVWXYZ abcdefghijklmnopqrstu
1234567890 +−×÷=#%&*,.:;!?()[]{}''""®©
ABCDEFGHIJKLMNOPQRSTUVWXYZ abcdefghijklmnopqrstuvw:
1234567890 +−×÷=#%&*,.:;!?()[]{}''""®©

11/16p

License	Open Font License	Link	fonts.google.com/specimen/Merriweather
Font tag	Sans serif, Screen, Chaparral, Google	Pair	Open Sans, Montserrat, Roboto, Source Sans Pro, Oswald

Deep into that darkness peering,
long I stood there, wondering, fearing, doubting,
dreaming dreams no mortal ever dared to dream before.
— **Edgar Allan Poe**, *Complete Tales and Poems*

Light 12/17p, 10 | SemiBold 10/14p, 0

Black 17p, 50

Light 8p, 100

Regular 10p, 100

Bold 16/22p, 50

Italic 9p, 0

Light Italic 11p, 100

Regular 10p, 30 | Light Italic 10p, 30 | Black 30/30p, 10 | Light 8/10p, 0

ADVENTURE FOR THE YOUNG AT HEART

Go outside and explore

At any rate, That is Happiness; To be dissolved into something COMPLETE AND GREAT.

Merriweather Regular 20.5p-Bold 19.9p-Black 26p, 20 | Regular 10p, 10

— Willa Cather, *My Ántonia*

"Stay close to anything that makes you feel you are glad to be alive. Plant the seeds for a sustainable future. *Connect, respect and listen to nature,* **for nature is our greatest teacher."**

Bold 10/15p, 30

LOOK UP, KEEP GOING

Black 14p, 100

Lorem ipsum dolor sit amet, consectetur adipiscing elit, sed do eiusmod tempor incididunt ut labore et dolore magna aliqua. Ut enim ad minim veniam, nostrud exercitation ullamco laboris nisi aliquip ex ea commodo consequat. Duis aute irure dolor in reprehenderit in voluptate velit esse cillum dolore eu fugiat nulla pariatur. Excepteur sint occaecat cupidatat non proident, sunt in culpa qui officia deserunt mollit anim id est laborum.

"Aliquam fermentum est. Praesent posuere lorem quis quam viverra tempus. Suspendisse varius nunc nec sapien convallis rutrum. Donec vitae tincidunt tortor, nec tortor."

Ultrices sagittis orci a scelerisque purus. Diam maecenas ultricies mi eget mauris. Nam aliquam sem et tortor consequat id porta nibh. Tempor orci dapibus ultrices in iaculis nunc sed augue lacus. Sit amet massa vitae tortor condimentum.

Regular 7/9p, 0 | Bold 8/11p, 50

Mi sit amet mauris commodo quis. Adipiscing at in tellus integer feugiat scelerisque varius morbi in enim. Elementum nibh tellus molestie nunc non. Nisi porta lorem mollis aliquam ut porttitor leo a. Sed sed risus pretium quam vulputate dignissim. Nunc mi ipsum faucibus vitae aliquet nec ullam corper. Scelerisque viverra mauris in aliquam sem fringilla.

In nisl nisi scelerisque eu. Odio facilisis mauris sit amet massa. Porttitor lacus luctus accumsan tortor posuere ac ut consequat. Nibh venenatis cras sed felis. Vestibulum sed arcu non odio euismod. Vitae aliquet nec ullamcorper sit amet. Amet mauris commodo quis imperdiet massa tincidunt nunc. Condimentum mattis pellentesque id nibh. Egestas purus viverra accumsan in nisl nisi scelerisque eu. Euismod in pellentesque massa placerat duis ultricies. Eget egestas purus viverra accumsan in. Id venenatis a condimentum vitae pellentesque habitant morbi. Dignissim convallis aenean et tortor Est ullamcorper eget nulla facilisi dignissim diam quis. Dui nunc mattis enim elementum sagittis.

Black 14/17p, 100 | Light 8/25p, 25

Noto Serif

Noto Serif Bold 65p, 0

Noto Serif Regular
Noto Serif Italic
Noto Serif Bold
Noto Serif Bold Italic

20/24p, 0

ABCDEFGHIJKLMNOPQRSTUVWXYZ
ABCDEFGHIJKLMNOPQRSTUVWXYZ
abcefghijklmnopqrstuvwxyz abc@gmail.com
abcefghijklmnopqrstuvwxyz abc@gmail.com
1234567890 +−×÷=#%&*, . : ; ! ? ( )[ ]{ } ' ' " " ®©
1234567890 +−×÷=#%&, . : ; ! ? ( )[ ]{ } ' ' " " ®©*

ABCDEFGHIJKLMNOPQRSTUVWXYZ
ABCDEFGHIJKLMNOPQRSTUVWXYZ
abcefghijklmnopqrstuvwxyz abc@gmail.com
abcefghijklmnopqrstuvwxyz abc@gmail.com
1234567890 +−×÷=#%&*, . : ; ! ? ( )[ ]{ } ' ' " " ®©
1234567890 +−×÷=#%&*, . : ; ! ? ( )[ ]{ } ' ' " " ®©

14/20p, 0

"I loved her against *reason*, against *promise*, against *peace*, against *hope*, against *happiness*, against *all discouragement* that could be."
— **Charles Dickens, *Great Expectations***

Regular 10/14p, 0 | Bold 9/14p, 10

| License | Apache License, Version 2.0 | Link | fonts.google.com/specimen/Noto+Serif |
| Font tag | Sans serif, Text, Velino Text, Google | Pair | Open Sans, Roboto, Montserrat, Roboto Slab, Playfair Display |

Deep into that darkness peering,
long I stood there, wondering, fearing, doubting,
dreaming dreams no mortal ever dared to dream before.
— **Edgar Allan Poe,** *Complete Tales and Poems*

Regular 12/17p, 10 | Bold 10/14p, 0

SPARKLING ARTS

www.sparklingarts.com

Founder

CAROLINE LEE

carolinelee@sparklingarts.com

010.2345.6789

Bold 18p, 50

Regular 9p, 100

Regular 10p, 100

Bold 16/20p, 50

Italic 9p, 0

Italic 11p, 100

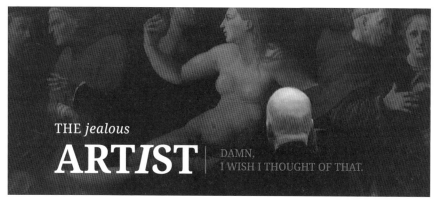

THE *jealous*
ART*IST*

DAMN,
I WISH I THOUGHT OF THAT.

Regular 10p, 30 | Italic 10p, 30 | Bold 30/30p, 10 | Regular 8/10p, 0

ADVENTURE FOR THE YOUNG AT HEART

Go outside and explore

At any rate, That is Happiness; To be dissolved into something COMPLETE AND GREAT.

— Willa Cather, *My Ántonia*

"Stay close to anything that makes you feel you are glad to be alive. Plant the seeds for a sustainable future. *Connect, respect and listen to nature,* for nature is our greatest teacher."

LOOK UP, KEEP GOING

Lorem ipsum dolor sit amet, consectetur adipiscing elit, sed do eiusmod tempor incididunt ut labore et dolore magna aliqua. Ut enim ad minim veniam, nostrud exercitation ullamco laboris nisi aliquip ex ea commodo consequat. Duis aute irure dolor in reprehenderit in voluptate velit esse cillum dolore eu fugiat nulla pariatur. Excepteur sint occaecat cupidatat non proident, sunt in culpa qui officia deserunt mollit anim id est laborum.

"Aliquam fermentum est. Praesent posuere lorem quis quam viverra tempus. Suspendisse varius nunc nec sapien convallis rutrum. Donec vitae tincidunt tortor, nec tortor."

Ultrices sagittis orci a scelerisque purus. Diam maecenas ultricies mi eget mauris. Nam aliquam sem et tortor consequat id porta nibh. Tempor orci dapibus ultrices in iaculis nunc sed augue lacus. Sit amet vitae condimentum.

Mi sit amet mauris commodo quis. Adipiscing at in tellus integer feugiat scelerisque varius morbi in enim. Elementum nibh tellus molestie nunc non. Nisi porta lorem mollis aliquam ut porttitor leo a. Sed sed risus pretium quam vulputate dignissim. Nunc mi ipsum faucibus vitae aliquet nec ullam corper. Scelerisque viverra mauris in aliquam sem fringilla.

In nisl nisi scelerisque eu. Odio facilisis mauris sit amet massa. Porttitor lacus luctus accumsan tortor posuere ac ut consequat. Nibh venenatis cras sed felis. Vestibulum sed arcu non odio euismod. Vitae aliquet nec ullamcorper sit amet. Amet mauris commodo quis imperdiet massa tincidunt nunc. Condimentum mattis pellentesque id nibh. Egestas purus viverra accumsan in nisl nisi scelerisque eu. Euismod in pellentesque massa placerat duis ultricies. Eget egestas purus viverra accumsan in. Id venenatis a condimentum vitae pellentesque habitant morbi. Dignissim convallis aenean et tortor Est ullamcorper eget nulla facilisi dignissim diam quis. Dui nunc mattis enim elementum sagittis.

Playfair Display

Playfair Display Bold 46p, 0

Playfair Display Regular *Italic*
Playfair Display Bold ***Bold Italic***
Playfair Display Black ***Black Italic***

18/24p, 10

ABCDEFGHIJKLMNOPQRSTUVWXYZ
abcdefghijklmnopqrstuvwxyz
1234567890 +−×÷=#%&*,.:;!?()[]{}''""® ©

ABCDEFGHIJKLMNOPQRSTUVWXYZ
abcdefghijklmnopqrstuvwxyz
1234567890 +−×÷=#%&,.:;!?()[]{}''""® ©*

ABCDEFGHIJKLMNOPQRSTUVWXYZ
abcdefghijklmnopqrstuvwxyz
1234567890 +−×÷=#%&*,.:;!?()[]{}''""® ©

ABCDEFGHIJKLMNOPQRSTUVWXYZ
abcdefghijklmnopqrstuvwxyz
1234567890 +−×÷=#%&*,.:;!?()[]{}''""® ©

ABCDEFGHIJKLMNOPQRSTUVWXYZ
abcdefghijklmnopqrstuvwxyz
1234567890 +−×÷=#%&*,.:;!?()[]{}''""® ©

ABCDEFGHIJKLMNOPQRSTUVWXYZ
abcdefghijklmnopqrstuvwxyz
1234567890 +−×÷=#%&*,.:;!?()[]{}''""® ©

14/18p, 0

| License | Open Font license |
| Font tag | Serif, Heading, Benton Modern Display, Google |

| Link | fonts.google.com/specimen/Playfair Display |
| Pair | Roboto, Open Sans, Montserrat, Lato, Oswald |

Deep into that darkness peering,
long I stood there, wondering, fearing, doubting,
dreaming dreams no mortal ever dared to dream before.
— Edgar Allan Poe, *Complete Tales and Poems*

Regular 13/18p, 10 | Bold 10/14p, 0

SPARKLING ARTS

www.sparklingarts.com

Founder
CAROLINE LEE

carolinelee@sparklingarts.com

010.2345.6789

Black 18p, 50

Regular 9p, 100

Regular 10p, 100

Bold 16/20p, 50

Italic 9p, 0

Italic 11p, 100

THE *jealous*
ART/ST

DAMN,
I WISH I THOUGHT OF THAT.

Regular 10p, 30 | Italic 10p, 30 | Black 30/30p, 10 | Regular 8/10p, 0

ADVENTURE FOR THE YOUNG AT HEART

Go outside and explore

At any rate, That is Happiness;
To be dissolved into something
COMPLETE AND GREAT.

Playfair Display Regular 23.4p·Bold 22.4p·Black 26.6p, 20 | Regular 10p, 10

— Willa Cather, *My Ántonia*

"Stay close to anything that makes you feel you are glad to be alive. Plant the seeds for a sustainable future. Connect, respect and listen to nature, for nature is our greatest teacher."

Bold 10/15p, 30

LOOK UP, KEEP GOING

Black 14p, 100

Lorem ipsum dolor sit amet, consectetur adipiscing elit, sed do eiusmod tempor incididunt ut labore et dolore magna aliqua. Ut enim ad minim veniam, nostrud exercitation ullamco laboris nisi aliquip ex ea commodo consequat. Duis aute irure dolor in reprehenderit in voluptate velit esse cillum dolore eu fugiat nulla pariatur. Excepteur sint occaecat cupidatat non proident, sunt in culpa qui officia deserunt mollit anim id est laborum.

"Aliquam fermentum est. Praesent posuere lorem quis quam viverra tempus. Suspendisse varius nunc nec sapien convallis rutrum. Donec vitae tincidunt tortor, nec tempor tortor."

Ultrices sagittis orci a scelerisque purus. Diam maecenas ultricies mi eget mauris. Nam aliquam sem et tortor consequat id porta nibh. Tempor orci dapibus ultrices in iaculis nunc sed augue lacus. Sit amet massa vitae tortor condimentum.

Regular 7/9p, 0 | Bold 8/11p, 50

Mi sit amet mauris commodo quis. Adipiscing at in tellus integer feugiat scelerisque varius morbi in enim. Elementum nibh tellus molestie nunc non. Nisi porta lorem mollis aliquam ut porttitor leo a. Sed sed risus pretium quam vulputate dignissim. Nunc mi ipsum faucibus vitae aliquet nec ullam corper. Scelerisque viverra mauris in aliquam sem fringilla.

In nisl nisi scelerisque eu. Odio facilisis mauris sit amet massa. Porttitor lacus luctus accumsan tortor posuere ac ut consequat. Nibh venenatis cras sed felis. Vestibulum sed arcu non odio euismod. Vitae aliquet nec ullamcorper sit amet. Amet mauris commodo quis imperdiet massa tincidunt nunc. Condimentum mattis pellentesque id nibh. Egestas purus viverra accumsan in nisl nisi scelerisque eu. Euismod in pellentesque massa placerat duis ultricies. Eget egestas purus viverra accumsan in. Id venenatis a condimentum vitae pellentesque habitant morbi. Dignissim convallis aenean et tortor Est ullamcorper eget nulla facilisi dignissim diam quis. Dui nunc mattis enim elementum sagittis.

↖ Black 14/19p, 100 | Regular 8/25p, 25

PT Serif

PT Serif Bold 86p, 0

PT Serif Regular
PT Serif Italic
PT Serif Bold
PT Serif Bold Italic

20/24p, 0

ABCDEFGHIJKLMNOPQRSTUVWXYZ
ABCDEFGHIJKLMNOPQRSTUVWXYZ
abcefghijklmnopqrstuvwxyz abc@gmail.com
abcefghijklmnopqrstuvwxyz abc@gmail.com
1234567890 +−×÷=#%&*,.:;!?()[]{}''""®©
1234567890 +−×÷=#%&,.:;!?()[]{}''""®©*

ABCDEFGHIJKLMNOPQRSTUVWXYZ
ABCDEFGHIJKLMNOPQRSTUVWXYZ
abcefghijklmnopqrstuvwxyz abc@gmail.com
abcefghijklmnopqrstuvwxyz abc@gmail.com
1234567890 +−×÷=#%&*,.:;!?()[]{}''""®©
1234567890 +−×÷=#%&*,.:;!?()[]{}''""®©

14/20p, 0

"I loved her against *reason*, against *promise*, against *peace*, against *hope*, against *happiness*, against *all discouragement* that could be."
— **Charles Dickens, *Great Expectations***

Regular 10/14p, 0 | Bold 9/14p, 10

| License | Open Font License |
| Font tag | Sans serif, Rusia, Utopia, Google |

| Link | fonts.google.com/specimen/PT+Serif |
| Pair | Open Sans, Roboto, Montserrat, Roboto Slab, Playfair Display |

Deep into that darkness peering,
long I stood there, wondering, fearing, doubting,
dreaming dreams no mortal ever dared to dream before.
— **Edgar Allan Poe, *Complete Tales and Poems***

Regular 12/17p, 10 | Bold 10/14p, 0

SPARKLING ARTS

www.sparklingarts.com

Founder
CAROLINE LEE

carolinelee@sparklingarts.com

010.2345.6789

Bold 18p, 50

Regular 9p, 100

Regular 10p, 100

Bold 16/20p, 50

Italic 9p, 0

Italic 11p, 100

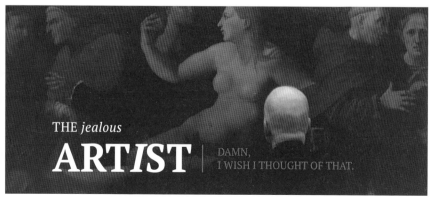

THE *jealous*
ART*IST* | DAMN,
I WISH I THOUGHT OF THAT.

Regular 10p, 30 | Italic 10p, 30 | Bold 30/30p, 10 | Regular 8/10p, 0

ADVENTURE FOR THE YOUNG AT HEART

Go outside and explore

At any rate, That is Happiness;
To be dissolved into something
COMPLETE AND GREAT.

— Willa Cather, *My Ántonia*

"Stay close to anything that makes you feel you are glad to be alive. Plant the seeds for a sustainable future. *Connect, respect and listen to nature,* for nature is our greatest teacher."

LOOK UP, KEEP GOING

Lorem ipsum dolor sit amet, consectetur adipiscing elit, sed do eiusmod tempor incididunt ut labore et dolore magna aliqua. Ut enim ad minim veniam, nostrud exercitation ullamco laboris nisi aliquip ex ea commodo consequat. Duis aute irure dolor in reprehenderit in voluptate velit esse cillum dolore eu fugiat nulla pariatur. Excepteur sint occaecat cupidatat non proident, sunt in culpa qui officia deserunt mollit anim id est laborum.

"Aliquam fermentum est. Praesent posuere lorem quis quam viverra tempus. Suspendisse varius nunc nec sapien convallis rutrum. Donec vitae tincidunt tortor, nec tortor."

Ultrices sagittis orci a scelerisque purus. Diam maecenas ultricies mi eget mauris. Nam aliquam sem et tortor consequat id porta nibh. Tempor orci dapibus ultrices in iaculis nunc sed augue lacus. Sit amet vitae condimentum.

Mi sit amet mauris commodo quis. Adipiscing at in tellus integer feugiat scelerisque varius morbi in enim. Elementum nibh tellus molestie nunc non. Nisi porta lorem mollis aliquam ut porttitor leo a. Sed sed risus pretium quam vulputate dignissim. Nunc mi ipsum faucibus vitae aliquet nec ullam corper. Scelerisque viverra mauris in aliquam sem fringilla.

In nisl nisi scelerisque eu. Odio facilisis mauris sit amet massa. Porttitor lacus luctus accumsan tortor posuere ac ut consequat. Nibh venenatis cras sed felis. Vestibulum sed arcu non odio euismod. Vitae aliquet nec ullamcorper sit amet. Amet mauris commodo quis imperdiet massa tincidunt nunc. Condimentum mattis pellentesque id nibh. Egestas purus viverra accumsan in nisl nisi scelerisque eu. Euismod in pellentesque massa placerat duis ultricies. Eget egestas purus viverra accumsan in. Id venenatis a condimentum vitae pellentesque habitant morbi. Dignissim convallis aenean et tortor Est ullamcorper eget nulla facilisi dignissim diam quis. Dui nunc mattis enim elementum sagittis.

Roboto Slab

Roboto Slab Regualr 60p, 0

Roboto Slab Thin
Roboto Slab Light
Roboto Slab Regular
Roboto Slab Bold

22/28p, 0

ABCDEFGHIJKLMNOPQRSTUVWXYZ
abcefghijklmnopqrstuvwxyz
1234567890 +−×÷=#%&*,.:;!? ()[]{}'' " " ®©

ABCDEFGHIJKLMNOPQRSTUVWXYZ
abcefghijklmnopqrstuvwxyz
1234567890 +−×÷=#%&*,.:;!? ()[]{}'' " " ®©

ABCDEFGHIJKLMNOPQRSTUVWXYZ
abcefghijklmnopqrstuvwxyz
1234567890 +−×÷=#%&*,.:;!? ()[]{}'' " " ®©

ABCDEFGHIJKLMNOPQRSTUVWXYZ
abcefghijklmnopqrstuvwxyz
1234567890 +−×÷=#%&*,.:;!? ()[]{}'' " " ®©

15/20p, 0

License	Open Font License
Font tag	Slab-Serif, text, FF Unit Slab, Google

Link	fonts.google.com/specimen/Roboto+Slab
Pair	Open Sans, Montserrat, Lato, Roboto Condensed

Deep into that darkness peering,
long I stood there, wondering, fearing, doubting,
dreaming dreams no mortal ever dared to dream before.
— Edgar Allan Poe, Complete Tales and Poems

Light 12/18p, 10 | Bold 11/15p, 0

SPARKLING ARTS

www.sparklingarts.com

Founder
CAROLINE LEE

carolinelee@sparklingarts.com

010.2345.6789

Bold 18p, 50

Light 9p, 100

Regular 10p, 100

Bold 16/20p, 50

Light 9p, 0

Thin 11p, 100

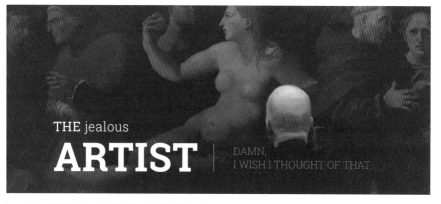

THE jealous
ARTIST | DAMN,
I WISH I THOUGHT OF THAT.

Regular 10p, 30 | Light 10p, 30 | Bold 30/30p, 20 | Light 8/10p, 0

ADVENTURE FOR THE YOUNG AT HEART

Go outside and explore

At any rate, That is Happiness;
To be dissolved into something
COMPLETE AND GREAT.

Roboto Slab Light 22.4 Regular 21.7 Bold 27.7p, 20 Regular 10p, 10   — Willa Cather, My Ántonia

Stay close to anything that makes you feel
you are glad to be alive. Plant the seeds for a
sustainable future. Connect, respect and listen
to nature, for nature is our greatest teacher."   Regular 10/15p, 30

LOOK UP, KEEP GOING   Bold 14p, 100

Lorem ipsum dolor sit amet, consectetur adipiscing elit, sed do eiusmod tempor incididunt ut labore et dolore magna aliqua. Ut enim ad minim veniam, nostrud aliquip ex ea commodo consequat. Duis aute irure dolor in lum dolore eu fugiat nulla pariatur. Excepteur sint occaecat cupidatat non proident, sunt in culpa qui officia deserunt mollit anim id est laborum.

"Aliquam fermentum est. Praesent posuere lorem quis quam viverra tempus. Suspendisse varius nunc nec sapien convallis rutrum. Donec vitae tincidunt tortor, nec tortor."

Ultrices sagittis orci a scelerisque purus. Diam maecenas ultricies mi eget mauris. Nam aliquam sem et tortor consequat id porta nibh in iaculis nunc sed augue lacus. Sit amet massa vitae tortor condimentum.

Light 8/10p, 0 Regular 8/11p, 50

Mi sit amet mauris commodo quis. Adipiscing at in tellus integer feugiat scelerisque varius morbi in enim. Elementum nibh tellus molestie nunc non. Nisi porta lorem mollis aliquam ut porttitor leo a. Sed sed risus pretium quam vulputate dignissim. Nunc mi ipsum faucibus vitae aliquet nec ullam corper. Scelerisque viverra mauris in aliquam sem fringilla.

In nisl nisi scelerisque eu. Odio facilisis mauris sit amet massa. Porttitor lacus luctus accumsan tortor posuere ac ut consequat. Nibh venenatis cras sed felis. Vestibulum sed arcu non odio euismod. Vitae aliquet nec ullamcorper sit amet. Amet mauris commodo quis imperdiet massa tincidunt nunc. Condimentum mattis vitae pellentesque habitant morbi. Dignissim convallis aenean et tortor Est ullamcorper eget nulla facilisi dignissim diam quis. Dui nunc mattis enim elementum sagittis.

Bold 14/17p, 100 Regular 8/25p, 25

Rokkitt

Rokkitt Bold 100p, 0

Rokkitt Thin

Rokkitt ExtraLight

Rokkitt Light

Rokkitt Regular

Rokkitt Medium

Rokkitt SemiBold

Rokkitt Bold

Rokkitt Extrabold

Rokkitt Black

18/22p, 0

ABCDEFGHIJKLMNOPQRSTUVWXYZ +−×÷=#%&*, . : ; ! ?
1234567890 abcefghijklmnopqrstuvwxyz ( )[ ]{ } ' ' " " ®©

ABCDEFGHIJKLMNOPQRSTUVWXYZ +−×÷=#%&*, . : ; ! ?
1234567890 abcefghijklmnopqrstuvwxyz ( )[ ]{ } ' ' " " ®©

ABCDEFGHIJKLMNOPQRSTUVWXYZ +−×÷=#%&*, . : ; ! ?
1234567890 abcefghijklmnopqrstuvwxyz ( )[ ]{ } ' ' " " ®©

ABCDEFGHIJKLMNOPQRSTUVWXYZ +−×÷=#%&*, . : ; ! ?
1234567890 abcefghijklmnopqrstuvwxyz ( )[ ]{ } ' ' " " ®©

ABCDEFGHIJKLMNOPQRSTUVWXYZ +−×÷=#%&*, . : ; ! ?
1234567890 abcefghijklmnopqrstuvwxyz ( )[ ]{ } ' ' " " ®©

ABCDEFGHIJKLMNOPQRSTUVWXYZ +−×÷=#%&*, . : ; ! ?
1234567890 abcefghijklmnopqrstuvwxyz ( )[ ]{ } ' ' " " ®©

ABCDEFGHIJKLMNOPQRSTUVWXYZ +−×÷=#%&*, . : ; ! ?
1234567890 abcefghijklmnopqrstuvwxyz ( )[ ]{ } ' ' " " ®©

ABCDEFGHIJKLMNOPQRSTUVWXYZ +−×÷=#%&*, . : ; ! ?
1234567890 abcefghijklmnopqrstuvwxyz ( )[ ]{ } ' ' " " ®©

ABCDEFGHIJKLMNOPQRSTUVWXYZ +−×÷=#%&*, . : ; ! ?
1234567890 abcefghijklmnopqrstuvwxyz ( )[ ]{ } ' ' " " ®©

12/16p, 0

| License | Open Font License |
| Font tag | Slab-Serif, Heading, Screen, Google |

| Link | fonts.google.com/specimen/Rokkitt |
| Pair | Open Sans, Lato, Ubuntu, Raleway |

Deep into that darkness peering,
long I stood there, wondering, fearing, doubting,
dreaming dreams no mortal ever dared to dream before.

— Edgar Allan Poe, Complete Tales and Poems

Light 13/16p, 10 | Bold 10/14p, 0

SPARKLING ARTS

www.sparklingarts.com

Founder
CAROLINE LEE

carolinelee@sparklingarts.com

010.2345.6789

Black 18p, 50

Light 9p, 100

Regular 10p, 100

Bold 16/20p, 50

Medium 9p, 0

Extralight 11p, 100

THE jealous
ARTIST
DAMN,
I WISH I THOUGHT OF THAT.

Medium 10p, 30 | Light 10p, 30 | Black 30/30p, 20 | Light 8/10p, 0

ADVENTURE FOR THE YOUNG AT HEART

Go outside and explore

At any rate, That is Happiness; To be dissolved into something COMPLETE AND GREAT.

Rokkitt Medium 24.2·Bold 24·Black 26p, 20 ⫶ Regular 10p, 10

— Willa Cather, My Ántonia

"Stay close to anything that makes you feel you are glad to be alive. Plant the seeds for a sustainable future. Connect, respect and listen to nature, for nature is our greatest teacher."

SemiBold 11/13p, 30

LOOK UP, KEEP GOING

ExtraBold 15p, 100

Lorem ipsum dolor sit amet, consectetur adipiscing elit, sed do eiusmod tempor incididunt ut labore et dolore magna aliqua. Ut enim ad minim veniam, nostrud exercitation ullamco laboris nisi aliquip ex ea commodo consequat. Duis aute irure dolor in reprehenderit in voluptate velit esse cillum dolore eu fugiat nulla pariatur. Excepteur sint occaecat cupidatat non proident, sunt in culpa qui officia deserunt mollit anim id est laborum.

"Aliquam fermentum est. Praesent posuere lorem quis quam viverra tempus. Suspendisse varius nunc nec sapien convallis rutrum. Donec vitae tincidunt tortor, tortor."

Ultrices sagittis orci a scelerisque purus. Diam maecenas ultricies mi eget mauris. Nam aliquam sem et tortor consequat id porta nibh. Tempor orci dapibus ultrices in iaculis nunc sed augue lacus. Sit amet massa condimentum.

Regular 8/9p, 0 ⫶ SemiBold 9/11p, 50

Mi sit amet mauris commodo quis. Adipiscing at in tellus integer feugiat scelerisque varius morbi in enim. Elementum nibh tellus molestie nunc non. Nisi porta lorem mollis aliquam ut porttitor leo a. Sed sed risus pretium quam vulputate dignissim. Nunc mi ipsum faucibus vitae aliquet nec ullam corper. Scelerisque viverra mauris in aliquam sem fringilla.

In nisl nisi scelerisque eu. Odio facilisis mauris sit amet massa. Porttitor lacus luctus accumsan tortor posuere ac ut consequat. Nibh venenatis cras sed felis. Vestibulum sed arcu non odio euismod. Vitae aliquet nec ullamcorper sit amet. Amet mauris commodo quis imperdiet massa tincidunt nunc. Condimentum mattis pellentesque id nibh. Egestas purus viverra accumsan in nisl nisi scelerisque eu. Euismod in pellentesque massa placerat duis ultricies. Eget egestas purus viverra accumsan in. Id venenatis a condimentum vitae pellentesque habitant morbi. Dignissim convallis aenean et tortor Est ullamcorper eget nulla facilisi dignissim diam quis. Dui nunc mattis enim elementum sagittis.

Black 16/17p, 100 ⫶ Regular 10/30p, 25

Source Serif Pro

Source Serif Pro Bold 45p, 0

Source Serif Pro Regular
Source Serif Pro SemiBold
Source Serif Pro Bold

24/30p, 0

AaBbCcDdEeFfGgHhIiJjKkLlMmNnOoPp
QqRrSsUuVvWwXxYyZz abc@gmail.com
1234567890 + − × ÷ = # % & * , . : ;! ? ( ) [ ] { } ' ' " " ® ©

AaBbCcDdEeFfGgHhIiJjKkLlMmNnOoPp
QqRrSsUuVvWwXxYyZz abc@gmail.com
1234567890 + − × ÷ = # % & * , . : ; ! ? ( ) [ ] { } ' ' " " ® ©

**AaBbCcDdEeFfGgHhIiJjKkLlMmNnOoPp
QqRrSsUuVvWwXxYyZz abc@gmail.com
1234567890 + − × ÷ = # % & * , . : ; ! ? ( ) [ ] { } ' ' " " ® ©**

14/20p, 0

"I loved her against reason, against promise, against peace, against
hope, against happiness, against all discouragement that could be."
— Charles Dickens, Great Expectations

Regular 10/14p, 0 | Bold 9/14p, 10

License	Open Font License	Link	fonts.google.com/specimen/Source+Serif+Pro
Font tag	Serif, Freight Text, Google	Pair	Source Sans Pro, Roboto, Open Sans, Roboto Slab, Montserrat

At any rate, That is Happiness; To be dissolved into something **COMPLETE AND GREAT.**

Source Serif Pro Regular 23.5·SemiBold 22.7·Bold 28.9p, 20 | Regular 10p, 10

— Willa Cather, My Ántonia

SPARKLING ARTS

www.sparklingarts.com

Founder

CAROLINE LEE

carolinelee@sparklingarts.com

010.2345.6789

Bold 17p, 50

Regular 9p, 100

Regular 10p, 100

SemiBold 15/20p, 50

Regular 9p, 0

Regular 11p, 100

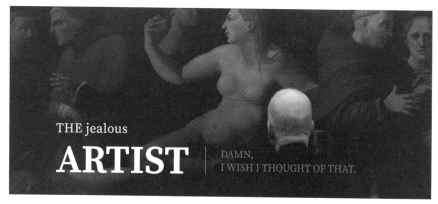

THE jealous

ARTIST | DAMN, I WISH I THOUGHT OF THAT.

Regular 10p, 30 | Bold 30/30p, 10 | Regular 8/10p, 0

261

Vollkorn

Vollkorn Bold 80p, 0

Vollkorn Regular
Vollkorn SemiBold
Vollkorn Bold
Vollkorn Black

Italic
SemiBold Italic
Bold Italic
Black Italic

18/24p

ABCDEFGHIJKLMNOPQRSTUVWXYZ abcdefghijklmnopqrstuvwxyz
1234567890 +−×÷=#%&*,.:;!?()[]{}'' " " ®©
ABCDEFGHIJKLMNOPQRSTUVWXYZ abcdefghijklmnopqrstuvwxyz
1234567890 +−×÷=#%&,.:;!?()[]{}'' " " ®©*

ABCDEFGHIJKLMNOPQRSTUVWXYZ abcdefghijklmnopqrstuvwxy:
1234567890 +−×÷=#%&*,.:;!?()[]{}'' " " ®©
ABCDEFGHIJKLMNOPQRSTUVWXYZ abcdefghijklmnopqrstuvwxyz
1234567890 +−×÷=#%&,.:;!?()[]{}'' " " ®©*

ABCDEFGHIJKLMNOPQRSTUVWXYZ abcdefghijklmnopqrstuvwx
1234567890 +−×÷=#%&*,.:;!?()[]{}'' " " ®©
ABCDEFGHIJKLMNOPQRSTUVWXYZ abcdefghijklmnopqrstuvwxyz
1234567890 +−×÷=#%&*,.:;!?()[]{}'' " " ®©

ABCDEFGHIJKLMNOPQRSTUVWXYZ abcdefghijklmnopqrstuv
1234567890 +−×÷=#%&*,.:;!?()[]{}'' " " ®©
ABCDEFGHIJKLMNOPQRSTUVWXYZ abcdefghijklmnopqrstuvw
1234567890 +−×÷=#%&*,.:;!?()[]{}'' " " ®©

11/16p

License	Open Font License	**Link**	fonts.google.com/specimen/Vollkorn
Font tag	Slab-Serif, Text, Heading, Arno Pro, Google	**Pair**	Open Sans, Roboto, Lato, Lora, PT Sans

Deep into that darkness peering,
long I stood there, wondering, fearing, doubting,
dreaming dreams no mortal ever dared to dream before.
— **Edgar Allan Poe, *Complete Tales and Poems***

Regular 12/17p, 10 | SemiBold 10/14p, 0

Black 17p, 50

Regular 8p, 100

SemiBold 10p, 100

Bold 16/22p, 50

Italic 9p, 0

Italic 11p, 100

Regular 10p, 30 | Italic 10p, 30 | Black 30/30p, 10 | Regular 8/10p, 0

ADVENTURE FOR THE YOUNG AT HEART

Go outside and explore

At any rate, That is Happiness; To be dissolved into something COMPLETE AND GREAT.

Vollkorn Regular 24.1p·Bold 21.9p·Black 27p, 20 | Regular 10p, 10

— Willa Cather, *My Ántonia*

"Stay close to anything that makes you feel you are glad to be alive. Plant the seeds for a sustainable future. *Connect, respect and listen to nature,* for nature is our greatest teacher."

Bold 10/15p, 30

LOOK UP, KEEP GOING

Black 14p, 100

Lorem ipsum dolor sit amet, consectetur adipiscing elit, sed do eiusmod tempor incididunt ut labore et dolore magna aliqua. Ut enim ad minim veniam, nostrud exercitation ullamco laboris nisi aliquip ex ea commodo consequat. Duis aute irure dolor in reprehenderit in voluptate velit esse cillum dolore eu fugiat nulla pariatur. Excepteur sint occaecat cupidatat non proident, sunt in culpa qui officia deserunt mollit anim id est laborum.

"Aliquam fermentum est. Praesent posuere lorem quis quam viverra tempus. Suspendisse varius nunc nec sapien convallis rutrum. Donec vitae tincidunt tortor, nec tortor."

Ultrices sagittis orci a scelerisque purus. Diam maecenas ultricies mi eget mauris. Nam aliquam sem et tortor consequat id porta nibh. Tempor orci dapibus ultrices in iaculis nunc sed augue lacus. Sit amet massa vitae tortor condimentum.

Regular 7/9p, 0 | Bold 8/11p, 50

Mi sit amet mauris commodo quis. Adipiscing at in tellus integer feugiat scelerisque varius morbi in enim. Elementum nibh tellus molestie nunc non. Nisi porta lorem mollis aliquam ut porttitor leo a. Sed sed risus pretium quam vulputate dignissim. Nunc mi ipsum faucibus vitae aliquet nec ullam corper. Scelerisque viverra mauris in aliquam sem fringilla.

In nisl nisi scelerisque eu. Odio facilisis mauris sit amet massa. Porttitor lacus luctus accumsan tortor posuere ac ut consequat. Nibh venenatis cras sed felis. Vestibulum sed arcu non odio euismod. Vitae aliquet nec ullamcorper sit amet. Amet mauris commodo quis imperdiet massa tincidunt nunc. Condimentum mattis pellentesque id nibh. Egestas purus viverra accumsan in nisl nisi scelerisque eu. Euismod in pellentesque massa placerat duis ultricies. Eget egestas purus viverra accumsan in. Id venenatis a condimentum vitae pellentesque habitant morbi. Dignissim convallis aenean et tortor Est ullamcorper eget nulla facilisi dignissim diam quis. Dui nunc mattis enim elementum sagittis.

Black 14/17p, 100 | Regular 8/25p, 25

Script

Adrenaline Regular 220p, 0

스크립트 폰트

펜으로 쓴 것 같은 스크립트 폰트는 인간적인 숨결을 불어 넣을 수 있는 디자인 요소입니다. 무료 폰트 중에서 감탄이 나올 정도로 품질이 좋은 스크립트 폰트는 찾기 힘들지만, 그래도 어렵게 찾아 다양한 스타일의 무료 스크립트 폰트 13종을 준비했습니다. 스크립트 폰트는 그 특성상 다양한 두께의 패밀리 폰트를 만들기 어렵습니다. 그대신 사람이 펜으로 쓴 것 같은 느낌을 살리기 위해서 다양한 변형 글자를 제공하고, 특별한 조합의 문자가 연달아 쓰였을 때 어울리는 모양의 글자들을 만듭니다.

Brush

브러쉬 폰트

붓으로 쓴 것 같은 브러쉬 폰트 역시 인간적인 숨결을 불어 넣는 특별한 요소입니다. 생생하게 살아 있는 질감은 화면보다 인쇄한 종이 위에서 더 멋지게 보입니다. 브러쉬 폰트도 품질이 좋은 무료 폰트를 찾기가 어려워서 7종을 준비했습니다. 브러쉬 폰트는 보통 굵기 때문에 섬세한 표현이 어려워 소문자나 다양한 기호를 빼고 대문자만 지원하는 경우가 많습니다. 물론 아래에 보인 Rockstar 폰트처럼 스크립트 폰트 같은 브러쉬 폰트도 있습니다.

Rockstar Regular 290p, 0

Adrenaline

Adrenaline Regular 78p, 0 ¦ 8 alt ② 74p -1°

ABCDEFGHIJKL
MNOPQRSTUVWXYZ

25/30p, 200

abcdefghijklmnopqrstuvwxyz
1234567890 + × ÷ = ...:·· ·˙ ˙ " " ™M

@ !?$% & < > « » ()[]{}[]\

25/30p, 0

a a	b b b	c c	d d d	e e
f f f	g g g	h h h	i i	j j j
k k k	l l l	m m	n n	o o	p p
q q	r r r	s s s	t t t	u u
v v	w w	x x	y y y	z z z

20/25p, 0

1 alt ①	1 alt ②	2 alt ①	2 alt ②	3 alt ①	3 alt ②
⌣	—	⌣	—	⌣	—
4 alt ①	**4 alt ②**	**5 alt ①**	**5 alt ②**	**6 alt ①**	**6 alt ②**
⌣	—	⌣	—	⌣	—
7 alt ①	**7 alt ②**	**8 alt ①**	**8 alt ②**	**9 alt ①**	**9 alt ②**
⌣	—	⌣	—	⌣	—

Adrenaline 폰트의 스와시 문자는 숫자(1~9)의 Alternate 문자로 2개씩 18개나 등록되어 있습니다. 따라서 어도비 앱에서는 글리프 패널에서 선택해서 입력해야 합니다.

10p

License	Free for commercial use	Link	www.pixelsurplus.com/freebies/adrenaline-free-script-font
Font tag	Script, Handwritten, Swash	Note	매끈한 곡선의 필기체가 매력적인 스크립트 폰트

Scene

100p, 0
24/24p, -10

a part of a play or film in which the action

Beach

Adrenaline Regular 90p, 0
9 alt ① 60p 4°

Scenery

Adrenaline Regular 80p, 0 │ 8 alt ① 60p   투명도 80%

Allexandrea Script

Allexandrea Regular 63p, 0

A A B C D E F G H I J K L M
N O P Q R S T U V W X Y Z

30/40p, Optical 300

abcdefghijklmnopqrstuvwxyz . . , ... ' " "
1234567890 ?!/%$&(){}//

30/40p, 0

Abella   Abella   abella   abella   abella
board   board   board   board
cheerful   cheerful   cheerful   cheerful
dragon   dragon   dragon   dragon
force   force   force   force
violet   violet   violet   violet
wonder   wonder   wonder   wonder

25/35p, 0

License	Free
Font tag	Script, Monoline

Link	www.behance.net/gallery/78783611/FREE-ALLEXANDREA-SCRIPT
Note	하나의 선으로 된 모노라인 타입의 필기체 스크립트 폰트

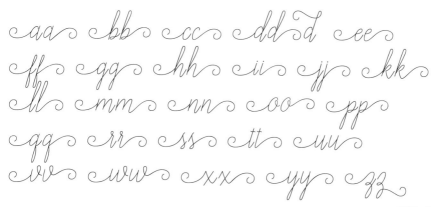

25/27p, 60

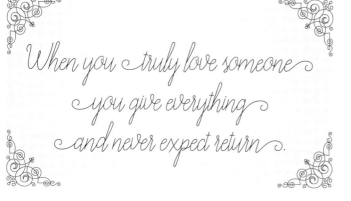

When you truly love someone
you give everything
and never expect return.

24/30p, 0

48/50p, 0

Open Sans Cond Light Italic 12p, 0

Ashfort Brush

Ashfort Brush Script Regular 68p, 0

ABCDEFGHIJK
LMNOPQRSTUVWXYZ

30/36p, 100

abcdefghij
klmnopqrstuvwxyz

30/40p, 100

1234567890Ø

@©®TM$£¥

.,:;…·°'"''""!?

#*%‰$(){}[]<>«»

+-±×÷=≠≈~≤<>≥≡≈–---

30/44p, 100

| License | Free |
| Font tag | Brush, Script, Handwirtten |

Link jeremyvessey.com/ashfort

Note 스크립트 폰트와 브러쉬 폰트의 특성을 모두 가진 필기체 브러쉬 폰트

Regular 80/56p, 0

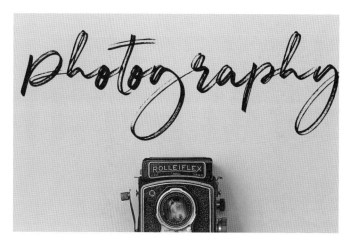

Regular 55p, 10

Regular 48/50p, 0

Open Sans Cond Light Italic 12p, 0

Barista

Barista Script Regular 79p, 0

ABCDEFGHIJKLM
NOPQRSTUVWXYZ

20/28p, 200

abcdefghijklmn
opqrstuvwxyz
1234567890
?!#&$€%@~
, . , : ' ‹ › + – = ( ) { } [ ]

20/28p, 200

Camera   Brown
Basic   School
build   Studio
Gindle   Colour
Much   Channels
Bikini   Collect
Drink   Pistou
Cream   Index

20/24p, 0

License	Free for commercial use
Font tag	Script, Modern, Caligraphy, Swash

Link	befonts.com/barista-script-font.html
Note	글자 아래쪽에 길게 배치되는 스와시 문자가 특징

55p, 0

일부 소문자(1자 혹은 2자 조합)를 입력하고 그 뒤에서 밑줄(_) 문자를 입력하면 자동으로 스와시(swash) 문자로 바뀝니다. 스와시란 글자의 획 끝이나 세리프를 과장되게 확장한 모양입니다.

윤곽선 만들기 기능을 이용하면 글자를 패스로 변환할 수 있습니다. 왼쪽의 예는 스와시 부분의 패스를 뒤쪽에 배치하고 그 중 일부를 가려서 보이지 않게 한 것입니다.

왼쪽의 예는 윤곽선 만들기 기능으로 글자를 윤곽선으로 바꾼 뒤에 직접 선택 도구를 사용하여 곡선의 포인트를 삭제하거나 이동하여 수정한 것입니다.

특정 조합의 두 문자가 만나면 자동으로 더 자연스러운 모양의 문자인 Ligature로 바뀝니다. Ligature란 활자를 사용하던 시대에 사용되던 용어로, 둘 이상의 글자를 하나의 글자로 주조한 활자입니다.

Different Governor Disrespect The Origin Wrangler

Different Governor Disrespect The Origin Wrangler

29/35p, 0

Beattingvile

Beattingvile Regular 141p, 0

ABCDÐEFGHIJKL
MNOPQRSTUVWXYZ

abcdefghijklmnopqrstuvwxyz

1234567890Ø

!?@$#%&<>()[]|/

40/40p, 0

a a ab ah b b c d d e e f g g h h i

i j j k k l l m m mm n n o o o p p q q

r r s s s s T T u u u v v w w x x y y z z

40/36p, -10

0 alt	1 alt	2 alt	3 alt	4 alt
5 alt	6 alt	7 alt	8 alt	9 alt

Beattingvile 폰트에서 스와시 문자는 숫자(0~9)의 Alternate 문자로 등록되어
있습니다. 따라서 어도비 앱에서는 글리프 패널에서 선택해서 입력해야 합니다.

40p

| License | Free for commercial use |
| Font tag | Script, Bold, Strong, Caligraphy, Swash |

| Link | www.behance.net/gallery/78343949/FREE-Beattingvile-Script-Font |

Try again,
Fail again,
Fail better.

60p, 0 | 65/50p, 0 | 75/60p, 0

Beautiful Mind

90p, 0 | ② 40p | ④ 50p

Seoul City Map

85p, 0 | ⑧ 46p

Be Precious!

116p, 0

Billenia

Billenia Regular 110p, 0 | ⑤

ABCDDEFGHIJKL
MNOPQRSTUVWXYZ

30/40p, 100

abcdefghijklmnopqrstuvwxyz

1234567890∅

!?@$#%&<>()(){}|||/+÷©®™

30/40p, 0

a a b b c c d d e e f f
g g g h h i v i j j k k l l
m m n n o o p p q q
R R R s s s t t t u u v v
w w x x y y y z z

30/35p, 0

① ② ③ ④ ⑤ ⑥

밑줄(_) 문자와 숫자(1~6)를 연달아 입력하면 그
에 대응되는 스와시 문자로 바뀌어 표시됩니다.

30p, 0

License Free for commercial use
Font tag Script, Handdrawn, Swash

Link www.pixelsurplus.com/freebies/billenia-free-script-font
Note 밑줄 스와시 문자를 키보드로 입력할 수 있는 스크립트 폰트

Alice's Adventures

40p, 0 i ①

in

30p, 0

Wonderland

50p, 0 | ⑥

단어 중간에 밑줄(_) 문자와 숫자(1~6)를 연달아 입력하면 그 위치를 중심으로 밑줄 스와시 문자가 삽입되어 표시됩니다. 위의 예에서 밑줄과 숫자가 있는 위치는 Ali와 ce 사이, Wo와 nder 사이입니다. 예: Ali_1ce's

숫자에 따라 달라지는 스와시 문자의 모양은 왼쪽 페이지의 아래 부분을 참고합니다. 한번 스와시 문자가 삽입되면 밑줄 문자와 숫자가 사라져 보이지 않게 됩니다. 다른 스와시 문자로 바꾸려면 밑줄과 숫자 사이에 커서를 넣고 스페이스 키를 눌러서 분리합니다. 그러면 밑줄과 숫자가 보입니다. 이제 숫자를 지우고 다른 숫자를 입력합니다. 밑줄과 숫자를 선택하여 문자 크기를 조정하면 스와시 문자의 크기를 조절할 수 있습니다.

20/28p, 0

*When you truly love someone
you give everything
and never expect return.*

BOSTHON BRUSH

BOSTHON BRUSH Regular 61p, 0

ABCDEFGHIJKLMN
OPQRSTUVWXYZ
1234567890

56/56p, 0

a	b	c	d
e	f	g	h
j	k	l	m
o	q	r	s
t	u		

BOSTHON Swash Regular 10p

BOSTHON Swash 폰트가 별도로 있습니다. 이 폰트를 적용하고 알파벳 소문자(대문자는 안됨)를 입력하면 그에 대응되는 스와시 문자가 입력됩니다.

| License | Free for commercial use |
| Font tag | Brush, Bold, Rough, Swash |

| Link | www.dafont.com/bosthon-brush.font |
| Note | 두껍고 거친 질감이 매력적인 브러쉬 폰트입니다 |

BOSTHON BRUSH 70p, 0 | 280p, 0 | BOSTHON Swash ⓐ 48p

BOSTHON BRUSH 100p | BOSTHON Swash ⓣ 30p

Briele brush

Briele Regular 92p, 0

Briele — Regular

Briele 2 — Italic에 해당

Briele 3 — Bold에 해당 40/40p, 0

ABCDEFGHIJKLMNOPQRSTUVWXYZ
abcdefghijklmnopqrstuvwxyz 1234567890
+-*/=_.,:;^!?#%&$ <> <<>> ()\/

ABCDEFGHIJKLMNOPQRSTUVWXYZ
abcdefghijklmnopqrstuvwxyz 1234567890
+-*/=_.,:;^!?#%&$ <> <<>> ()\/

ABCDEFGHIJKLMNOPQRSTUVWXYZ
abcdefghijklmnopqrstuvwxyz 1234567890
+-*/=_.,:;^!?#%&$ <> <<>> ()\/

23/24p,0

a	b	c	d	e	f	g	h	i	j	k	l	m

n	o	p	q	r	s	t	u	v	w	x	y	z

282　　Briele Swashes 폰트가 별도로 있습니다. 이 폰트를 적용한 상태에서 알파벳 문자(대소문자 동일)를 입력하면 그에 대응되는 스와시 문자로 바뀌어 입력됩니다.

Briele Swashes Regular 22p

License	Free for desktop commercial use
Font tag	Brush, Handwritten, Bold, Swash

Link	www.pixelsurplus.com/freebies/briele-free-script-font-trio
Note	스와시 문자가 매력적인, 붓으로 쓴 듯한 브러쉬 폰트

a a b b c c d d e e g g h h h
i i k k l l m m n n o o ʀ ʀ
s s t t u u v v y y

25/28p, 0

Bologra *Bologra*

Briele 60p, 0 | Briele Swashes ⓒ 80p

Mojave desert

Briele 70p, 0 | Briele Swashes ⓧ 80p, ⓞ 90p, ⓩ 60p, ⓝ 80p

Romanesque

Briele 70p, 0 | Briele Swashes ⓕ 100p, ⓖ 180p, ⓘ 80p

ellizabeth

Ellizabeth Regular 60p, 0

ABCDEFGHIJKLMNOPQRSTUVWXYZ

25p,60

ABCDEFGHIJKLMNO
PQRSTUVWXYZ

25/30p, Optical 300

abcdefghijklmnopqrstuvwxyz $ € £ ¥ $
1234567890 .,…:;'' " " !? #%& (){}[]

25/30p, 0

Abella Abella Abella Abella Abella Abella
Cherish Cherish Cherish Cherish Cherish
Elegance Elegance Elegance elegance
Bodacious Bodacious Bodacious Bodacious
Lullaby Lullaby Lullaby Lullaby Lullaby
Paradox Paradox Paradox Paradox
Surreptitious Surreptitious Surreptitious

25/30p, 0

License Free for commercial use
Font tag Script, Calligraphy, Elegant

Link befonts.com/ellizabeth-script.html
Note 무료 폰트로 상당히 귀한 우아한 곡선의 스크립트 폰트

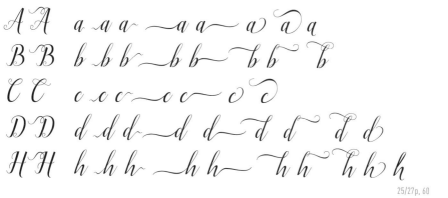

25/27p, 60

24/30p, 0

48/50p, 0

Open Sans Cond Light Italic 12p, 0

Fabfelt Script

Fabfelt Script Bold 68p, 0

ABCDEFGHIJKLM
NOPQRSTUVWXYZ
abcdefghijklm
nopqrstuvwxyz

30/36p, 100

1234567890½¼¾

@©®™$€£¥

.,:;....°'""`'""?

#*%&(){}[]<>«»

+−±×÷=−<>__ – – —

30/44p, 100

| License | Free |
| Font tag | Script, Bold, Handwritten |

| Link | www.behance.net/gallery/23900247/Fabfelt-script-Free-font |
| | fabiendespinoy.free.fr/typo-fabfelt.html |

Be Fearless

80/56p, 0

텍스트 프레임을 선택한 뒤에 '윤곽선 만들기' 기능으로 글자를 윤곽선으로 바꾸면 컴파운드 패스가 됩니다. 패스를 선택한 상태에서 이미지를 가져오면 아래의 예처럼 컴파운드 패스 내부에 이미지가 표시됩니다.

Be Fearless

Happiness is a choice.

44p, 0

When you truly love someone
you give everything
and never expect return.

21/32p, 0

Heavenfield

Heavenfield Regular 87p, 0

ABCDDEFGHIJKLMNOPQRSTUVWXYZ

abcdefghijklmnopqrstuvwxyz1234567890

22/30p, 0

+ − * = ~ @ # © !£ $%^& * ?.,.:: ∙ ' " ^ < > ( ) & 3[ ]|| \ / ©

22/30p, 100

b b   fff   g g   i i i i i i   jj

l l l   m m   n n   o o o o   r r r

s s s s   t t t t t t tt   w w

y y   3 3

22/30p, 0

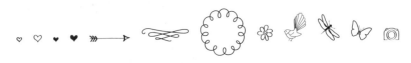

30/50p, 300

| License | Free for commercial use |
| Font tag | Script, Fancy, Handwritten, Dingbat |

| Link | fontlot.com/1755/heavenfield-wedding |
| Note | 결혼식 초청장에 쓰면 좋을 것 같은 스크립트 폰트 Havenfield Typewriter 폰트를 함께 받게 됩니다. 그런데 앱에서 보이는 폰트 이름은 Typewriter입니다. |

Be precious

72p, 0

When you truly love someone you give everything and never expect return.

22/34p, 0

• SAVE THE DATE •

Dina and Andy

• MAY 13, 2020 •

~ in beautiful ~
KAIVEN GARDEN HALL

formal invitation to follow

Heavenfield Regular 30p, 0 | 16p, 0 | 12p,0

Typewriter Regular 7p, 0 | 10p, 0 | 9p,0

Milles handwriting

Milles handwriting Regular 130p, 0

ABCDEFGHIJKL
MNOPQRSTUVWXYZ

40/40p, 200

abcdefghijklmnopqrstuvwxyz

1234567890 #@!?$%&(){}[]

40/40p, 0

A BBBl CcCh DD EEGGGGG FFFF
GG HH I J KK LlL MMMMi NNN OO
PP QQ RR SSSShSc TTh u N YY ZZ

a a ab ad ah and ant ar all aza ass ars aff aw ash aza — ag   bb bb bc bl bf   c ci ch cl ck

ddd dl dds   c ea ce en ef er es ev et eth ett ex ey ez ess eg el e   ff fo ffi fifl   g gh gt gg gi gg g

hhh ht   i il ia ill lt iz igs ish is uchi gi   j jjj jy   Rf fk   lflflll ls lb   m mm mm my mm m

nnn nit nk ng   o oo ott ok ot oss on oa oi ost ox oz oss OO ow osh or oh o   ppp phps   q gk gg

r rr ro rurs rj rl am ri   Ss ga si su sc sh ss st   TfftltyttstS

u ub ut ut ug us ass ash ur uh   v va vi vu ov ve   w   x   y yy yy yy yy   z zj

20/25p, 0

| License | Free for commercial use |
| Font tag | Brush, Script, Handwritten |

| Link | www.pixelsurplus.com/freebies/milles-free-script-font |
| Note | 브러쉬 폰트의 특성을 가진 필기체 스크립트 폰트 |

Elegants AND beautifull.

100p, 0
Lora Italic 10p, 0
110p, 0

Romeo and Juliet

Romeo and Juliet is a tragedy written by William Shakespeare early in his career about two young star-crossed lovers whose deaths ultimately reconcile their feuding families. It was among

50p, 0
20/25p, Optical 0

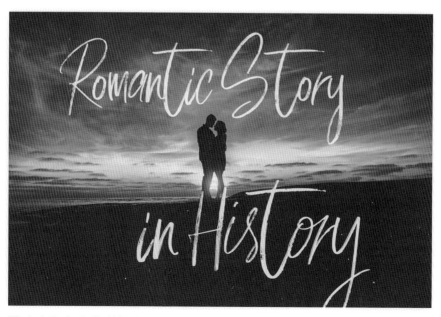

Milles handwriting Regular 75p, 0 | 100p, 0   투명도 80%

Ocean Six

Ocean Six Condensed 115p, 0

ABCDEFGHIJKLMNOPQRSTUVWXYZ

abcdefghijklmnopqrstuvwxyz

1234567890 ~+-*/=_ .,:,. •©®™

^!?#$%&@<>«»()[]{}\|/ `'"''""

36/40p, 0

300p, 0

License	Free for commercial use
Font tag	Brush, Bold, Rough, Condensed

Link	www.pixelsurplus.com/freebies/ocean-six
Note	두꺼운 획에 거친 질감이 매력적인 브러쉬 폰트

100p, 0   투명도 80%

Wildlife traditionally refers to undomesticated animal species, but has come to include all organisms that grow or live wild in an area without being introduced by humans.

Ocean Six Condensed 80p, 70 | Roboto Condensed Regular 10/12p, 0   투명도 90%

Oraqle Script

Oraqle Script Regular 97p, 0

● Oraqle Swash ① 60p, -5°

ABCDEFGHIJKLMNOPQRSTUVWXYZ
abcdefghijklmnopqrstuvwxyz © ® ™
1234567890 _+-=,.;:#$%&<>(){}[]!?@\|/   24/25p, 50

a a a a b b b c c c d d d d e e e g g g
h h h h h i i i i i j j k k
n n n n m m m m m n n n n n
p p q q r r t t t t u u u u u
v v w w y y y   24/25p, 0

	A	B	C	D	E	F	G	H
	⌐	⌐	~	⌐	⌐	~	⌐	⌐
	I	J	K	L	M	N	O	P
	⌐	⌐	⌐	⌐	~	⌐	⌐	⌐
	Q	R	S	T	U	V	W	X
	⌐	⌐	⌐	⌐	⌐	~	~	⌐
	Y	Z	a	b	c	d	e	
	⌐	⌐	⌐	⌐	⌐	⌐	⌐	
	g	h	i	j	k	l	m	n
	⌐	⌐	⌐	⌐	⌐	⌐	⌐	⌐
	o	p	q	r	s	t	u	v
	⌐	⌐	⌐	⌐	⌐	⌐	⌐	⌐
	w	x	y	z				
	⌐	~	⌐	⌐				

Oraqle Swash 20p

Oraqle Swashes 폰트가 별도로 있습니다. Oraqle Swash 폰트가 적용된 상태에서 알파벳 대소문자를 입력하면 그에 대응되는 스와시 문자로 바뀌어 입력됩니다.

License	Free for commercial use
Font tag	Script, Brush, Bold, Handwritten, Swash
Link	www.dafontfree.io/oraqle-script-font-free
Note	브러쉬 효과가 잘 표현된 볼드한 스크립트 폰트

atticism

concise and elegant expression, diction, or the like.

100p, 0
24/24p, 0

Beautiful ~ Foggy Scene

Oraqle Script 90/60p, 0 ┊ Oraqle Swash ⓒⓞ 50p

Oraqle Script 100p ┊ Oraqle Swash Ⓕ 70p 2°　투명도 50%

Rembank

Rembank Regular 93p, 0

Script font

70p,0

동일한 두 개 프레임을 0.5㎜ 차이로 배치.
위쪽 글자는 연청색 칠, 검정 획, 그림자 효과

ABCDEFGHIJKLMN
OPQRSTUVWXYZ

35/50p,100

abcdefghijklmnopqrstuvwxyz
1234567890!%$0[]&!?#&®©

a a a b b d d ggg hh i i

m m n n q q ssss t t th th

30/40p, 0

| License | Free for commercial use |
| Font tag | Script, Signature, Handwritten, Modern |

| Link | www.dafont.com/rembank.font |
| Note | 싸인 느낌이 나는 모던 스타일의 스크립트 폰트 |

Rockmusic festival

70/45p, 0

When you truly love someone
you give everything
and never expect return.

24/30p, 0

Christina Aguilera
singer-songwriter

48/50p, 0

Open Sans Cond Light Italic 12p, 0

Rockstar

Rockstar swashes ⑤ 1(
Rockstar Regular 100p,

Rockstar regular

Rockstar alternative regular

ROCKSTAR DISPLAY

40/50p, 0

ABCDEFGHIJKLMNOPQRSTUVWXYZ
abcdefghijklmnopqrstuvwxyz 1234567890
+-*/=_.,:;^!?#%£$@<><<>>()[]{}\|/

ABCDEFGHIJKLMNOPQRSTUVWXYZ
abcdefghijklmnopqrstuvwxyz 1234567890
+-*/=_.,:;^!?#%£$@<><<>>()[]{}\|/

ABCDEFGHIJKLMNOPQRSTUVWXYZ
ABCDEFGHIJKLMNOPQRSTUVWXYZ 1234567890
+-*/=_,;^!?#%£$@<><<>>()[]{}\|/

24/28p,0

License	Free for commercial use	Link	befonts.com/rockstar-handmade-brush-font.html
Font tag	Brush, Bold, Handwritten, Swash	Note	포토샵 브러쉬와 함께 여러 가지 이미지 파일도 포함

Rock and roll *Rock and roll*

Rockstar 50p, 0   Rockstar alt 50, 0

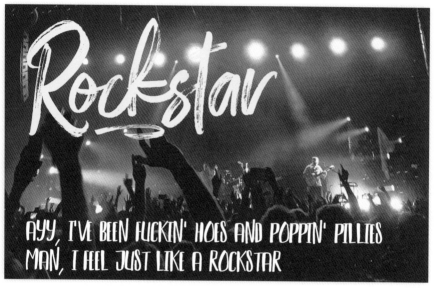

Rockstar 100p, 0 | Rockstar swashes ⓕ 40p | Rockstar Display 20/22p, 0

A	B	C	D	E	F	G	H
I	J	K	L	M	N	O	P
Q	R	S	T	U	V	W	X
Y	Z	a	b	c	d	e	f
g	h	i	j	k	l	m	n
o	p	q	r	s	t	u	v
w	x	y	z				

Rockstar swashes 20p

Rockstar Swashes 폰트가 별도로 있습니다. Rockstar swashes 폰트가 적용된 상태에서 알파벳 대소문자를 입력하면 그에 대응되는 스와시 문자로 바뀌어 입력됩니다.

Signatura Monoline

Signatura Monoline Script Regular 70p, 0

ABCDEFGHIJKLMNOPQRSTUVWXYZ

25p,90

abcdefghijklmnopqrstuvwxyz 1234567890

+−*/= _.,:; ' ' " " ^ !? #%&$ <>«»(){}[] \|/

25/30p, 0

a: a a a
b: b b b b b
c: c c

d: d d d d
e: e e

f: f f f ff f
g: g g g gg

h: h h h h
i: i i

j: j j j j
k: k k k k k

l: l l ll ll l
m: m m m
n: n n

o: o o o oo
p: p p p p pp p

q: q q q q
r: r r r rr r

s: s s ss s
t: t t t ttt

u: u u
v: v v
w: w w w

x: x x
y: y y y y yy y
z: z z z

25/27p, 0

| License | Free for commercial use |
| Font tag | Script, Monoline, Calligraphy |

| Link | ianmikraz.com/fonts/signatura-monoline-free-typeface |
| Note | 여성스러운 손글씨 느낌의 모노라인 스크립트 폰트 |

abella   abella   abella   classic   classic   classic

bulb   bulb   bulb   bulb   bulb

dialog   dialog   dialog   Dialog   dialog

future   future   future   future   future

trolley   trolley   trolley   trolley   trolley

halutz   halutz   halutz   halutz   halutz

paradox   paradoux   paradox   paradox

calligraphy   calligraphy   calligraphy

Photo studio   Photo studio   Photo studio

25/30p, 0

When you truly love someone
you give everything
and never expect return.

24/30p, 0

Storytella Regular 90p, 0

Storytella Regular ② 90p

ABCDEFGHIJKLMNOPQRSTUVWXYZ

abcdefghijklmnopqrstuvwxyz

28/36p,0

1234567890-_.,:;!?#&$()[]/ ' "

28/38p,70

a a   b b   d d   e e   f f   g g
h h   i i   j j   k k   l l   n n
o o   r r   s s   t t   y y   z z

28/36p,0

①　　　　　　②　　　　　　③

밑줄(_) 문자와 숫자(1~3)를 연달아 입력하면 그에 대응되는 스와시 문자로 바뀌어 표시됩니다. Storytella Regular 60p

License	Free, Seriously!	Link	letterhend.com/product/free-storytella-script
Font tag	Brush, Bold, Handdrwan, Swash	Note	거칠게 쓴 필기체 느낌의 브러쉬 폰트

Alice's Adventures
in
Wonderland

36p, 0
① 70p 4°

26p, 0 1°

60p, 0
③ 70p

Billenia 폰트에서처럼 밑줄(_) 문자와 숫자(1~3)를 연달아 입력하여 스와시 문자를 입력할 수는 없습니다. 별도의 텍스트 프레임을 만들고 그 내부에 글래프 패널을 이용하여 입력해야 합니다.

스와시 문자가 별도의 프레임에 있으므로 위에 보인 예처럼 회전을 시켜서 좀 더 멋지게 보이도록 조정할 수 있습니다. Alice 아래의 밑줄 스와시 문자는 반시계 방향으로 4도, Wonder 아래의 것은 반시계 방향으로 1도 회전한 것입니다.

20/28p, 0

When you truly love someone
you give everything
and never expect return.

THEME

THEME

THEME Regular 110/100p, 0

ABCDEFGHIJKLMNOPQRSTUVWXYZ

ABCDEFGHIJKLMNOPQRSTUVWXYZ

AaBbCcDdEeFfGgHhIiJjKkLlMmNn

OoPpQqRrSsTtUuVvWwXxYyZz

28/28p, 0

1234567890

¡?$#*%@&(){}[]‹›«»©®™

.,:;…•'"+−±×÷=≠~≈_---—

28/28p, 100

C ©   LL L̲L̲   NO N°

The THE   TT TT   TT TT

28/28p,

| License | Free for commercial use | Link | creativetacos.com/theme-textured-font |
| Font tag | Brush, Texture, Handwritten | Note | 소문자를 작은 대문자로 처리한, 볼드한 거친 브러쉬 폰트 |

TAKE THE RISK OR LOSE THE CHANCE

70p, 0

40p, 0

70p, 0

60p, 0

40p, 0

70p, 0

70/56p, 0

WAKE UP AND BE AWESOME

Tuesday Night

Tuesday Night Regular 65p, 0

Aa Bb Cc Dd Ee Ff Gg
Hh Ii Jj Kk Ll Mm Nn
Oo Pp Qq Rr Ss Tt Uu
Vv Ww Xx Yy Zz

abcdefghijklmnopqrstuvwxyz

1234567890 -,.!? #&@

24/50p, 0

Be Fearless

80p, 0

| License | Free for desktop commercial | Link | www.pixelsurplus.com/freebies/tuesday-night-free-signature-script |
| Font tag | Script, Handwritten, Signature | Note | 소문자가 매우 작은 시그니쳐 스타일의 스크립트 폰트 |

The wind whistles past my ears.
Closing my eyes, I lose all my fears.
The waves crash into the rocks.
Out here there is no time on my clock.

Tuesday Night Regular 20/40p, 0

The wind whistles past my ears.
Closing my eyes, I lose all my fears.
The waves crash into the rocks.
Out here there is no time on my clock.

Amiri Regular 10/14p, 0

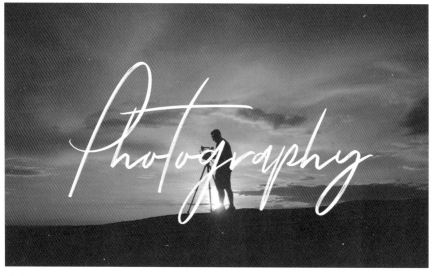

60p, 0

FUTU

Blanka Regular 180p, 0

퓨처리스틱 폰트

특별히 미래지향적인 폰트 같은 분류가 있는 것은 아닌데 진부하지 않은 모양의 무료 서체를 모으다 보니 SF 영화나 IT 관련 디자인에 쓰면 좋을 것 같은 폰트들이 모였습니다. 인간적인 부분을 제거하고 단순하고 심플하면서 뭔가 좀 신비한 느낌을 조성할 수 있는 폰트입니다. 스크립트나 브러쉬 폰트와 대비되는 포지션에 있습니다. 컨셉을 잡으면 만들기는 어렵지 않은 편이나 소문자와 기호까지 지원하는 폰트는 거의 없습니다. 11종을 준비했습니다.

Mode

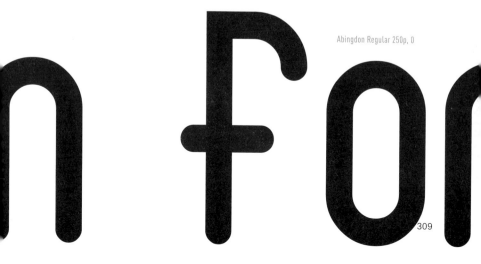

모던 폰트

모던 폰트란 과거에 보지 못하던 새로운 유형의 폰트란 뜻입니다. 여기에서 소개하는 4개의 폰트(Abingdon, Manrope, Quickpath, Redwing)는 좋은 품질의 무료 폰트를 찾는 과정에서 얻은 것으로 분류하기가 좀 애매하지만 미래지향적인 느낌이 있어서 여기에 함께 소개하게 되었습니다. 하지만 대소문자와 기호 등을 충실하게 지원하여 본문용으로 사용할 수도 있어 좀 다릅니다. Manrope 폰트는 96쪽에서 소개한 악치덴츠 그로테스크*Akzidenz Grotesk*의 대안 폰트이기도 합니다.

Abingdon Regular 250p, 0

Abingdon

Abingdon Regular 120p, 0

Abingdon Regular *Italic*

Abingdon Bold ***Bold Italic***

30/36p, 0

ABCDEFGHIJKLMNOPQRSTUVWXYZ
abcefghijklmnopqrstuvwxyz 1234567890
+−×÷=#%&*,.:;!?()[]{}'''""®©

ABCDEFGHIJKLMNOPQRSTUVWXYZ
abcefghijklmnopqrstuvwxyz 1234567890
+−×÷=#%&,.:;!?()[]{}'''""®©*

ABCDEFGHIJKLMNOPQRSTUVWXYZabc
abcefghijklmnopqrstuvwxyz 1234567890
+−×÷=#%&*,.:;!?()[]{}'''""®©

ABCDEFGHIJKLMNOPQRSTUVWXYZabc
abcefghijklmnopqrstuvwxyz 1234567890
+−×÷=#%&*,.:;!?()[]{}'''""®©

23/25p, 0

License	Free for commercial use	Link	befonts.com/abingdon-free-font.html
Font tag	Sans serif, Modern, Round, Display	Note	깔끔하면서도 둥글어 묘한 매력이 느껴지는 산세리프 폰트

Deep into that darkness peering,
long I stood there, wondering, fearing, doubting,
dreaming dreams no mortal ever dared to dream before.
— Edgar Allan Poe, *Complete Tales and Poems*

Regular 14/16p, 10 | Bold 12/15p, 0

SPARKLING ARTS

www.sparklingarts.com

founder
CAROLINE LEE

carolinelee@sparklingarts.com

010.2345.6789

Bold 20p, 50

Italic 9p, 100

Regular 10p, 100

Bold 16/20p, 50

Regular 9p, 0

Italic 11p, 100

THE *jealous*
ARTIST
DAMN,
I WISH I THOUGHT OF THAT.

Regular 10p, 30 | Italic 10p, 30 | Bold 30/30p, 10 | Regular 8/10p, 0

ADVENTURE FOR THE YOUNG AT HEART

Go outside and explore

At any rate, That is Happiness;
To be dissolved into something
COMPLETE AND GREAT.

Ablingdon Regular 31.5-31.4-Bold 40.5p, 20 | Regular 10p, 20

— Willa Cather, My Ántonia

"Stay close to anything that makes you feel you are glad to be alive. Plant the seeds for a sustainable future. Connect, respect and listen to nature, for nature is our greatest teacher."

Bold 10/15p, 30

LOOK UP, KEEP GOING

Bold 14p, 100

Lorem ipsum dolor sit amet, consectetur adipiscing elit, sed do eiusmod tempor incididunt ut labore et dolore magna ad veniam, nostrud exercitation ullamco laboris nisi aliquip ex ea commodo consequat. Duis aute irure dolor in reprehenderit in voluptate velit esse cillum dolore eu fugiat nulla pariatur. Excepteur sint occaecat cupidatat non proident, sunt in culpa qui officia deserunt mollit anim id est laborum.

"Aliquam fermentum est. Praesent posuere lorem quis quam viverra tempus. Suspendisse varius nunc nec sapien convallis rutrum. Donec vitae tincidunt tortor, nec tempor tortor."

Ultrices sagittis orci a scelerisque purus. Diam maecenas ultricies mi eget mauris. Nam aliquam sem et tortor consequat id porta nibh. Tempor orci dapibus ultrices in iaculis nunc sed augue lacus. Sit amet massa vitae tortor condimentum.

Regular 8/10p, 0 | Bold 9/11p, 50

Mi sit amet mauris commodo quis. Adipiscing at in tellus integer feugiat scelerisque varius morbi in enim. Elementum nibh tellus molestie nunc non. Nisi porta lorem mollis aliquam ut porttitor leo a. Sed sed risus pretium quam vulputate dignissim. Nunc mi ipsum faucibus vitae aliquet nec ullam corper. Scelerisque viverra mauris in aliquam sem fringilla.

In nisl nisi scelerisque eu. Odio facilisis mauris sit amet massa. Porttitor lacus luctus accumsan tortor posuere ac ut consequat. Nibh venenatis cras sed felis. Vestibulum sed arcu non odio euismod. Vitae aliquet nec ullamcorper sit amet. Amet mauris commodo quis imperdiet massa tincidunt nunc. Condimentum mattis pellentesque id nibh. Egestas purus viverra accumsan in nisl nisi scelerisque eu. Euismod in pellentesque massa placerat duis ultricies. Eget egestas purus viverra accumsan in. Id venenatis a condimentum vitae pellentesque habitant morbi. Dignissim convallis aenean et tortor Est ullamcorper eget nulla facilisi dignissim diam quis. Dui nunc mattis enim elementum sagittis.

Bold 14/17p, 100 | Regular 12/25p, 25

A.LEXANA.A

Alexana Regular 53p, 0

A.BCDEFGHIJKLM
NJPQRSTUVWXYZ.
A.BCDEFGHIJKLM
NJPQRSTUVWXYZ.
1234567890

27/37p, 0

대문자와 소문자가 같은 모양이지만 A, T, U, V, W,
X, Y에서는 점의 위치가 반대 방향입니다.

BIGHIT
TECHNOLOGY

50p, Optical 0 | 30/40p, -100

License	Free for commercial use
Font tag	Sans serif, Futuristic, Secret
Link	befonts.com/alexana-display-font.html
Note	외계인의 문자 같은 비주얼을 자랑하지만 가독성이 좋지 않음

34p, 0 투명도 80%

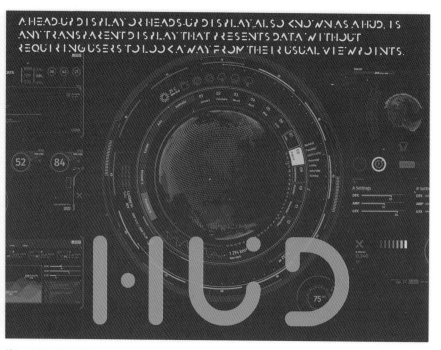

7/10p, -40 80p, 70 투명도 80%

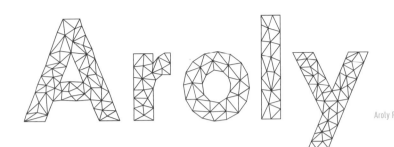

Aroly Regular 100p, -100

ABCDEFGHIJKLM
NOPQRSTUVWXYZ
1234567890+-=\/
!&?%@<>()[].,;"''""

30/35p, 0

50/60p, 0　외부광선: 표준 용지색 80%, 약하게, 크기 2㎜, 스프레드 10%, 노이즈 5%

License Free for commercial usage	**Link** befonts.com/aroly-font.html
Font tag Sans serif, Futuristic, Display, Line, Geometric	**Note** 내부를 기하학적 패턴으로 채운 특별한 폰트

42p, 0   투명도 80%

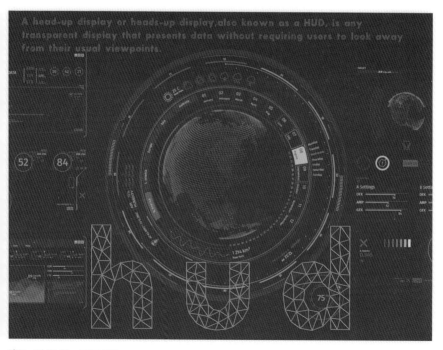

7/10p, -40 | 80p, 70   투명도 80%

BLANKA

Blanka Regular 89p, 0

ABCDEFGHIJKLM
NOPQRSTUVWXYZ
1234567890
!?#@()/.:;+ ‾ =

38/44p, 0

TECH TREND

61p, 0

DIGITAL
TECHNOLOGY

50p, 50 | 29/40p, 50

| License | Free for commercial use |
| Font tag | Sans serif, Bold, Futuristic, Minimalism |

| Link | www.behance.net/gallery/15451401/BLANKA-Free-font |
| Note | 미래지향적 느낌이면서도 가독성이 좋은 깔끔한 폰트 |

40p, 100 투명도 80%

8/11p, 0 | 80p, 70 투명도 80%

BLERN

Blern Regular 152p, 0

ABCDEFGHIJKLMN
OPQRSTUVWXYZ
1234567890$()/

56/56p, 0

50/60p, 0   외부광선: 표준 용지색 80%, 약하게, 크기 2㎜, 스프레드 10%, 노이즈 5%

License	Free for commercial use	Link	befonts.com/blern-typeface.html
Font tag	Slab serif, Condensed, Futuristic, Iirregular	Note	예상을 벗어난 모양이 미래지향적으로 느껴지는 폰트

50p, 0　투명도 80%

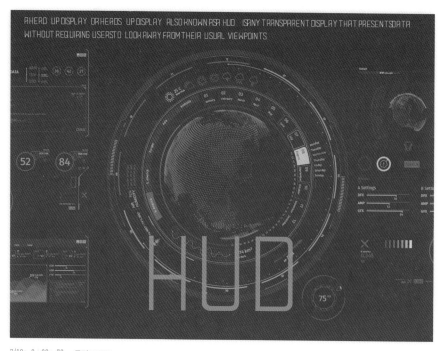

7/10p, 0 ｜ 80p, 70　투명도 80%

College Stencil

College Stencil Regular 47p, 0

ABCDEFGHIJKLMN
OPQRSTUVWXYZ
abcdefghijklmnop
qrstuvwxyz , .:;
1234567890 !?0 '""

34/40p, 50

Nunavut
college

50p, 0 | 50/53p, 80

License	Free for commercial use	Link	www.pixelsurplus.com/freebies/college-free-elegant-stencil-font
Font tag	Sans serif, Futuristic, Simbolic	Note	글자 모양의 일부를 생략하여 신비스럽게 보이는 폰트

50p, 0   윤곽선으로 바꾸고 내부에 이미지 삽입

50p, 0 ¦ 8/12p, 0   투명도 80%

EXAN

Exan Regular 149p, 0

ABCDEFGHIJKLM
NOPQRSTUVWXYZ
1234567890-

40/40p, 0

MONO AUDIO

30p, 50

42/50p,

50/60p, 0   외부광선: 표준 용지색 80%, 약하게, 크기 2mm, 스프레드 10%, 노이즈 5%

License	Free for commercial use
Font tag	Sans serif, Futuristic, Odd

Link	befonts.com/exan-3-font.html
Note	유일한 기호 문자 −를 키보드로 입력할 수 없습니다.

44p, 0　투명도 80%

7/10p, 0 ｜ 80p, 70　투명도 80%

KONTAKT

Kontakt Regular 65p, 0

ABCDEFGHIJKLM
NOPQRSTUVWXYZ
1234567890+-=
!?#@&[]_.,.::/\

34/38p, 0

TECH TREND

52p, 0

DIGITAL
TECHNOLOGY

50p, 0 | 29/40p, 50

| License | Free for any purpose |
| Font tag | Sans serif, Bold, Futuristic |

| Link | www.behance.net/gallery/51146151/KONTAKT-FREE-FONT |
| Note | 우주에서 영감을 받아 만들었다는 두꺼운 제목용 폰트 |

34p, 0   투명도 80%

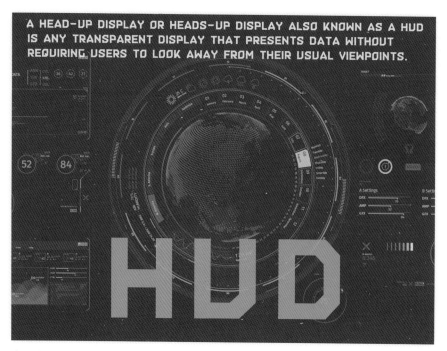

8/11p, 0 | 80p, 70   투명도 80%

Manrope

Manrope Bold 74p, 0

Manrope Thin
Manrope Light
Manrope Regular
Manrope Medium
Manrope SemiBold
Manrope Bold
Manrope Extra bold

20/24p, 0

ABCDEFGHIJKLMNOPQRSTUVWXYZ ⊙ ← → +–×=#%&*, . : ; ! ?
abcefghijklmnopqrstuvwxyz 1234567890   ( )[ ]{ } ' ' " " ®©™

ABCDEFGHIJKLMNOPQRSTUVWXYZ ⊙ ← → +–×=#%&*, . : ; ! ?
abcefghijklmnopqrstuvwxyz 1234567890   ( )[ ]{ } ' ' " " ®©™

ABCDEFGHIJKLMNOPQRSTUVWXYZ ⊙ ← → +–×=#%&*, . : ; ! ?
abcefghijklmnopqrstuvwxyz 1234567890   ( )[ ]{ } ' ' " " ®©™

ABCDEFGHIJKLMNOPQRSTUVWXYZ ⊙ ← → +–×=#%&*, . : ; ! ?
abcefghijklmnopqrstuvwxyz 1234567890   ( )[ ]{ } ' ' " " ®©™

ABCDEFGHIJKLMNOPQRSTUVWXYZ ⊙ ← → +–×=#%&*, . : ; ! ?
abcefghijklmnopqrstuvwxyz 1234567890   ( )[ ]{ } ' ' " " ®©™

ABCDEFGHIJKLMNOPQRSTUVWXYZ ⊙ ← → +–×=#%&*, . : ; ! ?
abcefghijklmnopqrstuvwxyz 1234567890 ( )[ ]{ } ' ' " " ®©™

ABCDEFGHIJKLMNOPQRSTUVWXYZ ⊙ ← → +–×=#%&*, . : ; ! ?
abcefghijklmnopqrstuvwxyz 1234567890 ( )[ ]{ } ' ' " " ®©™

11/15p, 0

| License | Open Font License | Link | www.fontsquirrel.com/fonts/manrope |
| Font tag | Sans serif, Modern, Grotesque | Note | 96쪽에서 소개한 악치덴츠 그로테스크의 대안 폰트 |

Deep into that darkness peering,
long I stood there, wondering, fearing, doubting,
dreaming dreams no mortal ever dared to dream before.
— **Edgar Allan Poe, Complete Tales and Poems**

Light 11/15p, 10 | Bold 9/12p, 0

SPARKLING ARTS

www.sparklingarts.com

Founder
CAROLINE LEE

carolinelee@sparklingarts.com

010.2345.6789

ExtraBold 18p, 50

Thin 11p, 100

Light 9p, 100

Regular 10p, 100

Bold 16/20p, 50

Medium 9p, 0

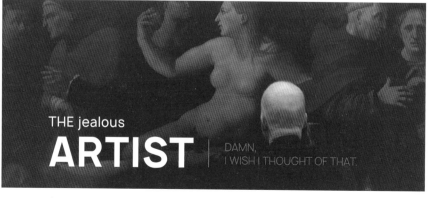

THE jealous
ARTIST
DAMN,
I WISH I THOUGHT OF THAT.

Medium 10p, 30 | ExtraBold 30/30p, 20 | Light 8/10p, 0

ADVENTURE FOR THE YOUNG AT HEART

Go outside and explore

At any rate, That is Happiness;
To be dissolved into something
COMPLETE AND GREAT.

Manrope Medium 21.4·Bold 20.3·ExtraBold 26.6p, 20 | Regular 10p, 10   — Willa Cather, My Ántonia

"Stay close to anything that makes you feel
you are glad to be alive. Plant the seeds for a
sustainable future. Connect, respect and listen
to nature, for nature is our greatest teacher."   Semibold 10/15p, 30

LOOK UP, KEEP GOING   ExtraBold 14p, 100

Lorem ipsum dolor sit amet, consectetur adipiscing elit, sed do eiusmod tempor incididunt ut labore et dolore magna aliqua. Ut enim ullamco laboris consequat. Duis aute irure dolor in sin reprehenderit in velit esse cillum dolore eu con fugiat nulla pariatur. Excepteur sint occaecat non proident, sunt in culpa qui officia deserunt mollit anim id est laborum.

"Aliquam fermentum est. Praesent posuere lorem quis quam viverra tempus. Suspendisse varius nunc nec sapien convallis rutrum. Donec vitae tincidunt tortor, tortor."

Ultrices sagittis orci a scelerisque purus. Diam maecenas ultricies mi eget mauris. Tempor orci dapibus nunc sed augue lacus. Sit amet massa vitae tortor viverra habitant tortor purus sed condimentum.

Regular 7/9p, 0 | SemiBold 8/11p, 50

Mi sit amet mauris commodo quis. Adipiscing at in tellus integer feugiat scelerisque varius mor in enim. Elementum nibh tellus molestie nunc non. Nisi porta lorem mollis aliquam ut porttitor leo a. Sed sed risus pretium quam vulputate dignissim. Nunc mi ipsum faucibus vitae aliquet nec ullam corper. Scelerisque viverra mauris in aliquam sem fringilla.

In nisl nisi scelerisque eu. Odio facilisis mauris sit amet massa. Porttitor lacus luctus accumsan tortor posuere ac ut consequat. Nibh venenatis cras sed felis. Vestibulum sed arcu non odio euismod. Vitae aliquet nec sit amet. Amet mauris commodo quis imperdiet massa tincidunt nunc. Condimentum mattis id nibh. Egestas purus viverra accumsan in a nisl nisi scelerisque eu. Euismod in pellentesque massa placerat duis ultricies. Eget egestas in a purus viverra accumsan in. Id venenatis a condimen vitae pellentesque habitant di morbi. Dignissim convallis aenean et tortor Est ullamcorper eget nulla facilisi dignissim diam quis. Duiisors mattis enim elementum sagittis.

ExtraBold 14/17p, 100 | Regular 8/25p, 25

NORDIC

Nordic Alternative Regular 85p, 0

ABCDEFGHIJKLM
NOPQRSTUVWXYZ
1234567890_ – —
+ – = ≪≫ .,...:;'´'" ()\|/!?

35/40p, 0

70p, 0 | 43/45p, 0

| License | Free |
| Font tag | Sans serif, Futuristic, Geometric |

| Link | www.behance.net/gallery/22172647/Nordic-(Free-Font) |
| Note | 암호나 외계어 분위기를 낼 때 쓰면 좋을 폰트 |

38p, 0 　투명도 80%

7/10p, -40 | 80p, 70 　투명도 80%

ONE DAY

ONE DAY Regular 87p, 0

ABCDEFGHIJKLM
NOPQRSTUVWXYZ
1234567890
!?#$%&@<>()[]{}|\/'"'.,:;

40/44p, 0

ONE DAY
TECHNOLOGY

50p, 0 | 30/40p, 40

License	Free for commercial use	Link	www.behance.net/gallery/23792563/ONE-DAY-Free-Font
Font tag	Sans serif, Futuristic, Stencil, Round	Note	모던하면서 가벼운 분위기의 스텐실 풍의 폰트

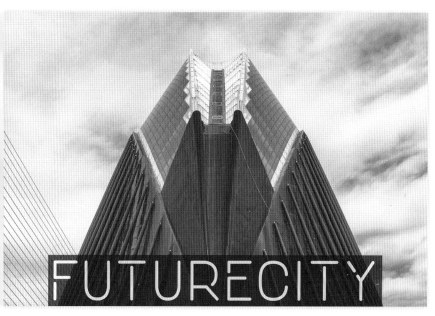

38p, 0   투명도 80%

8/11p, 0 | 80p, 70   투명도 80%

POTRA

Potra Light 109p, 0

ABCDEFGHIJKLM
NOPQRSTUVWXYZ
1234567890 _ - -
!?#$%&@<>(){}[]
+-×÷= ∞ .,;:'"" \|/

38/42p, 0

50/60p, 0   외부광선: 표준 용지색 80%, 약하게, 크기 2㎜, 스프레드 10%, 노이즈 5%

License	Open Font License
Font tag	Sans serif, Futuristic, Display, Round, Line

Link	rostype.com/en/potra_eng
Note	선과 점을 모티브로 만들어진 SF 느낌의 폰트

42p, 0　투명도 80%

7/10p, -40 ┊ 80p, 70　투명도 80%

QUANTUM

Quantum Regular 79p, 0

ABCDEFGHIJKLMN
OPQRSTUVWXYZ

ABCDEFGHIJKLMN
OPQRSTUVWXYZ

1234567890 !?

FUTURE IS COMMING!

33/37p, 0

QUANTUM

TECHNOLOGY

50p, 0 | 42/42p, 100

License	Free for commercial use	Link	befonts.com/alexana-display-font.html
Font tag	Sans serif, Bold, Futuristic, Stencil	Note	소문자는 작은 대문자에 대각선 방향 스텐실 무늬가 있는 폰트

34p, 0　투명도 80%

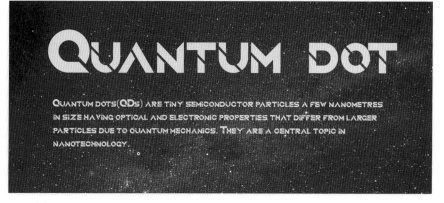

47p, -50 | 8/10p, -40　투명도 80%

Quickpath

Unisono Quickpath Regular 75p, 0

ABCDEFGHIJKLMN
OPQRSTUVWXYZ
abcdefghijklmn
opqrstuvwxyz
1234567890
~+-×÷=@'"'*''""
!?#$&<>()[]{},.;:/|_

36/40p, 0

Digital
technology

50p, 0 | 29/40p, 30

License	Free for commercial use	Link	www.pixelsurplus.com/freebies/quickpath-free-modern-font
Font tag	Sans serif, Modern, Cutout	Note	글자 일부를 잘라낸, 로고에 적합한 모던 폰트. 재배포와 변형 불가.

34p, 0　외부광선: 용지색 검정 100%, 정밀하게 10㎜, 노이즈 5%, 스프레드 40%

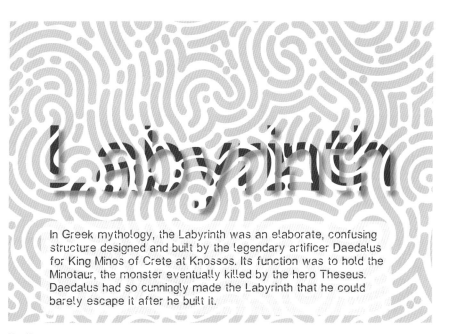

In Greek mythology, the Labyrinth was an elaborate, confusing structure designed and built by the legendary artificer Daedalus for King Minos of Crete at Knossos. Its function was to hold the Minotaur, the monster eventually killed by the hero Theseus. Daedalus had so cunningly made the Labyrinth that he could barely escape it after he built it.

70p, -25　그림자: 표준 검정 50%, 거리 2㎜ 135°, 크기 1㎜, 스프레드 10% 노이즈 5%
9/10p, 0　아래에 60% 용지색 사각형

Redwing

Redwing Medium 105p, 0

Redwing Light
Redwing Medium

40/50p, 0

ABCDEFGHIJKLMNOPQRSTUVWXYZ
abcefghijklmnopqrstuvwxyz abc@gmail.com
1234567890 +−×÷=#%&*,.:;!?()[]{}'' " " ®©

ABCDEFGHIJKLMNOPQRSTUVWXYZ
abcefghijklmnopqrstuvwxyz abc@gmail.com
1234567890 +−×÷=#%&*,.:;!?()[]{}'' " " ®©

19/24p, 0

"I loved her against reason, against promise, against peace, against
hope, against happiness, against all discouragement that could be."
— Charles Dickens, Great Expectations

Light 10/14p, 0 | Medium 9/14p, 10

| License | Open Font License |
| Font tag | Sans serif, Modern, Angled, Industrial |

| Link | fontesk.com/redwing-font |
| Note | 판매 버전은 8개의 패밀리 폰트로 구성되어 있습니다. |

Deep into that darkness peering,
long I stood there, wondering, fearing, doubting,
dreaming dreams no mortal ever dared to dream before.
— Edgar Allan Poe, Complete Tales and Poems

Light 14/18p, 10 | Medium 11/15p, 0

SPARKLING ARTS

www.sparklingarts.com

Founder
CAROLINE LEE

carolinelee@sparklingarts.com

010.2345.6789

Medium 20p, 50

Light 9p, 100

Light 10p, 100

Medium 16/20p, 50

Light 9p, 0

Light 11p, 100

THE jealous
ARTIST
DAMN,
I WISH I THOUGHT OF THAT.

Light 10p, 30 | Medium 30/30p, 10 | Light 8/10p, 0

ADVENTURE FOR THE YOUNG AT HEART

Go outside and explore

At any rate, That is Happiness; To be dissolved into something COMPLETE AND GREAT.

Redwing Light 30.5-30-Medium 36.7p, 20 ┆ Medium 10p, 10

— Willa Cather, My Ántonia

"Stay close to anything that makes you feel you are glad to be alive. Plant the seeds for a sustainable future. Connect, respect and listen to nature, for nature is our greatest teacher."

Medium 10/15p, 30

LOOK UP, KEEP GOING

Medium 14p, 100

Lorem ipsum dolor sit amet, consectetur adipiscing elit, sed do eiusmod tempor incididunt ut labore et dolore magna aliqua. Ut enim ad minim veniam, nostrud exercitation ullamco laboris nisi aliquip ex ea commodo consequat. Duis aute irure dolor in reprehenderit in voluptate velit esse cillum dolore eu fugiat nulla pariatur. Excepteur sint occaecat cupidatat non proident, sunt in culpa qui officia deserunt mollit anim id est laborum.

"Aliquam fermentum est. Praesent posuere lorem quis quam viverra tempus. Suspendisse varius nunc nec sapien convallis rutrum. Donec vitae tincidunt tortor, nec tempor tortor."

Ultrices sagittis orci a scelerisque purus. Diam maecenas ultricies mi eget mauris. Nam aliquam sem et tortor consequat id porta nibh. Tempor orci dapibus ultrices in iaculis nunc sed augue lacus. Sit amet massa vitae tortor condimentum.

Light 8/10p, 0 ┆ Medium 9/11p, 50

Mi sit amet mauris commodo quis. Adipiscing at in tellus integer feugiat scelerisque varius morbi in enim. Elementum nibh tellus molestie nunc non. Nisi porta lorem mollis aliquam ut porttitor leo a. Sed sed risus pretium quam vulputate dignissim. Nunc mi ipsum faucibus vitae aliquet nec ullam corper. Scelerisque viverra mauris in aliquam sem fringilla.

In nisl nisi scelerisque eu. Odio facilisis mauris sit amet massa. Porttitor lacus luctus accumsan tortor posuere ac ut consequat. Nibh venenatis cras sed felis. Vestibulum sed arcu non odio euismod. Vitae aliquet nec ullamcorper sit amet. Amet mauris commodo quis imperdiet massa tincidunt nunc. Condimentum mattis pellentesque id nibh. Egestas purus viverra accumsan in nisl nisi scelerisque eu. Euismod in pellentesque massa placerat duis ultricies. Eget egestas purus viverra accumsan in. Id venenatis a condimentum vitae pellentesque habitant morbi. Dignissim convallis aenean et tortor Est ullamcorper eget nulla facilisi dignissim diam quis. Dui nunc mattis enim elementum sagittis.

Medium 14/17p, 100 ┆ Light 8/25p, 25

Panto

Panton Rust Script Semibold Grundge 150p, 0

INTRODUCING
DEVIOUS
TYPEFACE
HANDMADE QUALITY

DEVIOUS Regular 30p, 0 | 80p, 0 | 20p, 0 | 28P

BERNIER Destressed 140p, 72

BERNIE

특수 폰트

다양한 스타일의 무료 폰트들(24종)을 특수 폰트로 분류하여 소개합니다. 여기에서 소개하는 폰트들의 상당수는 유료 폰트의 일부를 홍보용으로 공개한 것입니다. 이름 뒤에 Rust가 붙은 Intro Rust, Panton Rust, Zing Rust 폰트가 그 대표적인 예입니다.

본문용이 아닌 제목용이나 장식용 영어 폰트를 원한다면 여기에 소개된 폰트들을 살펴보기 바랍니다. 영어 폰트의 다양한 스타일을 확인해두면 디자인할 때 영어 폰트로 기대할 수 있는 것을 미리 상상할 수 있습니다. 또한, 그래픽 소프트웨어의 기능으로 영어 폰트를 표현하는 방법도 알아두면 좋습니다.

BERNIER

BERNIER Regular/Destressed/Shade Regular 95p, 100

BERNIER REGULAR
BERNIER DISTRESSED
BERNIER SHADE

36/36p, 0

ABCDEFGHIJKLMNOPQRSTUVWXYZ
ABCEFGHIJKLMNOPQRSTUVWXYZ
1234567890 „.,;!?()[]{}"''""@©+-*/=#%&

ABCDEFGHIJKLMNOPQRSTUVWXYZ
ABCEFGHIJKLMNOPQRSTUVWXYZ
1234567890 „.,;!?()[]{}"''""@©+-*/=#%&

ABCDEFGHIJKLMNOPQRSTUVWXYZ
ABCEFGHIJKLMNOPQRSTUVWXYZ
1234567890 „.,;!?()[]{}"''""@©+-*/=#%&

24/26p, 0

"I LOVED HER AGAINST REASON, AGAINST PROMISE, AGAINST PEACE, AGAINST HOPE, AGAINST HAPPINESS, AGAINST ALL DISCOURAGEMENT THAT COULD BE."

– CHARLES DICKENS, GREAT EXPECTATIONS

Regular 10/14p, 0 | Shade 9/14p, 10

| License | FFF EULA ver. 2.1 |
| Font tag | San Serif, Vintage, Old School, Distressed |

| Link | www.fontfabric.com/fonts/bernier |
| Note | 낡은 빈티지 느낌의 매력적인 폰트입니다 |

Destressed 42p, 0   투명도 60%

Destressed 50p, 0 | Regular 7/10p, -20   투명도 50%

BONDI

Bondi Regular 121p, 0

ABCDEFGHIJKLM
NOPQRSTUVWXYZ
1234567890

40/36p, 0

BLUE OCEON
SPECIAL TIPS
MEDITATIONS

50/50p, 0

ODD THINGS
SCARY MIND

50/50p, 0

| License | Open Font License | | Link | www.behance.net/gallery/72196735/Bondi-Free-Font-Typeface |
| Font tag | Sans Serif, Round, Contrast | | Note | 굵은 세로 기둥이 강한 대비를 보여주는 둥글둥글한 폰트 |

40p, 0   투명도 80%, 그림자: 표준 검정 90%, 거리 0.5㎜ 135˚, 크기 0.5㎜, 스프레드 5% 노이즈 3%

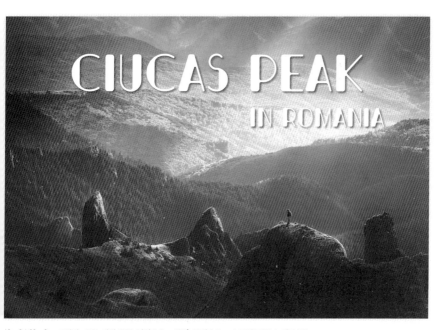

40p, 0 ┊ 20p, 0   그림자: 표준 검정 75%, 거리 0.5㎜ 135˚, 크기 0.5㎜, 스프레드 5% 노이즈 3%

CALIBRE SUPER CONDENSED

텍스트 프레임을 윤곽선으로 변환하여 컴파운드 패스를 만들고 그것을
선택한 상태에서 이미지를 가져오면 글자 내부에 이미지가 놓입니다.

Calibre Super Condensed Regular 145p, 0

ABCDEFGHIJKLMNOPQRSTUVWXYZ 1234567890

!?$¢£¤°%#(){}[]\\|/ ,.;:¡'"'"*∞®™

88/90p, 0

WHO IS THE MOST POWERFUL SUPERHEROS?

90p:80p, 0

License	Free for commercial use	Link	fontsrepo.com/calibre-super-condensed-free-font
Font tag	Sans Serif, Tall, Condensed, Round	Note	극단적으로 세로로 길고 홀쭉한 컨덴스드 폰트

150p, 0   그림자: 표준 검정 75%, 거리 1㎜ 135˚, 크기 1㎜, 스프레드 10% 노이즈 5%

200p, 0   경사와 엠보스: 내부 경사 크기 0.5㎜, 매끄럽게 0㎜, 놓기 80%, 각도 120˚ 높이 30˚   100p, 0   투명도 70%
밝은영역 표준 용지색 100%, 그림자 표준 검정 75%

Dan's Disney

Dans's Disney Regular 72p, 0

ABCDEFGHIJKLM
NOPQRSTUVWXYZ

abcdefghijklmnopqrstuvwxyz

1234567890 1234567890

!?#$%&©®™

+-×=«».,··●:; ' ' " "

~<>(){}[]\|¦/_-—

37/40p, 0

Cinderella Dress

Princess Bouquet

Spring Floral Picnic

40/42p, 0

License	Free for commercial use		Link	www.dafontfree.io/dans-disney-font
Font tag	Display, Disney, Casual		Note	디즈니 로고와 비슷하게 만든 폰트

34p, 0

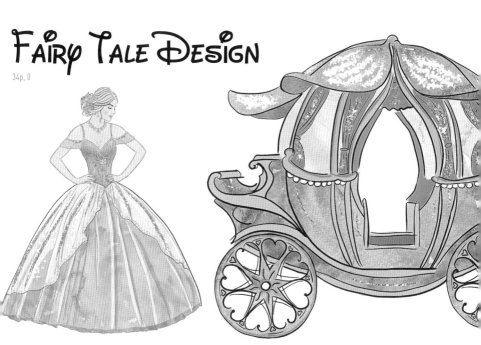

DEVIOUS

DEVIOUS Regular 158p, 0

ABCDEFGHIJKLMNOPQRSTUVWXYZ

AAA AJ AM AN AS AV AW AY BB C ÇA

DD ĐA EEE EJ EM EN ES EV EW EY FFF

FA FE FI FO FU HHHHH I IF IS IY J J

KK KA KE KI KO KU LLL LA LE LI LO LU

MMM MA ME MO MU NNN NA O OJ OM

ON OS OY PP PA QQ RR RA RE RI RO RU

SS TTT UUU UJ UM UN US UY VVV WW

WA WE XXXXX YYY YA YE YI YO YU ZZZ

1234567890 +-=!#$%&?<>()[]{}\|/@.,.:;"""'

30/40p, 0

License	Free for commercial use
Font tag	Serif, Vintage, Decorative
Link	www.dafontfree.io/devious-font-free
Note	장식적인 Ligature 조합이 멋진 고전적 분위기를 조성하는 폰트

30p, Optical 0   70p, 0   그림자: 표준 검정 50%, 거리 0.5㎜ 135°, 크기 0.5㎜, 스프레드 10% 노이즈 5%

30p, 0 | 80p, 0 | 20p, 20 | 28P, 0

Don José Black/Bigote/Raíces/Textil/Trayecto 80p, 0

DON JOSÉ BLACK
DON JOSÉ BIGOTE
DON JOSÉ RAÍCES
DON JOSÉ TEXTIL
DON JOSÉ TRAYECTO

25/25p, 0

ABCDEFGHIJKLMNOPQRSTUVWXYZ
1234567890+-×÷= _ ~©®™ ' " ' ' " "
@!?#$%&‹›«»()()[][]{}\|/*,.:;

ABCDEFGHIJKLMNOPQRSTUVWXYZ
1234567890+-×÷= _ ~©®™ ' " ' ' " "
@!?#$%&‹›«»()()[][]{}\|/*,.:;

ABCDEFGHIJKLMNOPQRSTUVWXYZ
1234567890+-×÷= _ ~©®™ ' " ' ' " "
@!?#$%&‹›«»()()[][]{}\|/*,.:;

ABCDEFGHIJKLMNOPQRSTUVWXYZ
1234567890+-×÷= _ ~©®™ ' " ' ' " "
@!?#$%&‹›«»()()[][]{}\|/*,.:;

ABCDEFGHIJKLMNOPQRSTUVWXYZ
1234567890+-×÷= _ ~©®™ ' " ' ' " "
@!?#$%&‹›«»()()[][]{}\|/*,.:;

21/20p, 0

| License | Open Font License |
| Font tag | Sans serif, Pattern, Bold, Black |

Link rostype.com/en/don-jose_eng
Note 글자 내부를 여러 가지 패턴으로 채운 특별한 폰트

70p, 0

200p | 70p, 0

FIREFLY

Firefly Regular 112p, 0

ABCDEFGHIJKLMNOPQRSTUVWXYZ
ABCDEFGHIJKLMNOPQRSTUVWXYZ
AABBCCDDEEFFGGHHIIJJKKLLMM
NNOOPPQQRRSSTTUUVVWWXXYYZZ
1234567890+−×÷= #!$%¿?,.;:©®~<>()[]{}\|/

26/30p, 0

VINTAGE GARDEN

55p/60p, 0   외부광선: 표준 검정 50%, 약하게 크기 1mm, 스프레드 20%, 노이즈 5%

License	Free for commercial use
Font tag	Serif, Handdrawn, Vintage
Link	befonts.com/firefly-hand-drawn-font.html
Note	소문자 대신에 대문자의 Alternative 문자를 제공합니다

50p, 0 | 20/28p, 0 | 50/50p, 0　　Top: 투명도 80% , Bottom: 투명도 오버레이 100% (텍스트 레이어를 2개 만들어 겹쳐 놓음)

40p, 20 | 10/12p, 0　　투명도 80%

FULBO

1234567890

Fulbo Argenta 118p, 0 | Fulbo Argenta/Champagne/Premier/Retro/Tango 60/70p, 0

FULBO ARGENTA   **1234567890**

FULBO CHAMPAGNE   1234567890

FULBO PREMIER   **1234567890**

FULBO RETRO   **12334567890**

FULBO TANGO   1234567890

15p, 0 | 29/35p, 0

ABCDEFGHIJKLMNOPQRSTUVWXYZ
ABCEFGHIJKLMNOPQRSTUVWXYZ
1234567890+-×÷=_–—ªºefİI
!⌗$%&?<>()[]{}\|/@©®™,.;:···'''

Fulbo 20/25p, 0

License	Free for commercial use
Font tag	San Serif, Number, Football

Link	www.pixelsurplus.com/freebies/fulbo-free-football-inspired-font
Note	축구 저지에서 영감을 받은 5가지 스타일의 번호가 있는 폰트

1234567890

1234567890

1234567890

1234567890

1234567890

50/50p, 0

Fulbo Argenta

Fulbo Champagne

Fulbo Premier

Fulbo Retro

Fulbo Tango

GAGALIN

Gagalin Regular 98p, 0

ABCDEFGHIJKLM
NOPQRSTUVWXYZ
1234567890+-=
!?#%&@()[]{}©™
——<< >>.,•:;''""\/

40/44p, 0

COMIC
SPEEDLINES

60p, 0 | 40p, 0

License	FFF EULA License ver2.1
Font tag	Sans serif, Bold, Retro, Comic, Vintage

Link	www.fontfabric.com/fonts/gagalin
Note	거친 스크래치에 빈티지 느낌의 코믹용 폰트

30p, 0 | 25p, 0 | 30/27p, 0   60/38p, 0   25p, 0 | 30/27p, 0

16/15p, 0 | 30p, 50 | 27p, 0   30p, 0 | 25p, 50 | 16/15p, 50

Gamine

Gamine Bold 110p, 0

Gamine Bold
Gamine Bold Italic

46/46p, 0

ABCDEFGHIJKLMNOPQRSTUVWXYZ
abcdefghijklmnopqrstuvwxyz fifffffiffl †‡
1234567890!?#$%&@(){}[],.·•;:''""""©®™■◇

ABCDEFGHIJKLMNOPQRSTUVWXYZ
abcdefghijklmnopqrstuvwxyz fifffffiffl †‡
1234567890!?#$%&@(){}[],.·•;:''""""©®™■◇

20/24p, 0

MOROCCO SAHARA DESERT

Few places on earth compare to the Sahara Desert, a natural wonder of vast plains and sun-baked dunes that dominates the south and east of Morocco. The world's largest hot desert, the Sahara stretches a

Gamine Bold Italic 30p, 0   투명도 80%   Gamine Bold Italic 10/12p, 0   투명도 60%

License	Free for commercial use	Link	www.dafontfree.io/gamine-typeface
Font tag	Serif, Small cap, Alternate, Ligature	Note	다양한 대문자(스몰캡, 어터너티브)가 매력적인 폰트

AaA̅ BʙB CcC DdD EɛE FғF GgG̲ HʜH IiI
JjJ KᴋK LʟL MᴍM NɴN OoO̅ PᴘP QǫǪ RʀR̄
SsS TᴛT UᴜU VᴠV WᴡW XxX̲ YʏY ZᴢZ

1ı 22 33 44 55 66 77 88 99 Oo ,,.. ;; ::
!¡ '' "" $$ %% && ?¿ *₊ @@ (()) [[ı]] // | \\

AWARD   A̅WARD   A̅ward
LIBERTY L̅IBERTY LIBERTY L̅iberty
LEOPARD L̅EOPARD LEOPARD L̅eopard
LLAMA   L̅LAMA   LLAMA   Llama

Configuration   Configuration
Superefficiency   Superefficiency
Insufficiency   Insufficiency
Afflictively   Afflictively
Hyperinflation   Hyperinflation

AWARD   A̅WARD   A̅ward
LIBERTY L̅IBERTY LIBERTY L̅iberty
LEOPARD L̅EOPARD LEOPARD L̅eopard
LLAMA   L̅LAMA   LLAMA   Llama

Configuration   Configuration
Superefficiency   Superefficiency
Insufficiency   Insufficiency
Afflictively   Afflictively
Hyperinflation   Hyperinflation

20/20p, 0

GIANT FONT

Giant Regular 91p, 0

ABCDEFGHIJKLM
NOPQRSTUVWXYZ
1234567890
0123456789
""!?$%/0/
+-=.:.:

50/50p, 0

ABCDEFGHIJKLM
NOPQRSTUVWXYZ
1234567890
0123456789
""!?$%/0/
+-=.:.:

50/50p, 0

License	Free for commercial use	Link	www.dafont.com/giant-2.font
Font tag	Sans Serif, Tall, Condensed, Outline	Note	무게 중심이 위에 있고 세로로 길쭉한 아웃라인 폰트

30p, 0   Top: 투명도 50% , Bottom: 투명도 오버레이 100%(텍스트 레이어를 2개 만들어 겹쳐 놓음)

96p, 0 | 30/35p, 0   외부광선: 표준 용지색 50%, 약하게 크기 1mm, 스프레드 10% 노이즈 3%

30p, 0   투명도 오버레이 100%

HAMURZ

Hamurz Regular 135p, 0

AABCDEEFGGHHIJ
KKLLMMNNOPPQ
RRSTTUUVWXYZZ
1234567890

50/55p, 0

DOL HARUBANG

60p, 0

LIFE IS SHORT AND ART IS LONG

36p, 0

License Free for commercial use
Font tag Sans Serif, Grit, Vintage

Link www.behance.net/gallery/34303959/Hamurz-Free-Font
Note 일부 대문자 자리에 Alternate 문자가 있고, 나머지 대문자는 없음

60p, 0 Top: 투명도 표준 70% , Bottom: 투명도 오버레이 80%, 그림자: 표준 검정 50%, 거리 0.5㎜ 135˚, 크기 0.5㎜, 스프레드 5% 노이즈 3%
(텍스트 레이어를 2개 만들어 겹쳐 놓음)

30p, 0 투명도 오버레이 80%, 그림자: 표준 검정 50%, 거리 0.3㎜ 135˚, 크기 0.3㎜, 스프레드 5% 노이즈 3%

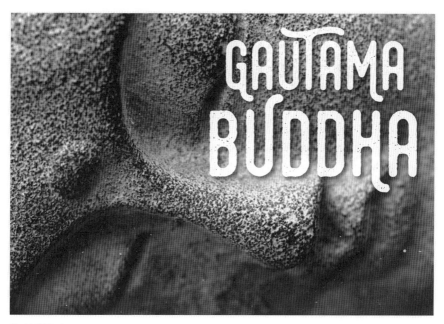

52p, 0 70/65p, 0 투명도 90%, 그림자: 표준 검정 75%, 거리 1㎜ 135˚, 크기 1㎜, 스프레드 10% 노이즈 5%

HIGHER

Higher Regular 190p, 0

텍스트 프레임을 윤곽선으로 변환하여 컴파운드 패스를 만들고 그것을
선택한 상태에서 이미지를 가져오면 글자 내부에 이미지가 놓입니다.

ABCDEFGHIJKLM
NOPQRSTUVWXYZ
1234567890-.

70/60p, 0

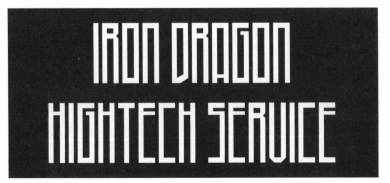

IRON DRAGON
HIGHTECH SERVICE

60/60p, 0

License	Free for commercial use	Link	www.behance.net/gallery/6797841/Higher-Free-Font
Font tag	Sans Serif, Tall, Condensed, Angled	Note	무게 중심이 극단적으로 위에 있고 세로로 길쭉한 폰트

30p, 0   그림자: 표준 검정 75%, 거리 0.5㎜ 135˚, 크기 0.5㎜, 스프레드 10% 노이즈 5%

96p, 0 ┊ 30/35p, 0   외부광선: 표준 용지색 50%, 약하게 1㎜, 스프레드 10% 노이즈 3%

Intro RUST

Intro Head R Base/Intro Script R H2 Base/Intro Rust G Base 2 Line 76p, 0

Intro Head R Base

Intro Script R H2 Base

INTRO RUST G BASE 2 LINE

30/35p, 0

ABCDEFGHIJKLMNOPQRSTUVWXYZ
abcefghijklmnopqrstuvwxyz
1234567890 ~+-*=,.:;...•-—''""
!#$%&?<>«»()[]{}\|/@©®™

ABCDEFGHIJKLMNOPQRSTUVWXY:
abcefghijklmnopqrstuvwxyz
1234567890 ~+-*=,.:;...•-—''""
!#$%&?<>«»()[]{}\|/@©®™

ABCDEFGHIJKLMNOPQRSTUVWXY
ABCEFGHIJKLMNOPQRSTUVWXYZ
1234567890 ~+-*=,.:;...••-—''""
!#$%&?<>«»()[]{}\|/@©®™←↑→↓↔↕

20/24p, 0

License	FFF EULA ver. 2.1	Link	www.fontfabric.com/fonts/intro-rust
Font tag	San Serif, Header, Script, Rust	Note	214개 패밀리 폰트 중 홍보용으로 폰트 3개 공개

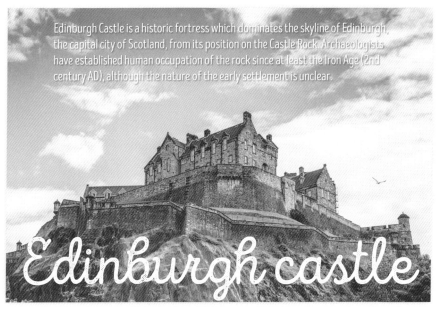

Edinburgh Castle is a historic fortress which dominates the skyline of Edinburgh, the capital city of Scotland, from its position on the Castle Rock. Archaeologists have established human occupation of the rock since at least the Iron Age (2nd century AD), although the nature of the early settlement is unclear.

Intro Head R Base 10/12p, 0   그림자: 표준 검정 50%, 거리 0.3㎜ 135°, 크기 0.3㎜, 스프레드 10% 노이즈 5%   Intro Script R H2 Base 50, 0

Therefore put on the full armor of God, so that when the day of evil comes, you may be able to stand your ground, and after you have done everything, to stand. Stand firm then, with the belt of truth

Intro Rust G Base 2 Line 66p, 0   투명도 60%   Intro Script R H2 Base 10/12p, 0

KOEBIS

Koebis Free Version Regular 120p, 0

A BCDE FGH IJK L M N O
PQR STU V WX YZ

ABCDEFGHIJKLMNOPQRSTUVWXYZ

1234567890

30/45p, 0

ABRAHAM LINCOLN EASTERN

HIGH BALL KISSES LA TIMES

MIGHTY PEOCOCK VOCAL

RISE OF SUN YES or NO ZOO

35p, 0

| License | Free for commercial use | Link | www.behance.net/gallery/30858683/Koebis-Typeface-Free-Font |
| Font tag | Sans serif, Vintage, Handrawn | Note | 유료 버전에는 Alternative 스타일이 하나 더 있음 |

35p, 25p, 0   투명도 70%

40p, 0

NEONEON

Neonon Regular 84p, 0 　외부광선: 표준 C100 50%, 약하게, 크기 2mm, 스프레드 30% 노이즈 3%

ABCDEFGHIJKLM
NOPQRSTUVWXYZ
1234567890+¬_⁂???
!?#%.&@<>()[]\/.,:::

40/42p, 0

　50/60p, 0 　외부광선: 표준 C100 80%, 약하게, 크기 2㎜, 스프레드 20% 노이즈 3%

| License | Free for commercial use |
| Font tag | Sans serif, Neon, 1980, Display |

Link www.behance.net/gallery/55332529/NEONEON-FREE-FONT
Note 80년대 스타일의 네온 효과를 제공하는 폰트

38p, 0 글자색 용지색, 그레디언트 페더: 정지점 초기값, 선형 90°

42p, 0 글자색 용지색, 외부광선: 표준 용지색 50%, 약하게, 크기 2㎜, 스프레드 40% 노이즈 2%
42p, 0 글자색 C100, 외부광선: 표준 C100 50%, 약하게, 크기 2㎜, 스프레드 40% 노이즈 2%   X=+0.5㎜ Y=+0.5㎜

379

Panton RUST

Panton Rust Script Semibold Grundge/Panton Rust Heavy Grundge Shadow 52p, 0

Panton Rust Script Semibold Gunge

32/32p, 0

PANTON RUST HEAVY GRUNGE SHADOW

32/32p, 0

AABCCDEEFGHHIJKKLLMM
NNOOPQRRSTUUVWXXYZZ
aabbccddeeßßgghhiijjkk
llmmnnooppqqrrssttuuvv
wwxxyyzz1234567890~+-×÷=
!#$%&?<>«»()[]{}\|//@©®™,.:;...··-—''""

ABCDEFGHIJKLMNOPQRSTUVWXY
112233445566778899000··.,.~+-=_
!#$%&?<>«»()[]{}\|//@©←↑→↓↖↘

20/24p, 0

License	FFF EULA ver. 2.1	Link	www.fontfabric.com/fonts/panton-rust
Font tag	San Serif, Script, Rust	Note	72개 폰트 패밀리 중 홍보용으로 폰트 2개 공개

Panton Rust Script Semibold Grundge 35, 0

Panton Rust Heavy Grundge Shadow 66p, 25   투명도 80%   Panton Rust Script Semibold Grundge 9/12p, 0

Peace Sans

Peace Sans Regular 59p, 0

AbCDEFGHIJKLM
NOPQRSTUVWXYZ
abcdefghijklm
nopqrstuvwxyz
1234567890+-=
!#$%&?,.•;:_©®™
~<>‹›«»()[]{}\|/""''""

33/36p, 0

ONE WAY
TICKET

55p, 0 | 55/60p, 20

License	Open Font License	Link	www.dafont.com/peace-sans.font
Font tag	Sans serif, Curve, Black, 8000 kern pairs	Note	둥근 곡선과 두꺼운 스타일이 결합한 블랙 폰트

60/60p, 100   투명도 60%

20/24p, 0   투명도 80%   그림자: 표준 검정 75%, 거리 1mm 135°, 크기 1mm, 스프레드 10% 노이즈 5%

Pilo Regular 90p, 150

Pilo Thin 90p, 0

Pilo regular

Pilo Regular 55p, 150

Pilo **Pilo** **Pilo** **Pilo** **Pilo** **Pilo**

30p, -25   30p, -10   30p, 0   30p, 50   30p, 100   30p, 150

ABCDEFGHIJKLMMNOPQRSTUVWWXYZ
abceeffghijklmnopqrstuvwwxyz
1234567890+-×÷=!?#$%&@©®○○ ¤ ™
‚‚·°:;≈«»()[]{}""''""°°*\|/_-==—

17/20p, 150

Pilo Thin

Pilo Thin 55p, 0

Pilo Pilo Pilo Pilo Pilo Pilo

30p, -25   30p, -10   30p, 0   30p, 50   30p, 100   30p, 150

ABCDEFGHIJKLMMNOPQRSTUVWWXYZ
abceeffghijklmnopqrstuvwwxyz
1234567890+-×÷=!?#$%&@©®®¤™
‚‚~‹›()[]{}""''""°°*\|/_--—

17/20p, 0

| License | CC0 1.0 Universal Public Domain | Link | fontesk.com/pilo-font-family |
| Font tag | Sans serif, Bold & Thin Duo, Inline | Note | 굵기와 스타일이 다른 두 폰트로 강한 대비의 디자인 가능 |

Pilo Thin 40p, 0 | Regular 50p, 0

Pilo Regular 70p, 30 | Thin 10/12p, 0   Thin 폰트는 외곽선 용지색 0.04㎜

PORAO GROTTESCHE

Porao Regular/Serif/Inline/Grottesche Regular 91p, 0

PORAO REGULAR
PORAO SERIF
PORAO INLINE
PORAO GROTTESCHE

ABCDEFGHIJKLMNOPQRSTUWXYZ
ABCDEFGHIJKLMNOPQRSTUWXYZ
ABCDEFGHIJKLMNOPQRSTUWXYZ
ABCDEFGHIJKLMNOPQRSTUWXYZ

52/40p, 0

HOROR STORY

130p, 0

| License | Free for commercial use |
| Font tag | Sans serif, Moody, Underground, Condensed |

| Link | befonts.com/porao-font-family.html |
| Note | 음침한 분위기에 적당한 폭이 좁은 폰트 |

Porao Grottesche 25p, 0   투명도 오버레이 100%

Porao Grottesche 70p, 0   투명도 오버레이 100%, 외부광선: 오버레이 검정 75%, 약하게 크기 2㎜, 스프레드 0%, 노이즈 0%

Rowan & Royal

Rowan & Royal Regular/**Brush**/Rough/**Round**/Stencil 67p, 0

Rowan & Royal Regular
Rowan & Royal Brush
Rowan & Royal Rough
Rowan & Royal Round
Rowan & Royal Stencil

40/38p, 0

ABCDEFGHIJKLMMNOPQRRSSSTUVWXYZ
aABcdefghijklmnopqrstuvwxyyzz
1234567890!?#$%.&&@<>()[]/|\-,.;:

ABCDEFGHIJKLMMNOPQRRSSSTUVWXYZ
aABcdefghijklmnopqrstuvwxyyzz
1234567890!?#$%.&&@<>()[]/|\-,.;:

ABCDEFGHIJKLMMNOPQRRSSSTUVWXYZ
aABcdefghijklmnopqrstuvwxyyzz
1234567890!?#$%.&&@<>()[]/|\-,.;:

ABCDEFGHIJKLMMNOPQRRSSSTUVWXYZ
aABcdefghijklmnopqrstuvwxyyzz
1234567890!?#$%.&&@<>()[]/|\-,.;:

ABCDEFGHIJKLMMNOPQRRSSSTUVWXYZ
aABcdefghijklmnopqrstuvwxyyzz
1234567890!?#$%.&&@<>()[]/|\-,.;:

18/16p, 0

| License | Free for commercial use |
| Font tag | Serif, Vintage, Blackletter |

| Link | fontesk.com/rowan-royal-typeface |
| Note | 빈티지 스타일을 포함하여 스타일 5개를 제공하는 장식 폰트 |

Royal Coat of Arms of the United Kingdom

Rowan & Royal Regular 20, 0

Brush 35p, 0 　Top: 문자색 C100, 투명도 90%

Bottom: 문자색 용지색, 투명도 100%
　　　X=+0.2㎜ Y=+0.2㎜

Rough 12p, 0 　투명도 60%

Speedball

Speedball Regular 66p, 0

ABCDEFGHIJKLM
NOPQRSTUVWXYZ
abcdefghijklm
nopqrstuvwxyz
1234567890 &

30/35p, 0

Time is short

35p, 0   외부광선: 표준 검정 80%, 약하게 크기 1mm, 스프레드 20%, 노이즈 5%

License	Free for commercial use	Link	dribbble.com/shots/3451824-SpeedBall-Regular-free-font
Font tag	Serif, Vintage, Studio Handbook	Note	세리프 폰트로는 흔치 않은 빈티지 스타일 폰트

30p, 0   투명도 오버레이 100%

30/30p, 0 | 40/50p, 0   Top: 투명도 70% , Bottom: 투명도 오버레이 100% (텍스트 레이어를 2개 만들어 겹쳐 놓음)

TRADESMITH

Tradesmith Regular/Rough/Round/Stamp 59p, 0

TRADESMITH REGULAR
TRADESMITH ROUGH
TRADESMITH ROUND
TRADESMITH STAMPE

33/35p, 0

AABCDEFGHIJKLMMNOPQRRSSTUVWX
1234567890 !?#$%&@‹›()[]/|\+-=,.;:

AABCDEFGHIJKLMMNOPQRRSSTUVWX
1234567890 !?#$%&@‹›()[]/|\+-=,.;:

AABCDEFGHIJKLMMNOPQRRSSTUVWX
1234567890 !?#$%&@‹›()[]/|\+-=,.;:

AABCDEFGHIJKLMMNOPQRRSSTUVWX
1234567890 !?#$%&@‹›()[]/|\+-=,.;:

20/24p, 0

License Free for commercial use

Font tag San Serif, Vintage, Industrial

Link fontsrepo.com/tradesmith-free-font

Note 빈티지와 인더스트리얼 스타일 4개를 제공하는 제목용 폰트

WORLD'S BEST FLAVOURED HERB & SPICE WINNER

RATSHERRN

WORLD'S BEST FLAVOURED HONEY & MAPLE WINNER

MAPLE VANILLA

WORLD'S BEST DARK BELGIAN STYLE DUBBEL WINNER

ST. BERNARDUS

Tradesmith Regular/Rough/Round 13p | Tradesmith Stamp 47/40, 0

BLACKSMITH

A BLACKSMITH IS A PERSON WHO WORKS WITH IRON AND STEEL. THE BLACKSMITH HAMMERS HOT IRON ON AN ANVIL TO CHANGE ITS SHAPE. BLACKSMITHS MAKE IRON AND STEEL TOOLS.

Tradesmith Stamp 40p, 0   투명도 90%   Tradesmith Rough 10/12p, 0   투명도 60%

ZI DE

Zing Rust Base 51p, 0   Zing Rust Diagonals2 Base 51p, 0   Zing Sans Rust Light Base 51p, 0

Zing Rust Shdow1 51p, 0   Zing Rust Line Horizontals1 Fill 51p, 0   Zing Script Rust SemiBold

ZING RUST BASE

ZING RUST SHADOW1

ZING RUST DIAGONALS2 BASE

ZING RUST LINE HORIZONTALS1 FILL

ZING SANS RUST LIGHT

Zing Script Rust SemiBold Ba

28/30p, 0

ABCDEFGHIJKLMNOPQRSTUVWXYZ
abcefghijklmnopqrstuvwxyz
*1234567890 !#$&?<>()[]{}/@+- *=,.;*

AA BB DD EE FF GG HH II JJ KKK
LL MM NN PP RRR TT UU VV WW
XX YY ZZ
aa bbbb cc dd ee gg hh iiii jjj kk ll
mm nn oooo pppp qq ss tt uu xxxx
yy zzzzz

Zing Script Rust SemiBold Base 20/22p, 0

| License | FFF EULA ver. 2.1 |
| Font tag | San Serif, Script, Rust |

| Link | www.fontfabric.com/fonts/zing-rust |
| Note | 10개 스타일의 521개 폰트 패밀리 중 홍보용으로 폰트 6개 공개 |

ABCDEFGHIJKLMNOPQRSTUVWXYZ
ABCEFGHIiJKLMNOPQRSTUVWXYZ
1234567890 !#$&?<>()[]{}/@+-*=,.;:

ABCDEFGHIJKLMNOPQRSTUVWXYZ
ABCEFGHIiJKLMNOPQRSTUVWXYZ
1234567890 !#$&?<>()[]{}/@+-*=,.;:

ABCDEFGHIJKLMNOPQRSTUVWXYZ
ABCEFGHIiJKLMNOPQRSTUVWXYZ
1234567890 !#$&?<>()[]{}/@+-*=,.;:

ABCDEFGHIJKLMNOPQRSTUVWXYZ
ABCEFGHIJKLMNOPQRSTUVWXYZ
1234567890 !#$&?<>()[]{}/@+-*=,.;:

26/26p, 0

ABCDEFGHIJKLMNOPQRSTUVWXYZ
ABCEFGHIiJKLMNOPQRSTUVWXYZ
1234567890 !#$&?<>()[]{}/@+-*=,.:

Zing Sans Rust Light Base 20/22p, 0

395

ZING RUST
ZING RUST
ZING RUST
ZING RUST

Top: Zing Rust Line Horizontal1 | Bottom: Zing Rust Base 40p,0
Y: +0,106mm

ZING RUST
ZING RUST
ZING RUST
ZING RUST

Top: Zing Rust Diagonals2 | Bottom: Zing Rust Base 40p,0

ZING RUST
ZING RUST
ZING RUST
ZING RUST

Top: Rust Base/Rust Diagonals2 | Bottom: Rust Shdow1 40p,0
X: −0,1mm, Y: +0,4mm

ZING RUST
ZING RUST

Top: Base | Middle: Diagonals2 | Bottom: Base 40p,0
X: 0,2mm, Y: 0,2mm X: 0,2mm, Y: 0,2mm

ZING RUST
ZING RUST

Top: Base | Middle: Diagonals2 | Bottom: Base 40p,0
X: 0,6mm, Y: 0,8mm X: 0,6mm, Y: 0,8mm

ZING RUST
ZING RUST

Top: Rust Line Horizontal1 | Bottom: Rust Shdow1 40p,0
X: −0,1mm

Korea   Regular   Zing
Korea   Regular   Zing
Korea   Regular

Zing Scirpt Rust SemiBold 36/38p,

Zing Scirpt Rust SemiBold Base 10/12p, 0   그림자: 표준 검정 50%, 거리 0.3mm 135°, 크기 0.3mm, 스프레드 5% 노이즈 3%

Edinburgh Castle is a historic fortress which dominates the skyline of Edinburgh, the capital city of Scotland, from its position on the Castle Rock. Archaeologists have established human occupation of the rock since at least the Iron Age (2nd century AD), although the nature of the early settlement is unclear.

EDINBURGH CASTLE

Top: Zing Rust Line Horizontal1 Fill 40p, 0   투명도 30%, Y=+0.106mm

Bottom: Zing Rust Base 40p,0   그림자: 표준 검정 75%, 거리 0.5mm 135°, 크기 0.5mm, 스프레드 5% 노이즈 3%

ARMOR

Therefore put on the full armor of God, so that when the day of evil comes, you may be able to stand your ground, and after you have done everything, to stand. Stand firm then, with the belt of truth

Top: Zing Rust Line Horizontal1 Fill 40p,0   Y: +0.3mm, 투명도 70%   Zing Scirpt Rust SemiBold Base 10/12p, 0   투명도 80%

Bottom: Zing Rust Base 40p,0

Font Index

한눈에 보이는
무료 글꼴 가이드 - 영어편

초판 1쇄 2020년 6월 1일

지은이   탁연상
펴낸이   윤명성
펴낸곳   상상하라 출판신고 제2016-000166호
주 소   서울시 영등포구 여의대로6길 17, B-1003
전 화   0505-737-0050
팩 스   0505-737-0051
메 일   imagine_book@naver.com
블로그   blog.naver.com/imagine_book
Facebook   www.facebook.com/imaginebooks
I S B N   979-11-959823-9-4   (13000)